Community Colleges on the Horizon

**Part of the American Council on Education
Series on Higher Education**
Susan Slesinger, Executive Editor

Community Colleges on the Horizon

Challenge, Choice, or Abundance

Richard Alfred, Christopher Shults,
Ozan Jaquette, and Shelley Strickland

Published in partnership with the

AMERICAN COUNCIL ON EDUCATION
® The Unifying Voice for Higher Education

Rowman & Littlefield Education
Lanham • New York • Toronto • Plymouth, UK

Published in partnership with
the American Council on Education

Published in the United States of America
by Rowman & Littlefield Education
A division of Rowman & Littlefield Publishers, Inc.
A wholly owned subsidary of The Rowman & Littlefield Publishing Group, Inc.
4501 Forbes Boulevard, Suite 200, Lanham, Maryland 20706
www.rowmaneducation.com

Estover Road
Plymouth PL6 7PY
United Kingdom

British Library Cataloguing in Publication Information Available

Library of Congress Cataloging-in-Publication Data

Community colleges on the horizon : challenge, choice, or abundance / edited
    by Richard Alfred . . . [et al.].
        p.   cm.
    ISBN-13: 978-1-60709-082-3 (cloth : alk. paper)
    ISBN-10: 1-60709-082-1 (cloth : alk. paper)
    ISBN-13: 978-1-60709-084-7 (electronic : alk. paper)
    ISBN-10: 1-60709-084-8 (electronic : alk. paper)
    1. Community colleges—United States—Forecasting.   2. Educational
leadership—United States.   I. Alfred, Richard L.
LB2328.C6916   2008
378.1'5430973—dc22   2008042325

∞ ™ The paper used in this publication meets the minimum requirements
of American National Standard for Information Sciences—
Permanence of Paper for Printed Library Materials, ANSI/NISO Z39.48-
1992. Manufactured in the United States of America.

*To community college leaders
today and tomorrow and throughout the organization*

Contents

Foreword

How is it possible that some community colleges thrive despite limited finances? Why do other colleges with sufficient assets sometimes struggle? Which is of greater value—money or people, numbers or ideas, or tangible or intangible resources? For those who regularly ponder issues like these, for those who refuse to be complacent about the need to confront change, and for those who desire a clear and compelling vision of the future for their institutions, there is much wisdom to be found in these pages.

Community Colleges on the Horizon takes us on a journey through three different scenarios of development or "wellness" for our colleges in the face of a dramatically changing landscape for higher education. Our world is a not-so-tightly knit family encompassing some 1,600 institutions. We are bound together through our collective roots as "colleges of the people," charged with making learning opportunities more accessible regardless of social class or economic status.

Families change as their members grow and take on new roles. Like any family, our individual members have grown up in different circumstances and with widely differing conceptualizations of themselves and their capabilities. Some members operate most comfortably in the status quo; others become overachievers. Some have clearly defined missions; others seek an elusive identity. Some have access to full resources; others work with austerity budgets. Some run smoothly; others encounter rough water. We have "come of age" at different times, and one size does not fit all. Yet in our quest to continuously move our institutions forward, there exists a natural tendency to measure our institutions' progress against each other. Call it sibling rivalry or whatever you would like, we are curious about how our numbers—enrollment, budget, facilities, and staff—

and our best practices and bottom lines compare. The similarities and differences we uncover inevitably lead to tough questions like those previously stated.

Geographic factors, funding mix, and public policy must be taken into account but only partially explain the dichotomies among us. How do we account for subtle or substantial differences in foresight, in community esteem, and in the fine line separating colleges that perform effectively versus those that are truly exemplary? It is this navigational gap that *Community Colleges on the Horizon* steps in to fill. What sets its content apart from other books and strategic planning guides is its conceptual framework and systemic approach to analysis. Traditional descriptors like "strengths/weaknesses" or "high performing/underperforming" have been replaced with a more nonjudgmental vocabulary—one capable of removing barriers that so often accompany introspection. The "lens" through which this book views community colleges consists of three states: challenge, choice, and abundance. Visualizing our organizations in this framework opens up a realm of possibilities for the kind of reflection that precedes healthy change.

For some years I have been a proponent of incorporating business best practices into the higher education arena. So it's fulfilling to find in these pages a kind of "good to great" model whereby community colleges, like private industry, can identify and activate their strategic potential. Like any business, our colleges are facing numerous external challenges that are influencing, for better or worse, organizational effectiveness. These include globalization, changing demographics, mass customization, and flattened financial resources. And if these forces aren't challenging enough, look at the competition we are facing. Leaders need to weigh and consider every possible solution to combat encroachment by hungry corporate providers with deep pockets who are entering the postsecondary education market.

Added to these concerns is the awareness that we as community colleges must reach beyond our traditional methodology and turn to innovation when contemplating the best ways to educate tech-savvy millennials. This new breed of digital native, one that seems almost unrecognizable when compared to past generations of students, has assumed its rightful place in our institutions and now demands engagement as part of a high-quality education. It will not be enough to tweak current practice. What we require more than ever are creative thinking and innovation to keep our colleges sustainable in the face of constant change.

This book's three-fold framework—challenge, choice, and abundance—inspires us to seek out those qualities we most desire for our future and then act to reconcile them to our mission, vision, and operations. An *abundant* college will most likely be sustainable and will be

guided by imaginative thinkers with transformational leadership qualities. And whereas a state of abundance is represented as a desirable goal
for community colleges, it should be noted that this state, like the others,
is always fluid rather than a fixed point of arrival. In fact, it's likely that
some colleges will possess aspects of all three states.

Those who recognize themselves as colleges of *choice* will find reassur-
ance . . . combined with reasonable cause to be shaken out of complacency
so they can reach beyond their comfort zone. And what about those *challenged* institutions that year after year are deadlocked in a struggle for
more resources or students? These pages offer real hope that they too can
ascend to the ranks of choice and ultimately abundance.

But be forewarned: as models of the three states are examined, some
"sacred cows" will be kicked over. For example, many would assume that
the leading benchmark for overall college well-being and success is a
steady increase in head count. This book, however, builds a solid case that
a college can experience continuous growth and prosperity and still need
to undergo major change to sustain itself. Positive numbers alone will not
be enough to ensure success. The community college of the twenty-first
century must search beyond growth for growth's sake and achieve vitality through new standards the authors propose: a capacity for leveraging,
a reassessment of leadership dynamics, a desire to substitute collaboration for competition, and more.

The strategic conversations generated by this book will be enhanced
through the added value of a model and tool for assessing abundance.
Rather than serving as a litmus test for which there are single defining
answers, the abundance tool is designed to provoke a disconnect between
what we wish to believe about our organizations versus the evidence of
who we truly are. The feedback generated through this tool can be the
impetus that turns your strategic plan into a living document.

All community colleges are capable of change; however, they must
individually and collectively understand *how* to transcend their current
state. *Community Colleges on the Horizon* serves as the compass that will
help leaders chart their own course for positive change.

Linda M. Thor, EdD
President
Rio Salado College
Tempe, Arizona

Preface

The book you are holding is the product of more than a decade of research on community colleges. It is based on conversations with leaders and staff on campus and stakeholders in external communities. It is also based on theories of organizational development and on environmental forecast data describing forces that are likely to emerge over the next decade. Together, these sources of information point to a future for community colleges unlike anything we have known or experienced. It is a future that can best be described through words like *turbulence, upheaval,* and *opportunity* in which institutions coping with rapid change and unpredictable resources perform well or poorly on the basis of their ability to leverage tangible and intangible resources.

Leveraging is a big word that only recently is beginning to find its place among community college leaders. As a concept, it refers to the achievement of superior performance through optimal use of resources. It is one of two pillars that we believe will be pivotal in the development of community colleges over the next decade. The other pillar is *abundance*—a state achieved by an institution when its resources are leveraged beyond a reasonable level of expectation. Together, these constructs form a grounded theory of organizational performance that can be used by community college leaders to guide institutional development.

Our interest in abundance had its genesis in a series of articles by Richard Alfred and Patricia Carter on the topic of organizational dynamics in community colleges that appeared in the *Community College Journal* between 1996 and 2004. These articles examined forces of change inside and outside of colleges and the extent to which leaders and staff were prepared for a future that would be markedly different. They were based on work currently underway in community colleges, and their intent was to portray dynamics of a new market and to urge leaders to think and act strategically. While ostensibly we were signaling an early alert to leaders and institutions, underneath something very different was happening. We were beginning to think differently about organizational development and leadership. While boundaries between institutions and their environments were changing and the role of leaders has always been important, leadership is about much more than navigating boundaries even in turbulent times. It is about change and optimization. An important but unexplored role of leaders is to bring out the very best in people and the organization, irrespective of conditions in the environment. This became a consuming interest for us, and it is what this book is about.

We became intrigued by institutional differences in outlook and performance often attributed to transparent factors, such as leadership, external conditions and regulations, resource availability, and the like. We discovered that simple explanations of effective or ineffective performance were not necessarily accurate because performance is often a function of unobtrusive root causes. For example, it is not uncommon for a college with full resources and favorable regional conditions to perform less capably than a college with lean resources and difficult operating conditions. What factors, we wondered, contribute most significantly to institutional performance? What circumstances dispose resource-lean colleges on occasion to perform beyond expectation and resource-plenty colleges to underachieve? What theory could explain how some colleges are able to leverage resources to achieve superior performance while others perform at or below expectation?

The marked differences we observed in performance could not be explained by incremental differences in operating resources or by obvious factors, such as the number and quality of staff. Something else was at work that presupposed a unique ability to leverage resources. As we examined the leadership and organizational dynamics of colleges identified as "high performers," we discovered that leaders and staff set ambitious goals and were accustomed to working at a pace and level that led to optimum performance. We saw leaders in these institutions engaging staff and making ambitious goals realistic and achievable while those in other institutions could not raise the sights of staff beyond workload and operations.

We concluded that leaders in high-performing colleges were capable of envisioning and interpreting opportunity in a way that impelled staff to see beyond the limits of their departments and their jobs. They spent less time on operations and more time generating ideas about where a college needed to be and the resources it would need to get there. Leaders in other colleges were more interested in problem solving and operating within the resources available to them. They took economic and market realities as a given, seldom reaching beyond the limits of their vision and resources. Change was a matter of convenience and performance goals were incremental—doing better than last year.

PURPOSE OF THE BOOK

The gap between institutional ambition, resources, and performance is what prompted us to develop this book. It is written at a time when community colleges are facing problems with increasing demand and limited resources that have forced them to search for efficiency and new ways of supporting growth. Our purpose is to open up a new way of thinking about institutional growth and development and the role and responsibility of leaders based on the concept of abundance—elevating dynamics in institutions that lead to extraordinary performance, outcomes that surpass expectations, and a decidedly positive effect. Our approach is to describe different circumstances that colleges will find themselves in as a function of their leadership, their resources, and the capabilities of their staff.

AUDIENCE

This book is a step into the future for community colleges. It has been developed for a reading audience of 1) those *inside* the nation's 1,300 plus community colleges who are in a position to make a difference by how they view the enterprise they are part of and how they approach their work and 2) those *outside* community colleges who study them, who create policy for them, and who have an interest in pursuing a career within them. It will be particularly useful to:

Community College Personnel

- Senior administrators (presidents, chancellors, vice presidents, provosts, and deans)
- Faculty (full-time and part-time instructors)
- Midlevel administrators (directors, coordinators, department chairs, and administrators in a supporting capacity)
- Support staff (staff performing operational tasks throughout the institution)

Community College Boards of Trustees

Educational Policymaking and Advocacy Organizations

- State coordinating board officials
- Accrediting agencies and advocacy organizations (American Association of Community Colleges, ACE, and regional accrediting associations
- State and federal government agencies

Faculty and Students in Graduate Programs for the Study of Higher Education

Management Consulting Organizations

Prospective Staff with a Career Interest in Community Colleges

We should indicate that *Community Colleges on the Horizon* is not for the complacent; it is not for those who are unwilling to look openly at their institutions. It will be a useful book for those who believe their institution can and should do better, for those prefer actions to words, for those who are unafraid to challenge convention, for those who are ready to pursue opportunity and change, and for those who believe that their institution has unexploited potential.

ORGANIZATION OF THE BOOK

The book is divided into three parts that describe the operating dynamics of community colleges and variable patterns of development: 1) *Community Colleges in Context,* 2) *Scenarios for Development,* and 3) *Looking Ahead.*

The prologue invites the reader into the book by presenting situation-specific accounts of community colleges facing different contextual conditions and, hence, traveling on different development paths. Some institutions lack the resources, capacity, and leadership to operate effectively. Others, powered by adequate resources and capable leadership, have the opportunity to grow and flourish but may not reach their full potential because of the choices they make. Institutions in this category are functional but not high achieving. A third category is comprised of institutions that emerge as exemplary because of their ability to achieve superior performance by stretching their resources beyond a level of reasonable expectation.

Part I, *Community Colleges in Context,* describes the relationship between forces in the external environment and institutional capacity that will shape college performance in the decade ahead. The opening chapter looks at community colleges in today's landscape and gauges their capacity for success from the standpoint of organizational dynamics that lead to advantage or disadvantage. A strategic thinking framework is used in chapter 2 to present a comprehensive scan of trends, forces, and conditions in the external environment impacting community colleges. Chapter 3 describes the internal capacity of colleges—their facility to produce, perform, and deliver value to stakeholders—using information from analytical reports, statistical summaries, and campus-based research. Three dimensions of capacity are examined—tangible resources, intangible resources, and leadership—and their implications for institutional performance are described. Chapter 4 identifies and describes development paths (challenge, choice, and abundance) that community colleges will follow in the decade ahead based on analysis of external forces and internal capacity.

Part II, *Scenarios for Development*, presents different developmental pathways for community colleges based on the extent to which institutions possess attributes of abundance. Chapter 4 presents a framework for abundance and shows how it can be operationalized in colleges. In chapter 5 ("Colleges of Challenge"), a development path is described for marginally performing institutions constrained by ineffective leadership, limited staff capability, and insufficient resources. Chapter 6 ("Colleges of Choice") profiles colleges further along the path to abundance as a result of leadership, staff capability, and resources that permit the option of choice. In chapter 7, colleges of abundance are described. These colleges have a unique capacity to leverage limited resources into high performance through leaders and staff, who possess highly developed strategic capabilities. Each chapter uses case study illustrations to show how the presence or absence of abundance affects performance.

Part III, *Looking Ahead*, moves to the hands-on world of performance in community colleges. The single chapter in this section (and the closing chapter in the book) describes the actions that community college leaders and staff must take to move their colleges on a path toward abundance.

Richard Alfred
Christopher Shults
Ozan Jaquette
Shelley Strickland

Ann Arbor, Michigan

Acknowledgments

This book was three years in development from its inception as a proposal in response to an invitation from the American Council on Education to the finished product that you are holding. It followed a path marked by twists and turns as we struggled to find an overarching theme that would pull together where community colleges are today and where they are likely to be tomorrow. The answer, as we painfully discovered, is that there is not a uniform place in the higher education universe that community colleges will occupy. Our colleges are diverse in origin, purpose, contextual conditions, and architecture, and they are going to be everywhere on the landscape of postsecondary education. What will distinguish them, however, is how effectively they perform in this landscape, and that is what this book is about.

We had help from many people who made significant contributions to the development of the book. At the top of the list are the presidents, senior administrators, faculty, and staff of the Strategic Horizon Network—a network of fourteen colleges committed to identifying and importing ways of business from organizations outside of education into practice on their campuses.

Member institutions in the *Strategic Horizon Network Colleges* are:

Anne Arundel Community College (MD)
Colorado Mountain College (CO)
Columbus State Community College (OH)
Community College of Beaver County (PA)
Lone Star College-Cy-Fair (TX)
Hawkeye Community College (IA)
Hocking College (OH)

Lorain County Community College (OH)
Metropolitan Community College (NE)
Mohawk Valley Community College (NY)
Northern Essex Community College (MA)
Owens Community College (OH)
Rio Salado College (AZ)
Tulsa Community College (OK)

The Network came together in 2004 under the sponsorship of the Center for Community College Development, and it flourished through interaction with counterparts from the corporate sector (Marriott, Caterpillar, SAS, Cisco, Lowes, and Whole Foods), the entertainment industry (Disney and Zingerman's Deli), health systems (Mott Children's Hospital/University of Michigan, Caritas Christi Health System, and Mercy Health System), and the transportation industry (Southwest Airlines, Honda, and Midwest Express Airlines) where different approaches to organizational design, development, and change were discussed. Leaders and staff in the Network colleges helped shape many of the ideas in this book by committing time to colloquia, interviews, and campus projects that helped us see the relationship between theory and practice, particularly the design and implementation of change. In the aggregate, personnel in the Network colleges contributed more than three thousand hours of time over five years to the creation of ideas that form the framework for *Community Colleges on the Horizon*. We thank them all and hope that this book reflects the scope and quality of their contribution and their expectations for a product that will make a difference.

In addition, we would like to acknowledge the important role that Kim Cameron at the University of Michigan Stephen M. Ross School of Business played in introducing us to the concept of abundance. Kim and his colleagues (Jane Dutton, Bob Quinn, and Gretchen Spreitzer) at Michigan have opened a new way of thinking about organizational performance called POS—Positive Organizational Scholarship. Over a period of two years, Kim worked with teams from the Horizon Network colleges to expand their horizon from performing effectively to superior performance—that is, to performing at a level beyond resources and reasonable expectation. Kim's work on abundance was the portal through which we learned about the importance of leveraging and related concepts such as authenticity, virtuousness, positive thinking, and engagement. We owe him an enormous debt of gratitude; he is a visionary, a scholar, a colleague, and a friend all in one.

We were very fortunate to have assistance from community college presidents and senior administrators engaged in organizational change who helped frame ideas through back-and-forth discussion in interviews, involvement in strategic planning projects, and casual discourse at conferences and professional gatherings. We will not identify these two hundred or so individuals by name, but they are the progenitors of the leadership evolution that is underway in community colleges. They are at the helm of colleges large and small, affluent and austere, rural and urban, challenged and abundant. More importantly, however, they are working with faculty and staff, who are the behind-the-scenes architects of what makes community colleges great: people who lead by doing— whose actions make change happen. Small things carried out every day by a lot of people make the real difference in moving colleges from effective to *superior* performance. We salute these leaders as the unsung heroes of the American community college.

We have benefited greatly from the work of prominent scholars and thinkers whose ideas fueled the early design of this book and, ultimately, its final shape. Our intellectual debt to the architects of Positive Organizational Scholarship—Kim Cameron, Jane Dutton, and Bob Quinn—is substantial, and it is more yet to the generation of community college administrators who are putting their ideas into practice. We are particularly indebted to Gary Hamel and C. K. Prahalad, whose 1994 book entitled *Competing for the Future* continues to shape our view of how organizations work and what they can do to improve their performance, and to Jim Collins, whose 2001 book titled *Good to Great* helped us understand, in compellingly simple language, factors that contribute to high performance in organizations. We would be remiss not to acknowledge the work of Fred Luthans, whose continuing scholarship on positive organizational behavior underscored the importance of putting ideas into action. It is one thing to think about the behavior and actions that go into high performance and something quite different to model this behavior. The bottom line is getting into motion, and this is the message that Luthans delivered.

Gratitude is expressed as well to thinkers, scholars, and practitioners who served as a source of ideas for specific sections in the book—Aran Caza in organizational virtuousness and abundance; Karl Weick, Kathy Sutcliffe, Deborah Ancona, Tom Malone, Wanda Orlikowski, and Peter Senge in the description of attributes of effective leaders; and Tamara Erickson and Lynda Gratton in organizational culture and imaging. The frameworks used to conceptualize and describe organizational behavior culminating in abundance owes much to their work.

As a team of authors, we owe much to our colleagues in the Center for the Study of Higher and Postsecondary Education at the University of Michigan whose teaching and scholarship have contributed significantly to our ability to shape ideas. We make special note of our colleagues in Organizational Behavior and Management—Marv Peterson, Mike Bastedo, John Burkhardt, Steve Desjardins, and Ed St. John—whose engagement in research on organizational dynamics in colleges and universities and understanding of practice furthered our understanding of community colleges as organizations. We acknowledge and deeply appreciate the support and assistance of Susan Slesinger, executive editor for the ACE Series on Higher Education at the American Council on Education. Susan read early drafts of the book and provided advice on form and content that made a significant difference in its design and presentation to the reader. Individually, we are deeply thankful for loved ones, colleagues, and associates who were and are an important source of inspiration and support:

Dick Alfred: My partner in life and work, Pat Carter, who is part of the brain trust behind this book, the editor of its content, and my deepest and most enduring support.

Chris Shults: The two ladies in my life: my beautiful wife Keiva and my lovely daughter, Niriel.

Ozan Jaquette: Erik Beecroft and David Fein of Abt Associates, who first aroused my interest in community colleges; the community college students who showed me it is possible to overcome great odds; and Glen Gabert, of Hudson County Community College, for creating an organization that helps students overcome great odds.

Shelley Strickland: Tim and Mitchell Strickland, David and Maxine Murphy, and my former students who taught me in return and continue to inspire.

We acknowledge how important you are and give our special thanks to you one and all!

Prologue

Like any industry, community colleges occupy different positions by virtue of the choices they make. Choosing smartly elevates performance and opens opportunities while choosing poorly closes doors and holds a college back from achieving its full potential. We open *Community Colleges on the Horizon: Challenge, Choice, or Abundance* with profiles of institutions that made different choices and, in so doing, created different futures for themselves.

A COLLEGE OF CHALLENGE

Patterson Community College is a single-campus community college located in a middle-income suburb of a large eastern city. Patterson depends on state aid and tuition for most of its operating revenue—a circumstance that has strained an already austere budget as rising costs for health care, K–12 education, and corrections have resulted in reduced state appropriations. The college has a new president, John Gales, an experienced administrator who served as the chief academic officer of two community colleges before coming to Patterson. Gales was heavily recruited by the Board of Trustees because of his experience with planning and change and his dedication to the general education mission that is the heart of the college. He has the earmarks of an outstanding CEO—impeccable credentials, an engaging personality, and energy to burn—but his early experience with Patterson has led him to question whether he made the right decision in taking the job.

Gales has discovered that Patterson is in much worse shape than he was led to believe. The primary reason, other than reduced state support, is a lack of talent. The college has a history of weak leadership at all levels in the organization. Administrators have routinely been appointed to positions for which they lack experience, resources are not sufficient to support professional development, and laissez-faire hiring practices and lax accountability standards have resulted in an organization that is unprincipled and devoid of rigor. Efforts toward change have been met by resistance from faculty and staff who have protected their interests by shifting the focus of their work from the institution to the operating unit. This has produced deep fissures within the college and reduced it to silos competing for shares of the operating budget. Morale is low, and a powerful sense of drift permeates Patterson that is beyond anything that Gales could have imagined. He needs to shift the direction of the college, but finding a starting point is difficult because the problems are so pervasive.

The talent void at Patterson can be traced back to two decades of ineffective leadership. The college has had three presidents (including Gales), and each has sought to mold the college into a specific image. The difficulty began under a president (1984–1998) who viewed leadership as the province of the CEO and operated with a belief that top-down management was the key to turning a college into an efficient and effective organization. Much of his time was spent on campus micromanaging staff, and little effort was made to establish ties with organizations in the community—especially business and industry. Kinship and loyalty were the primary criteria upon which staff were promoted into positions of power. Control was maintained through a centralized budget process and policies that closely regulated the work of employees. Little or no value was assigned to innovation, the result of which was a talent drain for Patterson as qualified faculty and staff left for greener pastures. Those who remained survived by detaching themselves from the institution and limiting their effort to the courses they were teaching and the services they were providing. After fourteen years in office, the president retired and left in his wake a shattered institution that was insulated from the larger world beyond the campus.

The next president served from 1998–2004 and was a collaborative and team-oriented leader. She did not like conflict and, working under the belief that only positive reinforcement was acceptable, refused to terminate ineffective administrators. When the state slipped into a deep recession and cuts were mandated, the operating budgets of all units were slashed using an across-the-board approach. Buyouts were offered to senior faculty, and those who left were replaced by part-time instructors. Under this president's watch, the proportion of credit hours taught by full-time faculty shifted from 60 percent to 40 percent, and temporary staff were brought in to help with the delivery of services. Trust between faculty and administrators waned, instructional quality declined, and services were inconsistently and haphazardly delivered. The Board became aware of the problem through informal contacts initiated by faculty and, after months of deliberation, chose not to renew the president's contract.

As the successor to two presidents and twenty years of marginal leadership, Gales inherited a dispirited institution with no universally understood direction. There was an absence of trust, innovation was sacrificed to the desire of faculty and staff to maintain the status quo, and increasing dependence on part-time faculty was eroding academic quality. While Patterson's mission placed student success at the center of its work, the leadership style of two presidents had induced faculty and staff to become the primary customer of their work. The declining economy exacerbated an already difficult situation by forcing the college to rely on poorly considered mechanisms for reducing the budget. Further complicating the financial picture was Patterson's isolation from external partners—a factor that severely limited its ability to create networks that could bring in new revenue and reduce operating costs.

Patterson is in a tough position, and Gales has been left with difficult choices. He has moved to address the most obvious problems by removing ineffective administrators and improving programs by adding new courses and curricula. He has also attempted to create a new direction for the college by consulting with a small number of carefully chosen individuals on campus and in the community. In doing so, he has developed a reputation among faculty and staff as a loner and a maverick. Opinion leaders freely express a yearning for the old days when at least they knew what to expect from the president. The fast pace pursued by Gales has taken them out of their comfort zone, and they are beginning to resist his initiatives. Frustrated by their recalcitrance, Gales has moved to assemble a new executive team—one capable of getting things done. Concerned by growing unrest, the Board has asked him to slow down and put the reorganization on hold. Gales is in the middle of a bad dream, and there is no easy way out.

Under its new president, Patterson is trying to find its soul, but it does not have the players or the energy to make the leap from stasis to action. There are questions in need of answers, but little help in answering them. What direction should Patterson pursue? How long will it take to experience visible success? Can a culture of distrust be transformed into a culture of trust? What opportunities lie outside of the college, and how can they be pursued? Can money be found to support growth and change? Can talented staff be attracted to a college with a marginal reputation? These questions and others like them speak to the viability of a college that is caught in a vortex of ineffective leadership, limited resources, and marginal staff capability—in a word, a *college of challenge.*

COLLEGES OF CHOICE

The main campus of *Great Lakes Community College* (GLCC) is located on 140 acres of land on the suburban outskirts of Springfield, a large city located in Great Lakes County. The college is located in the "Rust Belt" and has long been a contributor of training and skilled employees to manufacturing industries located throughout the region. In addition to its Uniondale and Hillsboro campuses, the college has a one-stop center located in Springfield Town Center and a collaborative agreement with Great Lakes Medical College that enables students to take advanced courses in the health professions.

Great Lakes' history as a postsecondary education provider in the region and the state is short and illustrious. While other colleges offer similar academic and technical programs, GLCC has emerged as a leader in workforce development. Its workforce mission is carried out through three organizations providing direct service to employers—the Entrepreneurship Institute, the Small Business Incubator, and the Center for Business and Technology. The primary function of the business incubator is to provide guidance to local entrepreneurs and business leaders on starting a company. It also provides small companies with meeting space, a printing and publishing center, high-tech conference rooms, and the ability to network with small businesses across the county. GLCC is not only a service arm to business and industry, it is also an innovator. Its award-winning Youth Entrepreneurship Program (YEP) connects youth and work at an early age by introducing elementary and middle school students to a range of career options in business and industry.

In Great Lakes' service region, conditions are anything but static in the manufacturing economy of the Rust Belt. With the regional economy in a shambles because of declining employment and deepening problems in the automotive industry, Great Lakes finds itself in the unusual position of being out of kilter with the changing needs of its constituents. For years the college had been living in the comfortable security of a predictable relationship between citizen needs, program and service offerings, and public support—a relationship that fueled growth in credit and noncredit enrollment. GLCC has reached a point, however, where students are being turned away from heavily enrolled courses due to inadequate space and funding. Worse yet, the resources needed to bring program and service offerings to fast-growing regions of the county are not available. Students have made use of distance education, but those traveling to the main campus are beginning to experience problems with unreasonable commute time, rising fuel costs, fewer evening sections, and increased class size.

Money that came easily to Great Lakes in the past is no longer available or requires considerable effort to procure. In 2004, the college attempted to pass a millage to increase the amount of funding from property taxes. To the chagrin of faculty and administrators who worked tirelessly to achieve a passing vote, the millage failed. After successfully passing three tax millages between 1990 and 2002, the failed millage appeared to mark a shift in public attitude toward support of the college. Surveys conducted annually of public perception had consistently found a 75 percent recognition rate and overwhelming support for GLCC's program and service offerings. Analysis of findings in the 2004 survey disclosed that citizens were beginning to view the offerings of competitors more favorably. Major inroads were being made in distance delivery, program and course cycles, customized services, and aggressive outreach to adult learners. Additionally, GLCC was on the receiving end of criticism for continuing to invest in programs that were outdated, failing to modernize systems and processes, and for carrying faculty and staff on payroll who were no longer effective.

Further complicating the resource problem is the start-up of new businesses in the county. These businesses expect Great Lakes to meet their training needs, but instead of a prime resource they are encountering a complacent organization. The college's traditional approach to program and course design is not effective because it is incapable of operating at a speed, standard of quality, and cost efficiency required by industry. To business executives looking ahead rather than in the rear view mirror, GLCC appears to be a victim of its own success. Growth has contributed to an illusion of security among faculty and administrators that has put GLCC two steps behind the needs of its most important stakeholders.

GLCC's evolution as an institution has paralleled the tenure and choices of its four presidents since its inception as Springfield Technical College in 1965. Each president contributed in unique ways to Great Lakes' growth and, in so doing, created an important legacy for the institution. The college started with small classes, limited resources, and a lack of respect from business and industry as well as other higher education entities. As Springfield Tech gradually evolved into a recognized player, enrollment and funding increased, and it morphed into Great Lakes Community College with all of the trappings of a "comprehensive community college." It didn't make a difference who the president was— GLCC's formula of open access, low cost, and comprehensive programming was the right strategy for the time, and the college was going to grow no matter what leaders did.

Great Lakes' early presidents worked hard to expand program and service offerings. The three presidents serving from 1965 to 2002 were top-down decision makers who did little to adjust their leadership style to the changing needs of staff in an increasingly complex institution. Inevitably this led to tension between subcultures that reached a zenith in 1998, when the president responded to the demands of faculty for more salary and reduced workload by moving to replace departing full-time instructors with lower-cost part-time teachers. This established a rift between faculty and administrators that continued into the term of the current president, who was hired in 2002.

Aware of the turmoil on campus and its potentially harmful effect on the community, the Board of Trustees moved carefully in selecting a new president. The next leader would bring a leadership style and experience conducive to building relationships, valuing people, and developing a compelling institutional vision. The Board chose Aileen Bass, a woman whose past experience included positions as a full-time instructor, department chair, division dean, and vice president of academic affairs at community colleges in Florida and California. In addition to broad experience in a variety of institutions, she possessed an open and participatory approach to leadership that was conducive to inclusion. Dr. Bass's expressed goal in regard to leadership was to create a collegial environment where she would be the "first among equals."

The conventional growth model and fractured relationships that President Bass inherited at Great Lakes were not immediately conducive to her open leadership style. The size and complexity of the institution had grown to a point where people no longer communicated across the institution, preferring instead to limit their communication to operating units. Nonstop growth of programs and services contributed over time to an inefficient administrative organization excessively reliant on cumbersome systems and processes and unable to respond to rapidly shifting needs. Faculty and staff had become the "owners" and primary customers of these systems and were part of a culture resistant to, and untrusting of, change. GLCC's size and complexity also made it difficult for President Bass to get a handle on the operating goals and performance of academic and administrative units. This was exacerbated by a poorly designed assessment system that measured too much and diverted attention from key performance outcomes.

The failed 2004 millage, the changing relationship with employers, and the rift between campus subcultures brought President Bass and the executive team to the conclusion that GLCC's early leaders had confused growth with success and deluded themselves into thinking the college was secure. In today's fast-paced market, success is more than growth, and GLCC's business model would need to change to put the college back on track.

Working with a heightened sense of awareness, the executive team moved to reconnect staff to the institution by decentralizing responsibility for decisions. It developed and installed systems for program planning and evaluation that produced continuous data about performance. It redesigned faculty hiring and incentive systems to retain and reward the best faculty and attract new talent. These and other steps produced a wave of growth in programs that now have waiting lists. Questions loom, however, about GLCC's future. Is growth an optimal strategy to pursue? Can the college continue to pursue a comprehensive mission? Where will resources be found to support new initiatives? How can the college optimize its capabilities and resources to achieve superior performance?

GLCC faces challenges, but it is a step ahead of Patterson Community College. Although it is not functioning optimally, it has options for the future that involve choice. Great Lakes Community College is a *college of choice*.

Capital Community College is located in Midland, an affluent county to the west of Great Lakes County. One of the twenty wealthiest counties in the country, Midland has a diversified economy, it is served by four higher education institutions, and it has a sophisticated labor base. Two elements of the county's economic infrastructure make it a fertile ground for postsecondary education: 1) the presence of a research university and a highly educated workforce which attract high-tech start-up ventures and 2) the diversification of industries, which shields the county from economic downturns that plague other regions of the state. The affluence of the county has created a natural niche for Capital as a low-cost workforce development and transfer engine for learners of all ages and backgrounds.

The financial condition of Capital is, in a word, comfortable. Roughly 60 percent of its operating revenue comes from local tax, and it has successfully passed eight tax levies over two decades. Although the state economy is up and down because of a failure to diversify, Capital has barely felt the impact of state aid reductions. Since its establishment in 1962, it has never had to downsize, cut programs, or offer buyouts to faculty. In fact, only 50 percent of its instructional hours are taught by adjuncts, and 60 percent of its credit courses are taught by full-time faculty whose average tenure is eighteen years. Salary and working conditions at Capital are so desirable that administrators joke that faculty have to be dragged out of the institution into retirement.

Money seems to be the organizational glue that holds Capital together. Its culture can best be described as disjointed. The effects of a faculty strike nearly two decades ago linger, and an aura of mistrust permeates the relationship between faculty and administrators. This schism prevents the college from collectively moving forward on almost any initiative. Sentiment aside, however, faculty and staff are the beneficiaries of generous salaries, they work with state-of-the-art equipment in attractive facilities, and they have no interest in leaving the college. The mistrust between faculty and administrators is not over money. It is about inclusion and the power to make decisions.

A downside of the resources that Capital enjoys is complacency born of a lack of urgency. The current president, like the one before him, is a self-directed leader with a lot of resources at his disposal. The Board of Trustees is comfortable with this mode of leadership because it produces visible results that make the college look good. When a new priority comes to the attention of decision makers, it is usually funded and there is little, if any, concern about how it fits into current operations. As a result, Capital's resources are poorly managed. The president is the "strategic plan" and priorities flow from the needs and interests of executive officers.

Because of its ample resources, Capital has the ability to pursue multiple priorities. It squanders its talent and resources on bad decisions, however, and does not have a capacity for leveraging. It has all of the tools necessary for becoming a high-performing college, yet its performance falls short of its resources. Like Great Lakes, Capital Community College is a *college of choice*.

A COLLEGE OF ABUNDANCE

Harrison College, or Harrison as students, employees, and community residents refer to it, is a multicampus urban college located in one of the largest cities in the West. Its service region has both been hurt and helped by the recent economic downturn as dying industries have disappeared and new sustainable industries have been attracted through tax breaks. The college is a proven ally of business and has been a major player in attracting new industries for more than a decade. Owen Jennings is the president of Harrison and, with five years of service, he is the newest member of the executive team. The vice president of student development has been at the college for twenty-five years, the vice president of academic affairs for thirty years, and the vice president of finance for thirty-five years. While the percentage of state aid reaching the college has decreased substantially over the past decade, the college has been able to maintain its stellar reputation through innovative practices, strong leadership, and cutting edge partnerships with profit and nonprofit organizations. Harrison is not affluent, but it has become a model of excellence for community colleges across the country through its ability to leverage resources.

A modest- to well-performing institution before Jennings arrived, Harrison has thrived under his leadership. He has used a continuous improvement model to turn a contentious relationship between faculty and administrators into one of collaboration. From his first day in office, he indicated that the college would focus on its highest potential through investing in the development of its faculty and staff. Jennings believes that transformation occurs through the efforts of faculty and staff in a culture of innovation. While not ruling out the adoption of best practices from other colleges, he feels that the best learning comes from organizations that, on the surface, appear to be different from education. The college has always sought input from community, business, and government leaders; however, Jennings believes that the college could do more with its resources by exploring opportunities beyond its visual horizon. In addition, he believes that leaders can be developed at all levels in the institution and that faculty and staff are capable of using strategic capabilities to achieve superior performance.

The president's vision could not come at a better time because major changes are taking place in the state and funding is in decline. Harrison will weather the storm because of steps it had taken early in Jennings's tenure. To reduce operating costs and leverage resources, Harrison flattened its administrative organization and developed a lean architecture, which put it in constant pursuit of opportunity through increased staff capacity. Additionally, through constant pursuit of partnerships with organizations within and beyond the service area, Harrison created a network that enabled it to generate new resources and reduce operating costs through collaboration.

Harrison does not have resources that are comparable to more affluent colleges like Capital Community College, but it is operating at full capacity. Unlike highly resourced colleges, it is able to optimize capabilities without having an abundance of resources. This is because it has a clearly articulated direction that is understood and valued by faculty and staff throughout the institution. Through focused programming and extensive collaboration, the college has been able to enhance its performance. Faculty and administrative subcultures do not always agree on new directions, but there is an appreciation for the transparent nature of decision making and the value placed on organizational learning. The president is focused on transparent processes—a form of servant leadership—and participatory management. His approach to institutional culture is transactional in nature; it is keyed to maintenance of a desirable continuity by emphasizing the best people have to offer and recognizing and rewarding positive achievement. Jennings believes that by maintaining and reaffirming the existing employee base, he will be able to identify players who will champion change and bring others along. In turn, goodwill and positive effort modeled by opinion leaders will catch on with others and lead to gains in performance.

Although Harrison is subject to the same state cuts and financial constraints that the vast majority of community colleges are facing, its performance is exemplary. Why—because it has been able to optimize the capabilities of its staff and stretch its resources to perform at a level that transcends expectations. Harrison is able to envision and pursue opportunities that are unseen by other institutions. It is constantly challenging itself by asking and answering questions like: What opportunities are on the horizon? How can we locate and pursue these opportunities? How can we build and sustain advantage? Harrison College has a built-in capacity to anticipate and adapt to change in the environment while remaining true to its mission. It is an institution of *abundance*.

CHALLENGE, CHOICE, OR ABUNDANCE?

Institutions of challenge, choice, and abundance, while malleable in form and permeable in boundary, represent alternative futures for community colleges. How can a college determine what its position in the future will be? A possible starting point would be to determine the capacity it has, or does not have, and to leverage resources through the capabilities of its leaders and staff. Look at your college. Think about where it is situated today. Think about changes in the market, both real and anticipated. Think about your college's vision, capabilities, and resources and consider its competitive position. Think about the issues and challenges that are occupying the attention of leaders and staff and consider your college's ability to shape the future in years to come.

Part I

COMMUNITY COLLEGES
IN CONTEXT

1

Three Ps for the Future: Prospect, Pitfalls, and Potency

Career professionals, the senior author among them, who broke in with community colleges in the early days, have never seen anything like it. The colleges we became part of—newcomers to the game and not to be taken seriously—have become colleges of choice. Lured by a winning formula of open access, affordability, convenience, and a focus on learners, enrollment is now approaching seven million students in 1,200 colleges—not bad for institutions once considered a "junior partner." Our colleges now enroll one out of every two first-time students, they are the primary portal of access for first generation learners, and they have become a preferred provider for K–12 students, workers and employers, and adult learners moving through life transitions. In itself, this is a remarkable achievement, but there is more. Community colleges are now bracing for a tidal wave of enrollment that will include more minority students, more lower-income students, and more underprepared students than ever before. Recent projections issued by the National Center for Education Statistics call for 7.5 million students to be enrolled in community colleges by 2016—an increase of almost 14 percent over the 6.5 million students enrolled in 2005 and more than 300 percent over the 2.3 million students enrolled in 1970.[1] Call them what you will: community colleges are a smash hit—they are institutions whose time has come.

CHALLENGE, CHOICE OR ABUNDANCE?

The ride into the future is going to be bumpy. Despite their enormous success, community colleges are caught in the vortex of a revolution as

3

profound as that which brought them onto the postsecondary education scene. It is a customer revolution, a service revolution, a learning revolution, a digital revolution, an information revolution, an industry revolution, and most significantly, a revolution in organizational dynamics. Learners are coming from every direction—from companies and K–12 schools, from regional communities and nations throughout the world, and from socioeconomic backgrounds ranging from affluence to poverty. These learners have expectations and needs, and they expect colleges to respond to them—not once, but again, and again, and again. Their needs include convenience; reasonable cost; state-of-the-art technology; courses anytime, anywhere, anyplace; service on demand; amenities like close-in parking and food service; learning that is relevant to life and a career; and outcomes that meet or exceed personal goals.

Ready or not, community colleges will be profoundly transformed. The future is now, and it is one in which learners swirling among and between institutions will drive academic schedules. Control over educational delivery will shift from instructors to learners as colleges and universities make learning materials available free of charge on the Internet. The learning experience will change as electronic information and personally tailored multimedia curricula replace books and lectures as the primary medium for pedagogy. Learning communities united by common interests and technology will cross geographical and political boundaries and creates "global classroom." Credentialing and alternative award structures will change the way learning is recognized and certified. Networks of profit and nonprofit organizations pursuing mutual benefit will reshape the way institutions organize and use their resources. These are just some of the forces that are coming together to reshape the postsecondary education industry.

The short term and long term are tightly intertwined in this market with no demarcation. What will happen five years from now is being determined by what institutions are doing today. Competencies are being developed, and alliances are being formed in the hope of cornering the market on tomorrow's opportunities. In this race to the future there are colleges that will be left at the starting gate because they are consumed by challenges, others that will run the race by creating choices for themselves, and a third group that will win the race through superior performance. We call these institutions colleges of *challenge, choice,* and *abundance.* Those that fail to achieve their potential—colleges of challenge—will forego opportunity because of limited talent and resources. Colleges of choice will pursue opportunity selectively by effectively using minimal resources or squandering resources on poor decisions. Institutions that perform at the highest level—colleges of abundance—will engage in freewheeling pursuit of opportunity because of their ability to leverage resources. Small in number but lofty in achievement, these institutions will be richly rewarded.

The question of which colleges succeed and why is far from academic. The stakes are high because resources, talent, and visibility depend largely on a college's performance. To perform at the highest level, leaders will need to learn the difference between managing strategically and managing operationally and allocating dollars and leveraging resources. They will also need to learn the difference between efficiency and stretch. The differences are profound, and they challenge traditional perspectives on leadership.

PROSPECT FOR THE FUTURE

Pick up any college's vision statement or marketing materials, and the focus will almost certainly be on growth through more and better service to learners. For most colleges, growth is not only sought, it is expected. And with good reason: the community college formula of open access, convenience, comprehensive offerings, and lower cost has been practically unbeatable when it comes to market share. Most colleges have had a long history of growth in a market with established rules and few surprises. It is well known what different providers will do to attract learners, what learners are willing to pay, the ease or difficulty they will encounter in accessing programs and services, and the benefits they can expect. Yet, community colleges are now beginning to encounter simultaneous forces of *opportunity* and *constraint* that will require new rules or, at the very least, a revision of existing rules. This vastly complicates the business of making strategic choices. More importantly, it leads to questions about the prospect for community colleges when the focus is on tomorrow rather than today.

Advantages versus Constraints

Often what prevents institutions from achieving their full potential is not competencies or resources, but missed opportunity. Leaders look at the future through the lens of the present and, in so doing, undercut their institutions' capability for growth and change. A sense of possibility is as important as a sense of foreboding in inducing a college to change. However unappealing the present, leaders are unlikely to abandon the past for the future unless they can envision an alluring vista of opportunities—an *opportunity horizon.*[2] The pursuit of opportunity in the future therefore must become as vivid and real as the pursuit of goals in the present for a college to reach its full potential.

Several aspects of the opportunity horizon for community colleges hold enormous promise. Each of them is premised on operating dynamics that lead to an advantage over competitors, but each has a price. These aspects—*advantages* for lack of a better word—are described below in terms of the leverage they provide for community colleges over rivals. The costs associated with each—*constraints*—can be understood as liabilities that work against institutional capacity to pursue opportunity.

Advantages

Cutting-Edge Innovation   A new outlook on education and learning has arrived—it is everyone's business. The term "learner" is no longer confined to youth in schools, adults taking college courses, or someone engaged in a formally organized learning experience. A learner is anyone engaged in the activity of learning, anytime, anyplace, and any way. Consumers are the newest and largest learning segment in today's market. As information technologies have become friendlier and smarter, they have become intrinsic to more and more of the products and services that consumers buy. People need to know more in a market driven by technology and continuous innovation. To know more, they need to spend more time on learning—particularly active learning—which enhances their capacity to choose between product and service offerings.

Community colleges have become an integral part of this progression by becoming a convenient knowledge purveyor. The progression began with community colleges expanding their mission to become a preferred provider for individuals needing literacy skills to access and work with information; for businesses needing skilled workers to compete in a global economy; and for communities needing to grow and prosper by providing a better quality of life. The progression is now moving into its next phase: community colleges partnering with consumers to create just-in-time learning experiences that meet time- and situation-specific needs. When an instructor can meet a learner electronically or face-to-face to craft a learning experience that will meet goals unique to the learner, that constitutes cutting-edge innovation. In the years ahead, community colleges will open new opportunities for learning by working directly with clients to cocreate learning and, in so doing, increase their value to the community. This will be accomplished by a commitment to innovation that will permeate every part of the institution. The medium will be a continuing influx of new staff with new ideas who will replace large numbers of staff retiring in the years ahead.

Speed, Flexibility, and Customization   Today, most economic activity is centered on delivering customized service. Colleges and universities are not exempt from this expectation—a circumstance that has enabled faster-moving institutions like community colleges and for-profit providers to extract market share from tradition-bound rivals. By intensifying their commitment to workforce education over the past decade, community colleges have established a capability for customization that will position them favorably for the future—a capability underestimated by competitors. Customized employee learning is more than just training and development. Businesses will spend billions of dollars on it in the years ahead, particularly in a global economy that is changing all of the rules of competition.

By itself, a capability for customization will not be enough to build and sustain an advantage. More will be necessary and the "more" for colleges and universities is speed and flexibility. Program development cycles are getting shorter, competitors are offering more and better choices, and learners expect almost instantaneous service. The ability to create and deliver a service to learners that is unmatched by rivals will depend on the pace at which a college can work and its capacity for change and innovation. This suggests an important difference between community colleges and postsecondary providers; namely, the prospect of creating immediate impact through customized learning. Instructional paradigms followed by traditional providers are likely to continue to be predicated on an instructor-controlled model in which learning is delivered in increments that produce a long-term impact. The paradigm followed by community colleges is more flexible with instructors organizing learning experiences to create both immediate and longer-term impact centered on the needs and capabilities of learners.

This is not to say that long-term impact is not important in education or that traditional providers do not organize and deliver learning experiences capable of producing immediate impact. It does mean, however, that community colleges have an advantage over traditional rivals in their ability to design and deliver customized learning. They do so with greater commitment and at a pace that responds more quickly to client needs.

Learner Centered Most institutions of higher learning espouse a student-centered philosophy. However, when one moves beyond mission and marketing statements to examine patterns of interaction between faculty, staff, and students, institutional variation is evident. There are institutions that prescribe the manner in which they will relate to students, institutions that listen to students and respond to their needs, and institutions that aggressively inquire into student needs and interests to improve their chances of success. Most community colleges fall into the second and third categories, but some are beginning to pursue a fourth approach. These colleges are focused on designing and delivering services that delight students by exceeding their expectations and amaze them by anticipating and fulfilling their unexpressed needs.

Conversations with currently enrolled students and recent leavers indicate that community colleges have successfully differentiated themselves from other institutions by employing practices that place students at the center of everything they do. They accomplish this by reaching out through instructors and staff to gain insight into what students want and need. For example, convenience—a frequently expressed need—can be delivered in many forms. A college can make all of its services available on the Internet 24 hours a day, 7 days a week, 365 days a year; a one-stop center can be developed to deliver a full battery of services at entry in one location; processes and systems can be reviewed and streamlined to make navigation easy; resources can be allocated for the design and delivery of hybrid and distance courses to enable students to take courses anywhere, anyplace, anytime. Community colleges offer convenience in all of these forms and have earned a reputation for learner-centeredness by constantly searching for new and novel ways to meet or exceed student needs.

Beyond convenience, there are other ways in which community colleges exceed the performance of rivals in meeting learner needs. Consider the following:

- Smaller classes taught by instructors who are focused primarily on teaching and learning
- One-stop facilities which provide integrated services to students at entry
- Cooperative programs with K–12 schools (dual enrollment, assessment, guaranteed tuition, etc.) and employers (tuition reimbursement) that ease the path to attendance
- Instructor sensitivity to variable learning styles and the need for varied instructional modalities
- Easy-entry/easy-exit procedures for students
- A focus on delivering value through service in contrast to making service available
- Engagement in programs like Six Sigma and CQI which streamline systems to make it easier for students to navigate the educational process

Advantage will reside with those institutions that strive to provide better service to the constantly changing needs of learners. Colleges that 1) learn how to empathize with rapidly changing learner populations by changing the lens through which learners are viewed and 2) broaden the angle of the lens to obtain information that can be used to design and deliver superior service will achieve the advantage over tradition-bound rivals.

Constraints

While these advantages would appear to position community colleges for continuing growth and success, nothing is guaranteed in a turbulent market. Every advantage is counterbalanced by constraints working singly or in combination that make growth an uncertain proposition. Consider the following forces at work in the environment surrounding community colleges:

- Economic conditions indicate a deepening recession and slow recovery in the years ahead. The shocking $2 a share Bear Stearns fire sale and government bailout in March 2008 combined with a volatile stock market, declining home values, and the credit crunch following the subprime mortgage meltdown have depressed household and business spending. Add to the mix news of rising prices for energy and food, slowing U.S. factory production and a weak U.S. dollar, and the result is a significant decline in activity spread across the economy extending into the foreseeable future.
- The relationship between state governments and public colleges and universities is in flux. Michigan withheld money from public colleges and universities in 2007 to address a budget deficit while simultaneously acknowledging the critical role community colleges perform in transforming the economy. In sharp contrast, the governor of Louisiana pushed for $57 million in new money for community colleges, and the governor of Massachusetts captured national attention with a proposal to make community colleges tuition-free for all of the state's high school graduates.
- Public policy is intensifying and becoming more invasive. The implications, real or perceived, of policy initiatives like the Spellings Commission Report have captured the attention of college leaders everywhere. In *A Test of Leadership: Charting the Future of U.S. Higher Education*, the Spellings Commission challenged the foundation of quality and effectiveness in American colleges and universities by advancing concerns about access, affordability, quality, and accountability.[3] Colleges and universities were cited for providing inadequate information to high school students about postsecondary education opportunities, doing too little to enhance access for students from families of modest means, being slow to embrace innovative ideas about new methods of teaching, failing to make timely changes in the structure of financial aid programs, neglecting to provide a rationale for rising costs, and making limited information available to the public about outcomes and costs.

Beyond these forces, the cumulative effect of decreased *public support* poses a serious challenge to community colleges. Appropriations have not kept pace with costs, forcing institutions to underwrite growth by doing more with less. The operating implications of doing more with less can be readily observed on almost any community college campus. The evening English 101 class that ten years ago enrolled twenty-two students and was taught by a full-time instructor today will enroll thirty students and be taught by a part-time instructor. The skills and experience of the instructor do not matter nor does the timing of the hire. The circumstantial truth is that resources are not sufficient to integrate part-time instructors into important aspects of campus life, including contact with full-time faculty, classroom support, and evaluation of teaching effectiveness.

Community colleges are also challenged by limits on their *capability*. "Capability" refers to the human dimension of a college—its people, talent and skills, and culture. Scholars and management researchers use terms such as "competencies" and "tacit knowledge" to describe this aspect of an organization. It is as important to success and vitality as are tangible resources. To grow and improve, staff need knowledge, skills, and motivation that unleash creative talent and enable achievement of stretch goals. Attracting and retaining staff that build this capability has a lot to do with the culture of an institution and its ability to perform at a high level.

Our work with community colleges has repeatedly shown that healthy cultures are more likely to develop in colleges that foster inclusion by continuously and consistently engaging staff in strategic activities. In colleges with healthy cultures, the commitment of staff is high, attitude toward work is positive, cooperation within and between units is the norm, and the fractious effect of silos is minimized through teamwork and collaboration.

In colleges with unhealthy cultures, the opposite is true: commitment is limited to the job or the work unit, morale is flat, change is resisted, and there is little evidence of teamwork. There is an almost irreversible drift toward fragmentation in these colleges as services are created to serve more needs and specialized staff are hired to deliver the services. Silos take hold and inhibit the efforts of leaders to move the institution forward. Unhealthy cultures are not inherently good or bad. They are a by-product of infrastructure that has not kept pace with organizational scale in fast-growing institutions. Like a child moving through a growth cycle, muscles lag behind bones and movement is clumsy and uncoordinated.

In the years ahead, a better understanding of culture will be necessary if community colleges are to grow and achieve stretch goals. If the infrastructure of a college is not aligned with its scale, performance will suffer and growth targets will be missed. There are a variety of symptoms of misalignment:

Breakdown of the Workplace

- The whole becomes the sum of its parts as an institution breaks down into multiple organizations comprised of work groups (faculty, support staff, senior administrators, and middle administrators) pursuing uniquely different interests.
- Work groups become isolated by developing a "group think" mentality that distances them from other parts of the institution.
- Greater importance is assigned to attributes that differentiate staff (length of service, race and ethnicity, work group affiliation, etc.) as opposed to those that unite them around a common purpose or goal.

Impersonality

- Impersonality prevails staff become costs or "mules" valued primarily in terms of the amount of work they can handle or responsibility they can bear without a corresponding increase in resources.
- Expediency is expected and planning is not rewarded; getting things done is more important than how well they are done.
- Additional responsibility is assigned, not negotiated; nor is it recognized or rewarded.

Lack of Organizational Glue

- A strategy or vision capable of binding staff in pursuit of a common goal is absent or buried under competing interests.

Revolving Leadership

- Changes in leadership are frequent as senior administrators come and go.

The cumulative result of misalignment between infrastructure and scale is a decline in capability. As staff withdraw from the center of the college to the security of their work units, tacit knowledge goes with them. The department or work unit becomes the "college" for them, and the ability of the institution to move forward as a whole suffers.

As daunting as these constraints are, the most significant obstacle standing in the way of growth and success for community colleges is *competition*. But not in a conventional sense because competition tomorrow will be different from what it is today. As an industry, postsecondary education will become less structured as institutional boundaries become more permeable, technology change accelerates, customers demand more, and more creative competitive tactics emerge. Learners' options will multiply as more providers offer more choices. Indeed, higher education will no longer be one industry but a collection of industries that are simultaneously converging and diverging.

Postsecondary education today is partitioned into five more or less distinct entities: 1) elite four-year colleges and universities that by name and reputation control a selective market comprised of college-age youth coming from higher socioeconomic status (SES) backgrounds; 2) less selective private four-year colleges competing for high school graduates on the basis of amenities and convenience; 3) less selective public colleges and universities competing for students on the basis of location, price, and convenience; 4) for-profit providers competing for adult learners using a formula of market-relevant curricula, convenience, and customized service; and 5) community colleges competing for learners of all ages and backgrounds based on a four-pronged strategy of cost, convenience, open access, and comprehensiveness. The problem for community colleges is that this terrain will become a map of the past and not of the future, and competitive strategies that distinguish different providers today will not distinguish them in the future.

A good example is the University of Phoenix. The Apollo Group, Inc., which oversees Phoenix, has indicated that it does not expect the double-digit enrollment and revenue increases in the future that it enjoyed in previous years. Sales figures have shrunk, increasing by only 10 percent in 2006 compared to 25 percent in 2005.[4] Traditional colleges and universities are targeting Phoenix using their own online courses at a cheaper price and subsidizing the cost with government grants not available to for-profit institutions. Phoenix has responded by turning to younger students—a move that will change the way it operates and put it into direct competition with community colleges. To sustain growth, Phoenix will need to spend more because the attrition rate among younger learners is very high. It will also need to work harder to nurture the brand identity it is trying to establish as a quality provider equivalent to a traditional university. The upshot of Phoenix's changing market position is a competitive strategy that will no longer be predictable and a change in the rules of competition with community colleges.

Phoenix is one of many examples of change in the pattern of competition among institutions. Others are evident in the actions of:

- Google striking a deal with twelve research universities to digitize ten million books
- Universities making course syllabi and learning materials available free of charge on the Internet

- Learning communities developing throughout the world to acquire knowledge and skills in specific subject fields
- Business products extending into education
- Instructors forming cartels to deliver education independently of institutions
- Skilled professionals in India and Europe delivering affordable tutorial services to American learners

All of these are examples of initiatives that could blur the boundaries of competition. Conventional ways of looking at competitors will be of little help to leaders in a progressively unstructured industry. Nor will linear approaches to strategic planning, which work well with the extant structure of the industry but ineffectively in periods of change. Strategy for community colleges in an unstructured industry will be as much about competing for tomorrow's market as it is gaining advantage in today's market. Thinking about competition as a quest to grab greater market share in an extant industry is a very different perspective than a view of competition as positioning an institution for market share in an emerging industry.[5] If the goal is growth, community college leaders will need to view competition as considerably more than maximizing enrollment and resources in today's market.

Today versus Tomorrow

Since their establishment, community colleges have viewed growth as success. Rising numbers—enrollments, budgets, programs, and staff—have been the primary criterion for measuring the strength of an institution's position. But what is the meaning of growth in a market that is evolving and beyond the visual horizon of leaders and staff? How will colleges grow in an industry where learner capabilities and preferences are changing, where competitors are constantly elevating customer expectations, and technology is reducing barriers to entry?

Hamel and Prahalad believe that growth in the future will involve competition for *opportunity* rather than numbers or market share.[6] It will involve efforts by institutions to maximize opportunities within an evolving market, be they market adult learners, new populations, workers, or something else. If this is correct, the question that must be asked and answered by leaders is: given our current resources and capabilities, what opportunities should we pursue in the future? This question leads to others: What customers will we be serving in the future? Through what delivery systems will we reach learners? Who will emerge as our competitors? What will be our basis for advantage? Taken as a whole, these questions boil down to one megaquestion that leaders will need to answer to understand prospects for the future: What new skills and competencies will we need to build to establish or maintain an advantage?

Achieving an advantage was easier when colleges and universities operated in a "closed system" with established rules. The door to advantage opened for institutions with enough resources and imagination to challenge convention—a different approach to program delivery, a new design for service, a unique approach to marketing, and so forth. An industry of clones is an advantage for any institution that is not locked into a conventional managerial frame. In the "open system" that community colleges operate in today, more than resources and imagination are required to gain advantage. By "more" we mean the foresight of staff that enables an institution to envision and pursue opportunity and, by extension, to leverage its resources. The extent to which foresight is in place can be assessed by asking the following questions:

- Do leaders and staff have a clear and collective view of forces in the environment that will make the future different?
- Are leaders spending as much time and energy on determining where advantage will be found in the future as to achieving advantage today?
- Do leaders and staff share a vision for the institution and a clear sense of what they are working to build?
- Is it clear to everyone in the institution how their individual contribution links to the institution's vision?
- Do staff throughout the institution possess a deep sense of urgency about the future and what the institution must do to succeed?
- Do leaders and staff have the foresight to envision opportunity?
- Do the opportunities envisioned extend beyond the boundary of existing markets?
- Is there an explicit process for identifying and pursuing opportunities that is understood and acted on by staff throughout the institution?
- Is innovation sufficient to ensure that the institution learns faster than competitors about future opportunities?
- Do leaders and staff possess the strategic capability to pursue opportunity when they see it?[7]

Rate the faculty and staff at your college. If most of your ratings are negative, the foresight of leaders and staff is probably limited. It takes a substantially developed strategic capability among staff throughout an institution to develop an informed view of the future. This capability is not likely to develop in institutions where staff are not included in strategic conversations or engaged in strategic tasks.

The most important asset a community college can have in a turbulent environment is a strategically capable staff. Yet this asset has not received the attention from college leaders that it deserves. Before leaders can understand the importance of a strategically capable staff, they will need to acknowledge that they are less than fully in control of their institution's future. They will also need to acknowledge that what they know today—the knowledge and experience that propelled them into positions of leadership—may not be sufficient to ensure the future of an institution that is larger and more complex. Acknowledging the importance of strategic capabilities and working to develop them in staff should also serve as an admission that top management does not have better headlights than anyone else and may not have a better sense of institutional direction. If community colleges are to fully realize the future that is in front of them, the strategic capabilities of all staff will need to be developed and fully utilized.

Numerator versus Denominator

The dramatic expansion of state and regional community college systems and the transition from simple to complex organizations has propelled community colleges into a different operating mode that can be described by words like *differentiation* and *disaggregation*. At the macro level, community colleges can no longer be viewed as a collectivity that constitutes a unified national movement. Different from one another in size and location and distanced from one another by variation in regional economic conditions, coordination, and funding, they have become freewheeling entrepreneurial organizations.

At the micro level, community colleges are a study in organizational growth and complexity. To cope with growth, most institutions have adopted centralized planning and decision support systems.[8] Executive officers have cast their jobs as making strategic decisions and delegated operating decisions to deans, department chairs, and a growing number of management specialists. For long-serving faculty and staff, the college is no longer the formative institution they affiliated with—it is larger, more impersonal, and staffed by large numbers of part-time personnel. Many have retreated to the comfortable security of departments and service units, and the sense of community that once prevailed has been replaced by a silo mentality that is typical of larger institutions. Walls divide administrative units, and discipline interests divide faculty. The institution that previously served as a "home base" for many has become a collection of silos with staff participating differentially according to their interests and responsibilities.

Imagine an executive team promoting a change agenda in a college that has grown rapidly and morphed into silos. Change has two components: a numerator—outcomes or results—and a denominator—with cost (time, money, people, technology, etc.). The team knows that improving outcomes is likely to be more difficult than allocating resources to the task of change. To generate a favorable outcome, they must engage staff in a change process, gain commitment to the process, and overcome resistance. So realizing that the numerator (eliciting a favorable outcome through change) will involve a lot of work, the executive team turns to the denominator. To grow the denominator, money and time are allocated to the change process and a mandate is issued that results must reflect a return on investment.

The migration to denominators at the expense of the numerator is a whole versus sum-of-the-parts problem in community colleges. Overburdened staff working faster in silos to keep pace with growth and change will invariably experience a loss of community. In lean institutions it is incongruous to tout the value of the individual to the institution when increasing distance from colleagues and diminished involvement in the strategic affairs of the institution is the reality. Working faster and apart from colleagues amounts to a lose-lose proposition: "If I do not do more, we will not be able to meet the needs of the students who are knocking on our door. If I do more, however, I will probably not meet their needs anyway because I will take on too much and not perform effectively." What faculty and staff hear is that they are the institution's most valuable asset; what they experience is that they are expendable.

Working harder and faster in silos may enable community colleges to conserve resources and to grow, but it will not result in performance enhancement. Enhancement comes primarily from producing results that make a difference (raising the numerator) in contrast to conserving resources (reducing the denominator). With a goal of conserving resources as an intended result rather than improving the result for given resources, denominator-driven leaders are more about maintaining growth than improving performance.[9] A college that stretches its resources at the expense of quality will find that productivity may improve—but only for a while. Unless new approaches to resource leveraging are found—delivering instruction through more effective deployment of full-time faculty, finding new ways to deliver service, using experienced adjunct instructors to supplement the work of full-time faculty, streamlining systems and processes—community colleges will face serious questions about quality as results fall short of stakeholder expectations.

Strategic versus Operational

In extended conversation, dialogue among faculty and staff on campus will invariably turn to problems they are encountering in their work. A focus on problem solving is important, but often it comes at the expense of opportunity. Many times what prevents colleges from pursuing new opportunities is not insufficient resources or uncertainty about the future but the tendency of leaders and staff to look at the institution through the narrow lens of operations. A focus on operations obscures a focus on strategy, and a focus on problem solving deflects attention from opportunity. What results is a substantially underdeveloped ability to envision and pursue opportunity.

To perform at a level equal to or better than competitors, community colleges will need to balance attention to strategic and operational aspects of organizational development. This will require strategic thinking that enables leaders and staff to envision the institution in a larger context of competitors, customers, and opportunity. Operational thinking typically concentrates on practical work-related issues to program and service delivery whereas strategic thinking involves knowledge of forces in the external environment and awareness of their impact. The two are not mutually exclusive, but more often than not leaders and staff have neither the background nor the time and inclination to think strategically. Operational efficiency is important in any college, but if leaders and staff equate success with doing the same things better and faster than last year, the institution will be tethered to a performance standard that falls short of what stakeholders want and what competitors are doing.

When one conceives of a college as a portfolio of strategic capabilities, a whole new range of opportunities opens up. Consider the example of Sun Valley College—a fast-growing community college in the Southwest. In 2002, Sun Valley reached a point in its development where additional space was required to absorb a continuing influx of learners. It was landlocked, however, by a bustling international airport holding land for future expansion that the college needed. Operationally focused staff viewed the airport as an impediment—a necessary inconvenience for travel, a place to avoid during peak periods of traffic, and an obstacle to growth. But for Sun Valley's strategically focused new president, the airport was something different. He saw its plans for expansion as an opportunity for partnering and collaboration. He wondered why the college was not doing more with the airport in workforce training and why only limited reference was made to the airport in its strategic plan. Conversations with faculty and staff revealed the extent to which operational thinking had resulted in a foregone opportunity. Looking at the present through the narrow lens of operations made the airport an obstacle to growth, whereas looking to the future through the broad lens of strategy made it an opportunity for growth and development.

The door to opportunity opens wide for colleges with broadly developed strategic capability. This represents the *opportunity horizon* for a college—its potential for envisioning and pursuing opportunity. Most colleges work hard to allocate time and resources to operations when their future lies in the strategic domain. Just as Sun Valley College squandered its opportunity horizon, too often strategic thinking is sacrificed in favor of operational thinking. If community colleges are to grow and succeed in turbulent times, the strategic domain will need to be much better developed than it is today.

Wellness versus Vitality

Borrowing from the work of Cameron, Dutton, and Quinn, imagine an institution in which growth and the absence of major issues are equated with well-being—that is, performing effectively.[10] Growth is the key indicator of success. Imagine that faculty and staff in this institution are characterized by disengagement, self-absorption, mistrust, fatigue, burnout, and feelings of being exploited. Self-preservation is part of most interactions and professional relationships. Imagine also that consultants working with this institution see evidence of strength indicated in numbers on the upswing—continuing enrollment growth, a budget in the black, new programs being added, services being modified to meet student needs, and an up-to-date technology infrastructure. The consultants also see evidence of dissatisfaction and low morale but attribute this to growth and change. On most counts, the institution is healthy—it is growing, it doesn't have any major problems, and nothing on the horizon would seem to pose a threat to its well-being.

For the purpose of contrast, now imagine another institution in which the well-being of students and staff is at the center of virtually everything it does. Leveraging resources and staff satisfaction are the key indicators of success. Imagine that faculty and staff in this institution are characterized by engagement, commitment to students, high levels of positive energy, the pursuit of change, and a feeling of connectedness.[11] Social relationships and interactions are characterized by honesty and candor, cooperation, respect, a can-do attitude, and a "we're in it together" mindset. Attention is given to ways of enhancing the educational experience of learners and the work experience of staff to create positive feelings of self-worth. Imagine that a visiting accreditation team is awestruck by the capacity of this institution to leverage limited resources—money, staff, facilities, and technology—into truly exceptional performance through the impassioned efforts of staff. This institution is more than healthy—it is flourishing.

The internal operating climate of most community colleges is more like the first context described above. They are unquestionably healthy organizations, if growth and positive numbers are used as indices of success. If other criteria are used, however, such as staff satisfaction, organizational health becomes questionable. This leads to a series of questions about organizational health and community colleges:

- What is *organizational health*—is it wellness, the absence of illness, or something else?
- Is organizational health the same or different from *organizational vitality*?
- What is organizational vitality?
- What are the attributes of a vital organization?

Following the logic of these questions, we wonder if community colleges may be deluding themselves into a false sense of security by equating growth with organizational health or, worse yet, with vitality. Growth is important, but it is a questionable index of vitality, particularly when achieved at the expense of satisfaction. Unlike wellness, which can be defined as "the absence of illness," vitality is a developmental state involving physical and mental rigor. It is a condition of superior health that lies beyond the well-being that leaders envision for their institutions when describing them in quantitative terms. The distinctions between wellness and vitality stand out when one compares their fundamental attributes, as shown in table 1.1.

Thinking differently about organizational wellness and vitality cannot be divorced from the need to think differently about success. Leaders who equate growth with success and earnestly believe their institutions to be in good health may hinder their colleges from achieving superior performance by neglecting the human dimension of the organization. Mobilizing staff around a shared vision, leveraging resources, envisioning and pursuing opportunity, building new competencies, and embracing change require new ways of thinking about success. Just as a focus on growth will not be sufficient to engender superior performance, neither will the efforts of leaders adhering to a quantitative conception of success.

PITFALLS

Pitfalls are an unfortunate reality for any and all organizations, and community colleges are not an exception. Today most of our colleges are fac-

Table 1.1.   Wellness and Vitality

	Wellness	*Vitality*
Meaning	Absence of major problems or issues	Presence of physical and mental rigor
Criteria for success	Growth	Satisfaction, individual well-being, and leveraged resources in addition to growth
Process	Resources are stretched to accommodate growth	Resources are leveraged to enhance performance and, ultimately, growth
	Improvement is defined in quantitative terms	Improvement is defined in qualitative terms
	Individual departments are the units of analysis	Institution is the unit of analysis
Resources	Money, space, and staff	People
	Leader-driven	Driven by the collective wisdom of leaders and staff
Results	Linear growth through operational efficiency	Abundance through leveraged resources

ing five challenges, largely of their own making, that make them vulnerable in the future. These challenges will not come as a surprise to leaders and staff: 1) inattention to organizational uniqueness, differentiation, and strategy: 2) falling into the trap of complexity; 3) missing or inconsistent emphasis on quality; 4) marginal staff involvement; and 5) slow pace of change and innovation.

What is striking about these challenges is not only their pervasiveness but that they are mainly management induced. Over the years, leaders in one college after another have faced them and allowed growth and complexity to obscure their importance. Leaders work hard and expectations for performance are high, but the task of leading will only become more difficult if colleges continue to operate in their current mode. Look at what is happening in our colleges. The pace of work is accelerating and has reached a point where no one has the time or the inclination to consider whether the organization is working more effectively. People are working on treadmills that are not only moving faster but also on an incline elevated by advancing technology, instantaneous communication, and the expectation for immediate action. In time, what are now challenges could become vulnerabilities, if steps are not taken to address them.

Inattention to Organizational Uniqueness, Differentiation, and Strategy

What an institution stands for, the ways in which it is unique, and how it is different from competitors is especially important in a fast-changing market. As community colleges have grown larger and more complex, the task of crafting a unique vision and a strategy that leaders and staff can share has become more difficult. The unique identity that faculty and staff created for community colleges in their formative period has eroded. New staff do not comprehend, nor do they necessarily care about, what the institution stood for when it began. Long-serving staff are so busy keeping up with the pace of work that they do not have the time necessary to reinforce enduring values. Leaders and staff are drifting away from core principles and relying on a tried and true strategy of access, cost, and convenience to capture market share.

The world is changing, and a strategy that works today may not differentiate an institution tomorrow. For example, Ohio community colleges have long enjoyed a competitive edge based on convenience in serving the adult learner market. In April 2005, however, a presentation by representatives of Indiana Wesleyan University challenged the foundation of their advantage. Indiana Wesleyan made learning accessible and affordable through a flexible academic schedule designed to move adult learners quickly through coursework while providing maximum financial aid through an online application system. Additionally, extensive library resources were made available to students over the Internet, a guaranteed schedule of courses was offered, and textbooks and course materials were delivered directly to students. Indiana Wesleyan encouraged course and program completion and made access to its programs and services even more convenient than that of community colleges.

Current strategies may not be sufficient to differentiate community colleges from competitors. The appeal of lower cost may diminish with a new generation of learners who will pay more to get what they want. Access and convenience can easily be duplicated by competitors as technology shatters barriers to entry and acquisition of service. New approaches to strategy are needed to identify a basis for differentiation that will work in tomorrow's market. A good place to look will be in the domains of experience and value. What kinds of learning experiences can community colleges offer to students that will distinguish them from competitors? What value can they deliver to students and stakeholders that will be different from the value competitors deliver?

The Complexity Trap

Organizations typically structure themselves to fit the complexity of the external environment. Complexity is determined by 1) the variety or extent of differentiation in the mission of an organization and 2) the number of different administrative and academic units needed to serve customers and fulfill the mission.[12] In response to increasing turbulence in the external environment, community colleges have expanded their mission and added staff to perform specialized functions. The administrative organization has grown larger with layers and walls separating work units. Complex structures and processes have been developed to get work done.

The consequences of complexity are significant for any organization, but for comprehensive institutions like community colleges, they are exceedingly important. The structures and processes developed to get work done in a fast growth organization overload the system with information, new problems on top of existing problems, and heightened expectation for how much can get done. This taxes the information-processing capacity of an institution and causes individuals to shut down and conserve their energy for important needs that may arise. We can see this in the words of staff who indicate that "communication is poor in this institution" and in the actions they take to eliminate information— namely, the delete button and the circular file. We can also see it in the actions of faculty who, barraged with competing demands for their time and attention, withdraw to the security of the courses they teach and venture no further than the academic department. And, we can see it in the actions of senior administrators who respond to complexity by creating more functions and adding staff to get more work done. In many cases, the "more" takes the shape of increasingly complex systems and processes that require time and effort for implementation.

As a result, nothing is simple anymore. If something appears to be simple, it is perceived as out of sync or ineffective, and efforts are made to change it to fit the environment. An example is the institutional effectiveness system designed for a large, urban multicampus community district in the mid-1990s. The district was a complex organization in every sense of the word—it served a host of constituencies in a diverse geographic region through an array of programs and services. The internal structure of the district and its colleges was equally complex with a differentiated staff performing functions that were disconnected from one another. In designing an effectiveness assessment system, two models were consid-

ered—one a simple system comprised of ten indicators that were important to a small number of high-profile stakeholders and the other a
complex model comprised of forty indicators that represented the interests of multiple constituencies. The case made for the "simple is beautiful" model was that a ten-indicator system would be much easier for staff
to understand and implement. The case made against it was one of inade-
quacy because the simple model could not cover all of the functions performed by the district nor could it represent the interests of the wide
variety of constituencies. The ease or difficulty of implementation was not
considered important. What was important was the perceived fit between
the system and the complexity of the environment. The district, of course,
opted for the complex model and almost immediately experienced difficulty in implementing it.

Confronting and working effectively with complexity is, and will
remain, a massive challenge for community colleges. It is an underlying
cause and a symptom of many problems being experienced, including
those involving communication, staff disengagement, and low morale.
There is no quick fix, but there are steps that colleges can take to limit and
channel complexity's harmful effects, including pushing decision making
down in the organization, streamlining and simplifying systems and
processes, and finding integrating mechanisms to bind staff in the collective pursuit of goals.

Missing or Inadequate Emphasis on Quality

The visible result of undocumented quality is pressure for evidence of
outcomes. Leaders focused on the bottom line well understand the importance of growth in a competitive industry. Trouble begins, however, when
the quantitative side of performance—more students and more
resources—takes primacy over the qualitative side—enhanced value and
better outcomes. Instructors and staff are the first to know when a college
is sacrificing quality for growth. They can improve performance by what
they do in the classroom and in service delivery, but they cannot allocate
resources to improve quality, so they follow the party line. Over time, the
entire institution compromises, temporizes, rationalizes, and settles for a
focus on numbers.

A "here and now" focus prevails in many colleges. Over four decades,
growth has been the primary indicator of success, and only recently have
stakeholders begun to ask questions about quality. With quality taking a
back seat to growth, leaders have taken on the mantle of acquiring
resources to support growth. They have become progressively detached
from academic departments and operating units and ceded responsibility
for quality assessment to middle managers. Other than obvious quality

indicators like graduation rates, transfer, and employer satisfaction, leaders are not engaged in quality assessment nor are they conversant with its results. The final nail in the coffin is the inconvenience of quality. It is difficult to define and measure with any degree of precision. There are numerous stakeholders for an outcome of any kind, and their interpretations of what constitutes a "good," "marginal," or "poor" result often are at odds.

To add to the problem, leaders are constantly being challenged to do more with less. We observed the dimensions of this challenge as part of a strategic planning project with a community college in a major metropolitan area. The project involved focus group meetings with business and industry leaders and senior and midlevel college administrators. The administrators concentrated their attention on problems related to growth and funding and the need for additional resources. The focus of the employers had very little to do with growth. They were feeling the full effect of global competition and finding their employees deficient in skills that would enable success. Their remarks were pointed and strong: "We're not getting what we need from the college in workforce preparation. The quality of the students who are coming to us is not sufficient to compete. We constantly hear about the college's growth and the need for resources. What is it going to do to enable us to compete globally?" The divide between college administrators and regional employers was not simply one of differing needs but of diverging commitment to quality. In the minds of administrators, growth and resources precede quality—give us the resources, and we'll grow and deliver quality at the same time. In the mind-set of employers, quality is a commitment that is fundamental to growth and success. Resources are important, but if a commitment to quality is lacking, the competitive position of the organization is constrained.

To balance growth and quality, community colleges will need to adopt new operating principles and emphasize different success criteria. There are actions they can take to improve quality, such as avoiding practices that subtract from value (hanging on to low-performing programs and investing in low-return projects) and encouraging practices that create value (developing new and better programs, streamlining systems and processes, and providing better service). They can also sharpen the focus on quality by changing the frame of reference for performance. For example, declining market share is almost always a sign of underlying problems with a college's offerings, the value it is delivering, or what competitors are doing. Which of these factors, however, is the biggest contributor to market share? By shifting its frame of reference for performance to value delivered to students, a college can map its position in the market against the value being delivered by competitors. How much convenience is it offering in relationship to competitors? What cost benefits are being delivered? How satisfied are its stakeholders compared to stakeholders being served by competitors?

These actions require community colleges to gain a better understanding of the competition, the value they deliver to stakeholders, and what they must do to improve quality. Every college compares itself with easyto-see competitors. Colleges that want to succeed will need to broaden the sample of comparison to include competitors they cannot see and measure themselves against new competitive tactics, such as culture, talent acquisition and retention, tacit knowledge, and value delivered. In addition, they will need to compare themselves to world-class organizations outside of education to determine their capability in relationship to best practices. The point is not to tweak performance standards but to set them at a level that will significantly improve performance.

Marginal Staff Involvement

In many colleges, faculty and staff are anchored in operations but not in the strategic development of the institution. Staff get most of their information through managers who are not linked to strategy or strategic planning. In effect, they are the foot soldiers who help students navigate a system that has been set up by decision makers detached from operations. If you ask students, "How important are staff in helping you navigate the system?" the answer will often come back, "They are very important, particularly in helping me get things done and stay on track." If you ask staff to assess their role, a typical response will be, "We are underlings in the institution, but we keep this place moving. We tie up the loose ends, we clean up after faculty and administrators, and we support each other. The college could not operate without us." When faculty are asked to assess their role, a different response will come back, but a theme emerges parallel to that of staff. They are detached from the strategic development of the institution but vital to its overall success.

Organizations that have captured the momentum in their industry have one common denominator: senior administrators with an operational understanding of the institution and staff engaged in planning and decision making. Conversations with leaders in industry-leading organizations, such as Southwest Airlines, Marriott, Caterpillar, Cisco, and SAS, reveal that they are more likely to lead by asking questions than by issuing directives.[13] They encourage staff to question current practice, instead of adhering to the status quo. They set robust goals but provide support staff with considerable latitude in how to get things done. They engage staff in decision making and make sure that personnel in all parts of the organization understand the industry environment, the organization's competitive position, and what needs to be done to improve performance. They are committed to helping staff succeed in contrast to catching mistakes and ensuring compliance.

Staff in these organizations have broad exposure to forces in the external environment. They are directly involved with customers and suppliers, and they are constantly working with information about product performance. They work long hours but mostly in teams where interactive processes are used to carry out operations. They have well-developed strategic capabilities—they know the business of the organization, what customers want, and what competitors are doing. They migrate to where the action is by seeking and immersing themselves in information about best practices in a variety of organizations. Most importantly, they are passionate about the business of the organization and committed to its future success.

There is much that community colleges can learn about high performance by studying best practices in organizations outside of education. A day spent with Southwest Airlines learning about its hiring, staff development, and retention practices could be a valuable investment in culture building. A conversation with the owners of Zingerman's Deli in Michigan could help leaders understand that staff members are an organization's primary customer and that motivated staff deliver great customer service. A day on-site with Marriott studying its approach to customer care could help colleges understand the importance of staff involvement in setting standards for service delivery to students. Community colleges and for-profit organizations have much in common, but one thing stands out: they are fast-responding organizations engaged in the business of transforming lives through great service. Engaged and committed staff are the vehicle for making this happen.

Slow Pace of Innovation and Change

A challenge for institutions that have experienced continuous growth is incrementalism—a belief that they should do today what they did yesterday, only do it better. Leaders and staff know that change is essential and that innovation is the conduit through which it happens. They also know that innovation most readily occurs in a culture where people are free to try out new ideas without fear of recrimination. The problem is that lip service to this simple logic is much easier than doing it.

Let's look at the approach to innovation followed by a fictitious community college in the Midwest called Opportunity Community College ("Opportunity"). Opportunity believes in and practices continuous innovation. Its approach begins with the president and executive team establishing a sense of urgency—an overarching theme on which to focus innovation. For example, making services provided to students the best in the region or dramatically improving quality to prepare the best-trained workers in the state. Managers at all levels set specific targets to guide innovation based on outperforming rivals on specific dimensions of competition. The targets aren't general like "redesign student services" or "develop a new delivery system for workforce education." Opportunity's managers and staff work together to set demanding goals like surprising and delighting students by delivering services that dramatically exceed their expectations. To get into motion, they create off-line project teams that identify specific actions that units need to take to design and deliver unparalleled service. These teams work with goals that are focused and demanding. At the same time, they enjoy considerable freedom to decide how to achieve a goal. Staff are encouraged to be creative and to channel innovation in specific directions, measured against rigorous goals and deadlines. Over time, innovation becomes a way of life within the college and transforms the operating environment.

In stark contrast are the operating environments of colleges that are organized to squeeze out efficiencies. They have produced economies of scale by proportionally reducing the number of full-time positions and expanding responsibilities, but they've retained the silos that thwart innovation. Moreover, the jury is out on the leadership academies many colleges have launched to spur engagement and innovation. Sustaining the momentum of programs in which personnel have been empowered to think and act as leaders is a tricky business, particularly when newly empowered leaders run into line managers who are playing by the old rules. Unless these programs are aimed at operationally relevant tasks, they leave staff wondering what they are being empowered to do. That is where results-driven for-profit organizations have a big edge. They know what drives results and adjust management systems and operating procedures accordingly.

A capacity for continuous innovation is critical in a fast-moving market. In community colleges, this capacity has been restrained by management practices that put operations ahead of opportunity and getting work done ahead of doing things differently. Leaders have not attended to the ingredients that go into a healthy culture—one capable of encouraging innovation. Leading and managing an innovation-driven work environment is not for the faint of heart. It will take perseverance, flexibility, and commitment. Leaders who adopt this framework will create a culture that attracts and retains talented staff. Ultimately, how leaders and staff think about their institution and their work is what makes a community college effective or ineffective. It's also the secret to avoiding pitfalls that constrain performance when colleges direct more energy to solving problems than creating opportunities.

POTENCY

The idea that the strength of an organization—its *potency*—may depend as much on the virtuous behavior of leaders as it does on its ability to solve problems, is a different way of thinking about organizations. Potency implies an ability to achieve or bring about a desirable result. In the operating context of community colleges, it is the capacity to produce a strong effect through the efforts of leaders and staff. It can perhaps be most easily understood as the difference between work and commitment. People will work for money, but they will commit to a cause. Institutions that are *potent* comprise committed people with a "collective efficacy" for results. Bandura defines collective efficacy as "a group's shared belief in its conjoint capabilities to organize and execute a course of action required to produce a desired level of attainment."[14] Leaders and staff in potent organizations use terms such as "attachment," "enjoyment," "belonging," and "community" to describe their experience in the organization. They express a strong sense of commitment, they ascribe meaning to their work, they gain satisfaction from it, and they hold positive feelings toward colleagues. Contrast this with the experience of leaders and staff in ineffectual organizations where feelings of frustration, divisiveness, fatigue, aggression, and dissatisfaction are commonplace.

Potency is an important aspect of organizational behavior in community colleges because it has a lot to do with the ability of a college to achieve favorable results. Potency increases when staff feel a strong sense of self-determination, in other words, when they have control over their lives, where they are going, and what they are doing. Only when leaders and staff feel congruence between their personal needs and the mission and objectives of the institution can they experience a sense of total involvement and commitment. Congruence leads to a sense of impact—a belief widely shared among staff that they have a voice in where the institution is going, that their actions make a difference, and that each individual has the power to affect organizational performance. It also leads to a sense of competence, realized in the personal growth and development that comes with exposure to new ideas and realms of experience—a feeling that one is learning new things. Organizations that are capable of generating positive feelings in staff are operating in an *abundance* mode.[15]

For the sake of contrast, let's describe an organization operating at a low level of potency—one that is delivering less than adequate results. Leaders and staff in this organization are part of a divisive culture. They take little enjoyment from their work and self-centeredness prevails. Staff are focused on taking care of their own needs and are not inclined to help others. There is a limited sense of belonging and a marginal sense of community. Interactions are marred by a lack of mutual respect, and people do not trust one another. This organization is operating in a *deficit* mode.[16] Staff cannot readily identify with the organization or their work, and they are not personally bound to its successes or failures. In this way, their perceptions of membership and belonging, or the lack thereof, diminish the ability of the organization to achieve favorable results.

The vast majority of thinking and dialogue about organizations approaches them from a deficit-correcting or problem-solving perspective. More attention is directed to problems inside the organization that affect performance such as inefficiency, low morale, or resistance to change than to attributes which produce positive outcomes.[17] This tendency extends to organizations of every kind, including business (positive terms like *caring, compassion,* and *goodness* seldom appear in business journals); medicine (studies of factors contributing to illness outnumber studies of factors contributing to health); and education (an emphasis on problem solving in organizations dominates the published literature and research).[18] The effect is to undercut the potential of an organization, and hence its capability, for producing superior outcomes. Institutions that work from a *deficit-correcting perspective* produce incremental gains as resources are committed to eliminating problems that stand in the way of getting work done.

Conversely, institutions that work from an *abundance perspective*— valuing strengths and leveraging resources—generate outcomes that are disproportionate to the resources they are working with. The difference between creating the positive and eliminating the negative is subtle but potentially powerful, and it has important implications for organizational development in community colleges.

We see a parallel between the deficit-correcting perspective and the capacity of community colleges to deliver superior results (that is, their potency). If a college has problems with its administrative organization or its personnel, correcting these problems is vitally important for its success and, quite naturally, becomes the focus of attention. Unfortunately, correcting problems may not be enough to achieve high performance. In the same way that a person's health is more than a lack of illness, the best possible outcome for a college may not lie in the correction of problems. For this reason, we view an abundance perspective on organizational development as vitally important to the future of community colleges. Differences between the deficit-correcting and abundance perspectives and their relationship to organizational potency in community colleges are illustrated in table 1.2.

A deficit-correcting approach to organizational development would attribute value to actions that resolve problems and maintain equilibrium. An abundance approach would attribute value to actions that enhance strengths and elicit favorable outcomes. Let's use a fitness analogy to

Table 1.2.   Perspectives on Organizational Development and Potency in Community Colleges

Dimension of Organizational Behavior	Perspective on Organizational Development	
	Deficit-Correcting	Abundance
Focus of Leaders	Eliminating problems	Valuing strengths
Objective	Operational efficiency	Leveraging resources
Method	Identify problems	Identify elements of success
	Analyze root causes	Determine enhancements
	Design interventions that solve problems	Design interventions create an ideal future
Change	Incremental	Optimization
Result	Stasis	High performance
Interpretation of Potency	*Institutions that are strong overcome major problems*	*Institutions that are strong embrace and enable highest potential*

illustrate the implications of these approaches for leadership and management in community colleges.

Physicians and psychologists have long concentrated on how to cure diseases—that is, how to take individuals from a negative state of illness to a neutral state called "normal." While curing disease is obviously a worthwhile endeavor, only recently have medicine and psychology paid attention to how individuals can achieve a positive state of well-being—that is, a state of excellence or "abundance." Physicians and psychologists are now making a distinction between wellness (the absence of illness) and superior health and describing it, in the words of Seligman, as "how to go from plus two to plus seven" and "not just how to go from minus five to minus three and feel a little bit better."[19] Applied to community colleges, a perspective of superior health would mean approaching leadership and management not in terms of how to make adjustments or improvements to take the institution from a negative to a neutral state. Rather, the goal would be to elevate the institution to a state of enhanced well-being and superior performance. As such, approaching organizational development from a perspective of abundance would assume that every college has a positive core that, if uncovered and tapped, would unleash positive energy.

The key to abundance is leveraging—the capacity of an institution to achieve superior performance through the optimal use of its resources. Having resources (people, money, facilities, and technology) is akin to having players and talent on a team. Leveraging is about how to coach and manage these players to get the most out of them and optimize a team's chances for victory. Resources will enhance the ability of an institution to produce superior outcomes, but their effect will be multiplied by leaders who know how to leverage them to their fullest potential.

PATHWAYS TO THE FUTURE

Are all colleges abundant?—the answer is *no*. Are all colleges capable of achieving abundance?—the answer is *maybe*. The path to the future will not be uniform for community colleges. They have grown apart from one another as they have become larger and more complex. In contrast to a tightly coupled national movement, they are evolving into a loosely coupled regional movement. This evolution will involve different futures for colleges based on variation in their operating resources, their demographic and economic circumstances, the quality of their leadership and management, and the talent and motivation of their staff. A small number of institutions, identified as *colleges of challenge*, will experience a future marked by continuing threats to their survival rooted in conditions of resource deprivation, marginal staff capability, and ineffective leadership. A significantly larger number of institutions, termed *colleges of choice*, will have access to resources through ascription or achievement but will perform at a level that falls short of their ability. Finally a select group of institutions with a combination of favorable external conditions, leveraged resources, and strong leadership will achieve superior performance outcomes and achieve a state of prosperity. These institutions, identified as *colleges of abundance*, will become exemplars for community college development.

Existing approaches to the study of organizations do not focus on superior performance as a corollary of abundance and leveraging. They have helped institutions and leaders understand factors that contribute to poor performance but have failed to address those that lead to abundance. Our objective in the chapters that follow is to create a picture of what abundance is in community colleges and alternative futures that community colleges will encounter based on their ability to achieve abundance.

We begin the journey by examining the external environment in which community colleges operate (chapter 2) and their capacity to respond to forces in this environment (chapter 3). In chapter 4 we describe the concept of abundance as a foundation for depicting alternative futures for community colleges. The different futures we envision are described in chapters 5, 6, and 7 using illustrations derived from institutional case studies, interviews with community college leaders, and campus projects. We bring the concept of abundance to life as a tool for organizational development in chapter 8 by describing actions that community college leaders and staff will need to take to elevate performance.

NOTES

1. National Center for Educational Statistics, *The Condition of Education, 2007* (Washington, DC: U.S. Department of Education, 2007).

2. G. Hamel and C. K. Prahalad, *Competing for the Future* (Boston: Harvard Business School Press, 1994), 71.

3. The Secretary of Education's Commission on the Future of Higher Education, *A Test of Leadership: Charting the Future of U.S. Higher Education* (Washington, DC: U.S. Department of Education, 2006).

4. "Growth at University of Phoenix Slumps as Competition Rises," *Community College Week* 19, no. 21, (June 18, 2007): 17.

5. Hamel and Prahalad, *Competing for the Future,* 42.

6. Hamel and Prahalad, *Competing for the Future,* 31.

7. The framework for these questions is derived from the work of Hamel and Prahalad in *Competing for the Future.*

8. R. Alfred and P. Carter, "Organizational Change and Development in Community Colleges," *Higher Education Handbook of Theory and Research* (New York: Agathon Press, November 1997).

9. Hamel and Prahalad, *Competing for the Future*, 159.

10. K. Cameron, J. Dutton, and R. Quinn, "Foundations of Positive Organizational Scholarship," in *Positive Organizational Scholarship*, eds. K. Cameron, J. Dutton, and R. Quinn, 1–19 (San Francisco: Berret-Kohler, 2003).

11. Cameron, Dutton, and Quinn, "Foundations of Positive Organizational Scholarship," 1–19.

12. K. Dooley, "Organizational Complexity," in *International Encyclopedia of Business and Management*, ed. M. Warner, 5013–5022 (London: Thompson Learning, 2002).

13. Conversations with executive officers of high performing corporations were carried out between 2003 and 2007 as part of learning site visits conducted by the Strategic Horizon Program and sponsored by the Center for Community College Development.

14. A. Bandura, *Self Efficacy: The Exercise of Control* (New York: W. H. Freeman, 1997).

15. Cameron, Dutton, and Quinn, "Foundations of Positive Organizational Scholarship," 1–5.

16. Cameron, Dutton, and Quinn, "Foundations of Positive Organizational Scholarship," 1–5.

17. K. Cameron and A. Caza, "Contributions to the Discipline of Positive Organizational Scholarship," *American Behavioral Scientist* 47, no. 6 (2004): 731–738.

18. Cameron and Caza, "Contributions to the Discipline," 731–738.

19. M. Seligman, *Authentic Happiness* (New York: Free Press, 2002).

2

Portrait of a Changing Landscape

Community colleges are operating in a landscape today that is beyond anything they envisioned or have encountered. What makes this landscape special is the intersection of demographic, economic, technological, and competitive forces that are reshaping life patterns and fundamentally altering the terrain upon which institutions work. Think for a moment about the dramatic changes in our lives created by electronic devices that provide instant access to people, information, goods, and services. Consider the effect of domestic policies on our movement in space and time. Marvel at the transparency of behavior in organizations, states, and nations in a world made smaller by technology. Reflect on the stories that command our attention now and compare them to those that commanded our attention fifteen years ago:

- Soviet Union dissolves as individual nations declare independence
- United States commences military operations against Iraq in the first Gulf War
- Apartheid is repealed in South Africa
- Racial conflict in America plays out through the beating of Rodney King
- Eastern Airlines and Pan Am cease operations
- Exxon oil spill in Alaska brings environmental awareness to the forefront
- Magic Johnson announces that he has contracted HIV
- Jack Kevorkian brings assisted suicide into the national debate

- Sexual harassment becomes front-page news through Anita Hill's testimony in the Clarence Thomas hearings

BACK TO THE FUTURE

In 1990, CNN was new, and the primary venues for information were telephone, television, and radio. E-mail was in a stage of infancy, and written information was communicated via first-class mail; FAX was used for time-sensitive information. Today, news is delivered instantaneously to desktops and cell phones. Before e-mail and blogs, elected officials and governments could choose their own timing for the release of information. Today, technology-enabled news media deliver information about events and circumstances as they unfold. In the early 1990s, money was made through traditional pathways in established organizations. Today, money is just as likely to be made through entrepreneurial opportunities in start-up organizations. Yesterday, teachers controlled the content and logistics of instructional delivery. Today, students expect instruction to be delivered when they want it, where they want it, and how they want it. Services once offered through direct contact with staff between 8 and 5 during the workweek are now available 24 hours a day, 7 days a week, 365 days a year on the Internet.

Lines between personal and professional spaces have blurred as learners expect continuous access to instructors and staff through e-mail, cell phones, and PDAs. Staff and learners alike carry Blackberries to receive and view instant messages. Those who work in colleges are not only part of an educational community—they are principals in a 'business' in which timely service to *customer* needs is a must. Postsecondary education has become market driven. Learners exposed to fast-moving, fast-changing organizations—restaurants, hotels, big box stores, hospitals, airlines, Amazon, and E-Bay—expect market-savvy service. As educational delivery becomes more consumer-oriented, systems and processes must meet consumer expectations. The information colleges deliver to the public must be engaging and attractive or face the prospect of being ignored. Learners face an avalanche of information every waking minute. They have too many choices and too little time—only the most compelling information will capture their attention.

Finally, and perhaps most importantly, community colleges are serving a populace that is increasingly diverse. To thrive, colleges must engage learners of varying backgrounds, persuasions, and interests while competing with educational providers throughout the world. Thinking globally and acting locally have never been more important. The emergence of world-class companies in developing nations is a shift that will pose a major challenge to the supremacy of established economies. Rather than competition among three or four countries that have long dominated global commerce, the landscape is one of multiple geographies involving fierce competition from firms in China, India, Brazil, Mexico, and Russia. These firms are challenging entire industries—from farm equipment and appliances to aircraft and telecom services—and will become influential players in a global higher-education industry. They can tap into large pools of talented workers and low-cost resources and bring to the market an unseen level of diversity. Diversity is not simply about changing demographics through birth rates and in-migration. It is also about the expansion onto Western soil of multinational firms staffed with expertly trained workers who are products of rapidly developing school systems in different parts of the world.

The implications of these forces for community colleges are clear: To anticipate the future, forces of change will need to be better understood. What leaders and staff know about, and how they react to, forces swirling around their institutions have a lot to do with performance.

EXTERNAL TRENDS AND FORCES

A Knowledge Economy

National and global economic forces in the last two decades have hastened the demise of manufacturing and ushered in a knowledge economy. Workers who prospered in the predictable pace of the manufacturing economy without the benefit of postsecondary education face an uncertain future. A worldwide market has developed in which low-wage work is being outsourced to countries with large numbers of skilled workers willing to work for less. For most of the twentieth century the United States could take pride in having the best educated workforce in the world. Over the last thirty years, however, one country after another has surpassed us in the proportion of their entering workforce with the equivalent of a high school diploma, and many more are on the verge of doing so.[1] At one time, the United States could lay claim to having 30 percent of the world's college students. Today, that proportion has fallen to 14 percent and is continuing to fall.[2] Yesterday, a high school diploma, a strong work ethic, and a connection with organized labor were the currency for attainment in an industrial economy. Today, advanced education aimed at producing critical thinking skills is the currency of attainment in a knowledge economy.

Community colleges will bloom in role and importance in the knowledge economy. The diminished power of regions and nations to control economic competition will force them to engage in a global war for knowledge. Education will become increasingly important as work shifts away from occupations rooted in production to occupations emphasizing knowledge and information.[3] Individuals will find work skills becoming obsolete at a faster pace and will be impelled to embrace lifelong learning as a means for keeping up with advancing technology. Their employment will change often as firms and industries compete globally and adopt new technologies and approaches to the organization of work.

Economic Globalization

Economic globalization involves the worldwide integration of markets for goods, services, labor, and capital. Research points to the capability of globalization to undermine the ability of governments to directly influence the economy. Prior to globalization, increasing labor costs—wages, regulation, and social benefits—were passed on to consumers in the form of higher prices.[4] This is no longer possible as low-cost imports undercut the price of goods made by American workers. Additionally, because capital is globally mobile and technological advances reduce geographic barriers to market entry, corporations often have profit incentives to relocate their operations to countries where lower wages can be paid for an equal or higher level of quality.[5]

Free trade, foreign investment, and the proliferation of technology enabling work to be done anywhere are three facets of economic globalization that have helped the economies of developing countries. Liberal market economies like the United States and the United Kingdom will continue to be successful because of their ability to lead innovation in new industries, such as biotechnology.[6] However, innovation can be replicated at lower cost by highly skilled workers in countries with lower labor costs. In *The World Is Flat* Thomas Friedman aptly describes the global transformation to a knowledge economy and the success of developing countries in transitioning from unprofitable manufacturing to innovative knowledge-intensive industries.[7]

These nations have made massive investments in education that are beginning to bear fruit. The 'Asian Tiger' economies of Singapore, Taiwan, and South Korea have used education as the cornerstone of economic policy to move from low-value-added manufacturing to white-collar industries. These economies are not alone in using education policy as the handmaiden of economic policy. In England and the United Kingdom, policymaking is increasingly dominated by economic concerns as economically attractive industries are identified, and institutions of higher learning and students are given financial incentives to supply and enroll in relevant courses and curricula.[8]

These global trends have important implications for American community colleges. As education plays an increasingly prominent role in economic competitiveness, national governments have a stronger incentive to integrate education and economic policy. These prospects are limited in federalist countries like the United States and Germany where state education policy is more powerful than national education policy. However, the passage of No Child Left Behind (NCLB) signaled a stronger role for the federal government in K–12 education policy. Part of the rationale behind NCLB was the declining competitiveness of America's youth in comparison to other countries. These concerns were first voiced in 1981 with the publication of *A Nation at Risk*.[9] Given the increasingly competitive nature of the global economy, cross-national comparisons of educational achievement have become important indicators of future economic prosperity.

The Organization for Economic Cooperation and Development (OECD), a global leader in international research on education, has developed the Programme for International Student Assessment (PISA) test, which is designed to compare achievement across nations.[10] Administered to representative samples of fifteen-year-olds in OECD countries and in non-OECD countries, results of the 2003 PISA tests in math and reading reveal that in math, U.S. students ranked twenty-fourth out of twenty-nine OECD countries and twenty-ninth out of forty participating countries.[11] U.S. students scored higher than their peers in Brazil, Turkey, and Italy but lower than students in Hungary, Latvia, Poland, the Slovak Republic, China, Korea, and Japan. U.S. students fared only slightly better in reading, ranking sixteenth out of twenty-nine OECD countries and nineteenth out of forty participating countries. Additionally, U.S. students evidenced higher variance in their scores than other countries. A small proportion of U.S. students score very high, and a large proportion score very low.

These peer comparisons raise important questions about the capability of the United States to compete in a global economy. The obvious question is one of preeminence—will the United States be able to maintain its position as a world economic leader? Subsidiary questions arise about the capability of K–12 education to prepare youth for a changing world order and the resources available to colleges and universities to prepare a world class workforce. As cross-national comparisons of achievement proliferate, concerns about international competitiveness will grow, and more aggressive policy initiatives can be expected from the federal government.

The Spellings Commission on Higher Education is precursor to a changing federal position on higher education. The recommendations in its 2006 report have clear implications for colleges and universities:[12]

- Better academic preparation in K–12 schools for postsecondary education
- Simplified and restructured financial aid
- A robust culture of accountability and transparency, including a new 'unit record' database that would track student progress
- Provision of grants to colleges and universities that test their students and report the results
- Targeted federal investment in knowledge arenas critical to America's competitiveness, such as science, math, and foreign languages
- Strategy to promote lifelong learning

Policymaking initiatives can be surmised from these recommendations. As linkages between K–12 and higher education are tightened, an increased focus on ensuring that high school graduates are ready for college-level work can be anticipated. Policymakers are likely to channel students with significant remediation needs toward community colleges rather than baccalaureate institutions—implying an even greater remediation role for community colleges. Interestingly, illiteracy/innumeracy is given high government priority in the United Kingdom as both an economic and social problem. Colleges are provided with stipends to enroll basic skills students, whereas in the United States basic skills are accorded low priority by states and the federal government.[13] To the degree that community colleges can recast low literacy and numeracy rates as an economic issue, federal and state governments may be more likely to provide special funding for basic skills and remediation.

Community colleges will also be expected to show robust evidence of student learning outcomes. Initial drafts of the Spellings Commission report went as far as to recommend replacing the accreditation system with state regulatory agencies. Accreditation agencies serve as a buffer between postsecondary education institutions and state and federal agencies that demand more accountability.[14] As the federal government has pushed for more evidence of accountability, accrediting agencies have been constrained to require evidence of student learning outcomes from colleges and universities. The current system of accreditation will likely continue unchallenged if lawmakers feel the response of regional agencies to government policy initiatives is sufficiently rigorous. A clear outcome of this push-pull interplay, however, will be an increase in demands for evidence of program effectiveness. Community colleges with well-developed assessment systems will be in a strong position to adjust to these changes while those with inadequate systems will find themselves scrambling to put systems in place to meet government mandates.

Outsourcing and Offshoring

Economic competition is most often discussed in terms of nations, but in a global economy dominated by multinational corporations, the economic development of local communities is a more pertinent focus. Should Toyota locate its new plant in Georgetown, Kentucky; Livonia, Michigan; or Tianjin, China? This decision depends on a complex set of factors including labor costs, the availability of skilled labor, and access to job training programs in the local community.

Offshoring refers to the performance of domestic work in a foreign country whereas *outsourcing* refers to hiring a third party to perform the activities. Offshoring has received more media attention than outsourcing because it involves jobs lost to foreign competition. Offshoring typically refers to white-collar jobs as opposed to manufacturing jobs. Goldman Sachs has estimated that offshoring accounted for a half million layoffs in the United States from 2002–2004, while Forrester, an information technology consulting firm, expects the number of outsourced U.S. jobs to grow from 400,000 in 2004 to 3.3 million in 2015.[15] Focusing on service-sector jobs, the McKinsey Global Institute downplayed the impact of offshoring on the U.S. economy:

> We estimate that a total of 9 percent of jobs in services in the United States could theoretically be performed remotely. However, it is unlikely that all potentially transferable jobs will move offshore over the next thirty years, because of the considerable barriers to offshoring . . . Assuming that half the potentially transferable service jobs—a more realistic estimate, although still high—are actually relocated offshore over that period, the resulting job turnover would be around 225,000 jobs per year—or 1–2 percent of the 16 million jobs created per year in the U.S. economy.[16]

Outsourcing, offshoring, and the loss of manufacturing jobs clearly has important implications for the nation and for community colleges, the effects of which are distributed unevenly throughout the country. For example, "Rust Belt" states, such as Ohio and Michigan, have been particularly hard hit by manufacturing losses. California has more to lose from offshoring because a higher proportion of workers are employed in information technology, which is particularly vulnerable to offshoring. Community colleges face daunting challenges in localities where the void left by departed manufacturing jobs has not been filled by service-sector jobs. Depressed states are often unwilling or unable to sufficiently fund community colleges although these colleges are a primary engine for economic growth. This can easily culminate in a vicious cycle in which emaciated regional economies fail to adequately fund community colleges, which in turn fail to help stimulate the economy, which in turn leads to further stagnation.

LABOR MARKET TRENDS

Labor market trends are a critical dimension of the external environment because they provide timely information about careers and jobs that community colleges use to calibrate programs and curricula with market needs. In today's turbulent work environment, jobs and careers are anything but static. The green movement and advancing technology, particularly digitization and miniaturization, are opening up new industries, and jobs are being reconfigured to match changing knowledge and skill requirements. The design of work is changing, and more and more work is being carried out in digitized form. From X-rays used for medical diagnostic purposes to songs, movies, architectural drawings, and technical papers, work is saved in memory files and transmitted instantly over the Internet to someone near or far who makes use of it in a variety of ways. Employers have access to a worldwide workforce comprising people who do not have to move to participate in global work teams. American workers are now in direct competition with workers throughout the world.

Growth Occupations

Projections about occupations in which the most jobs will grow are an important source of information for enrollment planning and program development. Information about occupational growth and "hot jobs" is in ample supply through industry reports and projections, think tank projections, and government reports, including projections of occupational growth published annually by the Bureau of Labor Statistics (BLS). If colleges choose to focus on hard numbers, the Bureau of Labor Statistics projections of occupational growth show that, consistent with trends in the global economy, major growth is expected in computer and mathematical occupations, education and training occupations, health care occupations, and "green jobs."[17]

Growth in health-related occupations reflects, among other things, an aging population that requires more care and medical advances that permit more aggressive treatment of health-related problems. The "green movement" is creating jobs in renewable energy and sustainability, including wind and solar technicians, eco-friendly construction managers, clean energy auditors, waste disposal managers, air quality engineers, agricultural inspectors, and environmental health and safety technicians. The U.S. Department of Labor has yet to project the number of jobs that could be created by the green movement, but industry reports predict growth ranging from conservative to a jobs bonanza similar to the information technology boom a decade ago. An analysis by the Apollo Alliance, a leading coalition of labor and environmental leaders, projected that an investment of $30 billion per year in sustainable energy has the potential to create 3.3 million jobs and boost the nation's gross domestic product by $1.4 trillion. The same analysis found that twenty-one jobs are created for every $1 million invested in the energy efficiency industry.[18] These trends suggest that job growth and transition will occur in new and existing occupations, and community colleges, as a preferred provider, can expect pressure for skilled workers from employers and for market share from competitors.

General labor market data are helpful as a predictor of job growth and decline, but trends for specific occupations yield better information for program planning in community colleges. Bureau of Labor Statistics data for jobs that typically require an associate's degree or an occupational certificate show that the fastest rate of growth will occur in midlevel occupations that provide trained technical assistance to higher level professionals. Registered nurses are projected to have the fastest growth rate, adding more than 703,000 jobs between 2004 and 2014.[19] Nursing aides, orderlies, and attendants rank second, with an expected growth of 325,000 jobs. Preschool teachers, auto mechanics, and LPN/vocational nurses round out the top five.[20] Rapid growth is also expected in the fields of medical assisting, information technology, secretarial support, and automotive repair.

The picture changes when the universe of occupations is expanded to include fields requiring an associate degree or bachelor's degree (not including graduate or professional degrees). Twenty-one of the twenty-five fastest growing occupations require a bachelor's degree with nursing the top ranked occupation followed by computer-oriented professions and education.[21] Occupations projected to have the largest decline from 2002–2012 are lower-level occupations requiring on-the-job training in contrast to formal education—farming, office clerks, computer operators, office machine operators, word processors, and the like.[22] Job losses for these occupations are due primarily to automation and competition from low-cost foreign labor. Workers in these and related occupations will face high unemployment and will need further education to prepare for new careers. Community colleges will be a major resource for limited skill workers if they are aware of what colleges have to offer.

Manufacturing does not appear on the list of occupations projected to undergo decline because it is divided into two strands: *old* manufacturing that is declining and *new* manufacturing which is growing.[23] Old manufacturing encompasses industrial-age technologies, and new manufacturing encompasses high-tech technologies, such as nanotechnology. According to the Council on Competitiveness, there is strong demand for skilled workers in high-tech manufacturing.[24] Similarly, the National Association of Manufacturers has projected a need for ten million new skilled workers in high-tech jobs by 2020.[25] The implications for community colleges engaged in manufacturing technology are significant and will require that they monitor occupational projection data and technology advances in different manufacturing fields as a requisite for identifying occupations in high demand.

DEMOGRAPHIC TRENDS

Age Distribution

Information about demographic trends is important because of its utility as a benchmark for enrollment and program planning in community colleges. U.S. census data show that from 2000 to 2050, the United States population is expected to increase from 280 to 420 million.[26] A breakdown of population by age group reveals that the percentage of people sixty-five or older is expected to rise from 12 percent in 2000 to 20 percent in 2030.[27] The percentage of persons eighty-five or older is also expected to rise due to medical advances. These trends will have profound implications for the labor market and for community college enrollments. As baby boomers reach retirement age, the number of persons retiring annually will grow dramatically as will the number of people over sixty-five who continue to work. Demand for customized training will intensify, and community colleges offering retraining programs and leisure and recreational learning opportunities will flourish.

Race and Ethnicity

Demographic projections from the U.S. Census Bureau (2004) show the percentage of the U.S. population that is nonwhite will increase dramatically in the next fifty years.[28] African-American, Asian, and mixed race populations will continue to increase, but the increase in the nonwhite population will be dominated by growth of the Hispanic population. Community colleges are generally more diverse than the U.S. population as a whole, and these population projections suggest that they will become even more diverse in the future.

K–12 AND POSTSECONDARY ENROLLMENT

Projections related to K–12 enrollments are also important for enrollment and program planning. Total K–12 enrollment was approximately forty-six million in 1990 and is projected to rise to fifty-seven million by 2014.[29] Growth will be stagnant between 2007 and 2014, and for grades 9–12 there is even a predicted decline in enrollment. These projections have profound implications for community colleges because a substantial proportion of enrollment is derived from graduating high school students. Finding ways to attract a greater number of high school graduates and to increase the number of dual enrollment students will be important. These trends differ dramatically among states and localities within states, thereby increasing the importance of regional projection.

High School Graduates

The number of students projected to graduate from high school, many of which will attend community colleges, is another important statistic for community colleges. Nationally, a 10.7 percent increase in the number of high school graduates from 2000–13 is expected, but this figure is down from a 14.1 percent gain between 2000 and 2007.[30] The percentage change varies dramatically from state to state. For example, between 2000–2013, the number of high school graduates is expected to increase by 70 percent in Nevada and 30 percent in Florida and Arizona but is expected to decline by more than 20 percent in South Dakota, Montana, Wyoming, the District of Columbia, and North Dakota.

Postsecondary Education Enrollment

Overall, postsecondary enrollment totaled fourteen million in 1990 and is expected to grow to nineteen million by 2014.[31] Public two-year and four-year colleges are expected to maintain their position as the dominant postsecondary institutions in terms of enrollment. Public community colleges are projected to enroll 7.1 million students by 2014 while public four-year colleges and universities will enroll 7.7 million students, and private four-year colleges will enroll 4.3 million students.[32]

TECHNOLOGY

Technology is radically changing the knowledge industry and opening postsecondary education to new competitors. A distance education provider from San Francisco or Singapore can compete for students in Oklahoma and Florida, new players using innovative technology can enter the market, and incentives abound for market entry of for-profit corporations. Two examples reveal the leveraging effect of technology: 1) companies previously publishing textbooks are now developing and offering entire online courses and 2) the entry of the Washington Post into postsecondary education through its subsidiaries, Kaplan Test Prep and Kaplan Higher Education, offering degree and certificate programs throughout the country.

Technology and Economies of Scale

Economies of scale enabled by technology could lead to oligopolies in distance education. The idea behind economies of scale is simple—the fixed costs for designing a distance education course are quite high, while the variable costs are much lower than classroom delivery. This means that the cost per customer will decline rapidly as the number of customers grows. Currently, community college instructors design their own courses or collaborate with colleagues in course design. The health division at Monroe County Community College in Michigan, for example, teams with a network of regional colleges in designing online courses. When a faculty member at one college designs an online nursing course, students at other colleges are eligible to enroll in the course, thereby eliminating the cost of course design for network colleges.

It is not unreasonable to imagine a corporate competitor raising equity over time to develop distance education courses in allied health. It would hire the best medical researchers, curriculum designers, programmers, and human computer interaction (HCI) experts available and, over the long term, deliver a market-leading product to a large consumer base. In 2003, for-profit corporations controlled 41 percent of the then $3.5 billion online education market.[33] Although for-profit providers enroll only 4 percent of postsecondary students, they serve 33 percent of all distance education students.[34]

Open Sourcing

Why not take the 'Race in America' class from Cornell West or economics from Paul Krugman? This is the promise of open sourcing—the act of releasing previously proprietary software, in this case educational materials, under an open source/free software license. The Massachusetts Institute of Technology has been the pioneer of open sourcing and defines its OpenCourseWare project as follows:

> Welcome to MIT's OpenCourseWare: a free and open educational resource for faculty, students, and self-learners around the world. OCW supports MIT's mission to advance knowledge and education, and serve the world in the 21st century. It is true to MIT's values of excellence, innovation, and leadership.[35]

MIT OpenCourseWare is easy to access and has received rave reviews from users throughout the world. One begins by selecting a discipline from a list of disciplines and clicking a class to gain free access to the class calendar, readings, lecture notes, assignments, exams, and discussion groups. Open Sourcing has unlimited potential, and other institutions are following suit and opening up their courses and curricula on the Internet. Predicated on the assumption that distance and financial barriers should not stop people from learning, open sourcing is a potential threat to the financial viability of synchronous delivery. Prospective students may choose to learn online for free instead of enrolling at a community college for face-to-face or distance classes. One drawback of open sourcing is that "free learners" cannot get feedback from teachers or credentials to show employers. However, it is not difficult to imagine scenarios where these drawbacks could be overcome, or at least minimized.

Pedagogy and Modes of Education

Contemporary researchers indicate that students learn best when experience is active and engaging. Distance education has the potential to engage learners in ways that are not possible through classroom instruction. For example, video games are now being used as learning tools. These games follow a 'play, fail, and play again' format which can be used to learn new languages and overcome learning obstacles. Research indicates that students learn most effectively when they are entertained and challenged but not overwhelmed; when they can creatively work toward complex goals; and when consequences of their actions can be observed.[36] In video games, consequences are success, failure, and "high scores" that can be one form of assessment. Classrooms often fail to provide this learning environment because students are often required to memorize lists of facts. In contrast, educational video games may be more entertaining and engage students as active participants in learning.

Video games, and, more generally, technology-driven education will have important implications for community colleges. As game formats become mainstream, players (such as video game designers) who are more adept with technology than instructors will enter the market and could alter the role of faculty. A distance education course could be designed by a company specializing in learning technology rather than an instructor. A video game could automatically calculate student "scores" on a test, thereby eroding the assessment/grading role of the instructor. Instructors could be relegated to the role of leading online discussion and answering questions.

Expert knowledge of a discipline will still be of paramount importance. However, in ubiquitous subject areas, such as an introduction to statistics or principles of microeconomics, the need for specialized faculty expertise may be diminished. A 2002 report on the role of IT in higher education identified "helping faculty integrate technology into their instruction" as the single most important IT issue.[37] Considering that personnel costs are typically 75 to 85 percent of an operating budget, greater cost efficiencies may be found by reducing the role instructors play in online education. The potential for conflict is great, however, because teachers have a strong incentive for protecting their role in curriculum and instructional design, and cost efficiency is a tough idea to drive home with entrenched faculty.

The Digital Divide

Prensky discusses the differences in learning styles between "digital immigrants"—those who grew up in a predigital world—and "digital natives"—those who have been immersed in a world of cell phones, video games, computers, and the Internet since birth.

> It is now clear that as a result of this ubiquitous environment and the sheer volume of their interaction with it, today's students think and process information fundamentally differently from their predecessors. [38]

Digital immigrants are engaged in the difficult process of learning the new language:

> As Digital Immigrants learn—like all immigrants, some better than others—to adapt to their environment, they always retain, to some degree, their "accent," that is, their foot in the past. The "digital immigrant accent" can be seen in such things as turning to the Internet for information second rather than first, or in reading the manual for a program rather than assuming that the program itself will teach us to use it. Today's older folk were "socialized" differently from their kids, and are now in the process of learning a new language.[39]

A similar vein of research has described the arrival of the millennials—students who would rather learn through online webcasts or MP3s of lectures than through traditional lectures.[40] Prensky suggests that the biggest problem facing education today is that digital immigrant instructors speak an outdated language that digital native students do not understand. To digital natives, "school often feels pretty much as if a population of heavily accented, unintelligible foreigners has been brought in to lecture them."[41]

The digital native/digital immigrant divide has more important implications in community colleges than four-year institutions because community colleges have a higher proportion of older students who are digital immigrants and younger students who have been less exposed to digital technology because of their socioeconomic background. In addition, a rift between digital native instructors, the majority of whom will be young and newly hired, and digital immigrant instructors, the majority of whom will be older and longer tenured, is likely to develop in the future. The challenge posed by the diversity of learning styles and the range of comfort that instructors will have with technology suggests the importance of a strong technology plan and professional development program to bridge instructors to newly developed technologies.

POLICYMAKING TRENDS

A trend toward increased accountability and decreased funding is a reality and not a passing phase for colleges and universities. Four stakeholders are key players in public policy for community colleges: state governments, local governments, the federal government, and accrediting agencies. The federal government has historically been concerned with consumer protection against diploma mills but has recently turned its attention, through initiatives like the Spellings Commission, to strengthening accountability and fostering economic development. States are increasingly concerned with maximizing economic benefit in return for a given financial input. And, local governments are concerned with regionalized economic development and meeting community needs.

The interests of accrediting agencies can be broken down into regional and professional accrediting associations. The relationship between community colleges and regional accreditors is typically friendly because the board of governors of accrediting bodies comprises college and university presidents. Regional associations accredit entire institutions. They seek to ensure a minimum baseline of quality and to maximize quality, especially in student learning outcomes. Professional associations accredit programs, such as nursing, teacher education, and engineering. Their goals are to ensure that curricula are continually updated to meet changing industry standards and to ensure that graduates are adequately qualified to practice.

Changing Emphasis on Accountability

Most accountability programs are motivated by economic development. As competition intensifies and education achieves recognition as a catalyst for economic growth, interest grows in college and university operations. Accountability systems hold colleges responsible for improving performance on specific goals, which are measured using indicators such as graduation rates, transfer rates, and job placement. Performance accountability—a topic of great interest to state governments—is exercised through three kinds of programs: performance funding, performance budgeting, and performance reporting.[42] Performance funding automatically ties funding to institutional performance on specified indicators. Performance budgeting allows institutional performance to be considered in budget allocations. Performance reporting more typically creates incentives for institutional improvement by publicizing institutional performance.

Performance reporting is currently the dominant form of accountability. The most common reporting indicators used by states are student transfer, enrollment rate, graduation rate, retention, tuition and fees, job placement, remedial activity and effectiveness, and enrollment by program.[43] Information can leverage accountability by inducing institutions to align their behavior with state goals to put a favorable spin on performance data published by state agencies. As student tracking systems improve, states will bore deeper into the core operations of community colleges and report results to the public. When unflattering, these results can undermine public support, which explains why community colleges are often reticent to provide performance information. More often than not, performance indicators are a poor measure of quality, and are not useful as a guide for enhancement efforts at the campus and unit level.

State Governments and Coordination

Contrary to the rhetoric of higher education leaders, the last ten years have seen a general rise in higher education appropriations, with the exception of 2002–2005 when state tax revenues were in decline.[44] Funding varies dramatically across states. For example, higher education funding in Colorado rose only 10 percent between 1997 and 2006, but rose by 150 percent in Nevada over the same time period. The increase in Nevada is partly due to a population boom, but differences among states reveal an important reality about funding for public institutions—variation between community colleges in different states may be greater than variation between community colleges and four-year colleges in the same state. Regardless of location, community college budgets are strained because the cost of educating students has outstripped state appropriations. Furthermore, state funding is coming with accountability strings attached.

State coordinating systems create different power relationships between states and community colleges. States with centralized coordinating systems typically have the capacity to mandate stringent accountability from individual colleges. Among state coordinating systems nationally, there are three forms of control: twenty-four states utilize consolidated governing boards that have legal management and control responsibilities for all aspects of higher education, twenty-four states have coordinating boards that have review and approval authority over institutional budgets and programs, and two states (Michigan and Delaware) use planning agencies that serve in information gathering and advising roles.[45]

Richardson identifies four state policy roles on a continuum from state-provided postsecondary education to market-provided higher education.[46] In the role of "resource provider," the state subsidizes higher education with little regard for the market, as in low-tuition/low-aid states. In the "regulator" role, the state specifies the relationship between institutions and the market by controlling user charges, constraining administrative discretion in using resources, and eliminating or attenuating incentives for efficient operation. In the "consumer advocacy" role, the state redirects some allocations for higher education to students, thereby increasing the influence of their market choice on institutional behavior, as in high-tuition/high-aid states. In the "steering role," states restructure the market for higher education by creating market incentives for institutions to behave in ways that are consistent with government priorities—a model popularized by the book *Reinventing Government*.[47]

Community college leaders can use this information as a guide for analysis of the strength of policymaking agencies in their states. States like Florida have strong policymaking powers, while others, like Michigan, hardly have any. The ability of community colleges to resist deleterious accountability policies is determined to a significant extent by the powers granted to coordinating boards.

Local Government

In 2006, community colleges received 19 percent of their operating revenue from local government, but only half of community colleges receive local funding.[48] Predictably, states receiving a higher amount of funding per FTE from local sources typically receive less state funding per FTE. For example, in 2005 Connecticut received $7,197 in state appropriations per FTE and nothing in local appropriations. At the other end of the spectrum, Arizona received $1,396 in state appropriations per FTE, but $3188 in local appropriations. Generally, community colleges that receive both local and state funding have higher total revenue than those that do not receive local funding.[49]

Conflicts between state and local goals play an important role. For example, imagine a college in a state with a strong performance-reporting system that receives a larger share of its operating revenue from the state in contrast to the local tax district. The objective of the performance-reporting program is to encourage colleges to allocate their resources in a manner consistent with state goals. The local community, however, has signaled that it cares more about dual enrollment programs and performing arts programs than state economic development programs. Allocating resources toward state goals may undermine local community goals while failing to comply fully with state mandates that may endanger long-term funding. Financial support from the community must be continually nurtured through evidence of value delivered on goals deemed important by the community. State performance indicators that do not correspond with local needs may hamper community colleges that rely on local funding for a significant portion of their operating budget. Community colleges will need to find ways to ensure that state goals, embodied by performance indicators, are not in conflict with local goals.

Federal Government

Like the states, the federal government has a strong economic incentive to increase its control over postsecondary education. The basis for state control is the power to fund and to regulate—a power the federal government does not have. Federal policy initiatives, Perkins funds, and student aid, however, shape the flow of resources to colleges and are not to be neglected as a mandate for performance. Consider, for example, the potential impact of the Spellings Commission on policy related to accountability. Charged with recommending a national strategy for reforming postsecondary education with an emphasis on how well colleges and universities are preparing students for the twenty-first-century workplace, the Commission's September 2006 report focused on four key areas: access, affordability, standards of quality in instruction, and institutional accountability to constituencies.[50]

Access

Access to higher education is unduly limited by inadequate preparation, lack of information about college opportunities, and persistent financial barriers. A lack of communication between colleges and high schools is one source of the problem. Early assessment initiatives that determine whether students are on track toward college are recommended to link the expectations of college professors for incoming students to criteria required for high school graduation. Additionally, greater use of open content and open source at the collegiate level is encouraged to increase access for learners.

Affordability

Minorities and learners from low-income families experience more difficulty with access to higher education than their affluent peers with similar qualifications. Shortening the financial aid application is recommended to encourage more learners to apply for financial aid, and greater efficiency and productivity is called for in the financial aid system.

Quality

Colleges and universities are urged to embrace innovative ideas for new approaches to teaching, such as distance learning, to improve the quality of education. Modification of curricula and assessment systems is recommended to enhance student outcomes during and after college.

Accountability

A public database should be created where statistics and other information about colleges and universities can be viewed by all in order to clarify the haziness of accountability. The information that should be made available in the database includes cost, price, admissions data, and college completion rates. Eventually the database should contain data describing the learning outcomes of students.

The mystique surrounding college costs and learner outcomes has befuddled federal government agencies and officials for more than three decades. If one accepts the argument that postsecondary education will inevitably follow the same path of reform that organizations in health and the for-profit sectors have followed, the point of origin will likely be a shift in federal policy to mandate greater accountability for access, cost, and learner outcomes.

The Future of Funding

The capability of tax revenue to support community college operations will depend on economic prosperity at the local, state, and federal levels. Education has a long-term impact on the economy, but tax revenue is based on short-term economic prosperity. During periods of fiscal downturn, community college funding from public sources will inevitably decline. Political persuasion will also have an impact on funding as elected officials react differently to taxes depending on their platform for election. To the extent that voters elect officials friendly to education and voters can be convinced that public postsecondary education is in their best interest, community college funding may be favorable. However, postsecondary education must compete with "mandatory" programs, such as K–12, corrections, and Medicaid. As Medicaid spending for an aging population increases, arguments in favor of additional public funding for postsecondary education will be increasingly difficult to make.

A vein of hope for the future is that community college education will be seen as a universal catalyst for economic prosperity. Books such as *The World Is Flat* may help to create a paradigm shift in public support for community colleges as a regional and national resource for the economy. In today's political climate, funding is dependent on showing stakeholders value for their money. Increasingly, value-added performance indicators that are meaningful to stakeholders will be important to gain and retain community support. They will need to reflect the needs and goals of important stakeholders and be within the capability of institutions to measure and deliver. This synergy does not exist in practice, but it will improve to the degree that community colleges align the needs and interests of internal and external stakeholders.

Lobbying for community college interests will be central to maximizing funding and autonomy. This implies a need for cooperation between colleges at both the state and national level. Position papers that lobby for increased funding on equity grounds are given little weight by policymakers. Community colleges could, however, use the rationale underlying performance reporting—information as a weapon—to build a case for increased support. States compare information on college outcomes against prespecified performance benchmarks or against the performance of other colleges. In theory, this produces a "name and shame" response in which colleges, embarrassed that their performance has been made public, have an incentive to do better. This strategy can work both ways. Most states have not fulfilled their funding responsibilities nor have they provided sufficient resources to stimulate economic development through workforce programs. This phenomenon has been well documented in research by the Education Commission of the States and by the National Center for Public Policy and Higher Education.[51] Community colleges could use this information as a strategic weapon at the lobbying table just as states use performance reporting to induce colleges to follow mandates.

COMPETITION AND COMPETITORS

If you get on the Internet and click on www.nasdaq.com to find stock quotes for APOL, the Apollo Group, Inc., you will find that as of April 3, 2008, the Apollo Group had a market value of $7.8 billion.[52] Their total FY

2007 revenue was $2.7 billion, compared to $1.3 billion in FY 2003. Net income rose from $278 million in FY 2004 to $409 million in FY 2007. Clearly, business is booming. Their main subsidiary, the University of Phoenix, is the largest university in the world.[53]

In a world where education increasingly determines national prosperity and individual standard of living, education has become an attractive industry. In 2003, five for-profit providers—Apollo, Corinthian Colleges, Career Education, Strayer Education, and ITT Educational Services—ranked in the top twenty-five of Business Week's "Hot Growth Companies."[54] Today there are thousands of noncorporate for-profit education providers playing in an industry previously dominated by community colleges, public four-year colleges, and nonprofit institutions.

Over the next fifteen years, new providers will enter the market, and providers unable to adapt will be forced to reduce the scope of their operations or to exit. Porter's classic "Five Forces" model of strategy is at play in the knowledge industry.[55] Competitive rivalry in an industry increases when there is an increase in any of the following: 1) the threat of new organizational entrants to the industry, 2) the bargaining power or control of suppliers of key resources, 3) the bargaining power of customers who purchase products or services, 4) the threat of substitute products or services from new organizations, and 5) innovations in the core technology of organizations in an industry.

Competitors

Community colleges have typically considered public four-year institutions to be their primary competitors, while for-profits have been accorded the status of a minor threat.[56] In the next few pages, emerging patterns of competition for community colleges will be examined by comparing public four-year teaching institutions and for-profit institutions on different dimensions of student choice. In-depth case studies of DeVry University and the University of Phoenix—both corporate for-profit institutions—will be used to illustrate the impact of for-profit institutions on enrollment in tomorrow's market.

Public Four-Year Teaching Institutions

Public four-year teaching universities are motivated by financial stability, institutional prestige, enabling personal and professional growth for students, and delivering value to the region in which they are located. The baccalaureate degree is central to their mission, but they also provide occupationally specific graduate degrees in professional fields such as education, health, and business. Their target customers are full-time traditional college-age students who fall between the fiftieth and seventy-fifth percentile in terms of academic achievement. They also serve working professionals who seek a graduate degree or skills to complement an existing degree.

Teaching universities differentiate themselves from competitors on the basis of features that cannot be duplicated. They use the traditional appeal of the baccalaureate degree and campus life to distinguish themselves from community colleges and reasonable cost, a comprehensive curriculum, and campus life to distinguish themselves from for-profit institutions.

For-Profit Institutions

The percentage of all postsecondary students enrolled in for-profit institutions increased from .5 percent in 1976 to 1.5 percent in 1983.[57] This percentage remained static between 1983 and 1993 but jumped from 1.6 percent in 1993 to 3.6 percent in 2002, and 5.1 percent in 2004.[58] These numbers understate for-profit enrollments because they only include for-profit institutions that are eligible for Title IV funding.

It is unwise to make generalizations about how for-profit institutions operate due to the heterogeneity of institutions and students enrolled in them. At one extreme are billion-dollar corporations such as Apollo (University of Phoenix) and ITT, each owning hundreds of campuses and serving several hundred thousand students. At the other extreme are single-campus training schools serving three hundred or fewer students.

A better understanding of for-profit institutions can be gained by looking at the students they serve. Students at for-profits are disproportionately female compared to other postsecondary institutions.[59] They are also disproportionately minority—43 percent of for-profit students are African American or Hispanic compared to 21 percent of students enrolled in not-for-profit institutions. For-profit students are older, less likely to be dependents, and more likely to have dependents. They are also less affluent, have lower high school grades, and are more likely to delay college enrollment than students at other institutions.[60] Compared to their nonprofit counterparts, for-profit students are more likely to enroll in IT or technical/professional programs—a statistic which reveals the extent to which for-profit institutions are in direct competition with community colleges for less-educated, working adults.

Enrollment statistics show that for-profit students are likely to attend institutions that are much smaller than students enrolled in traditional colleges and universities. Four out of five are enrolled in an institution with fewer than one thousand students. Looking at highest degree offered, the vast majority (85 percent) of these students attend campuses where the highest degree offered is less than a baccalaureate degree. This is important because it implies that a high percentage of students attending for-profit institutions are capable of receiving the benefit of customized service at small, single-campus institutions offering career-focused occupational degrees.

Competing for Students

Community colleges, public four-year teaching institutions, and for-profits are increasingly competing for overlapping target populations. In the pages that follow, competition is analyzed along three dimensions of student choice: price, convenience, and value-added.

Price

Price is among the most important factors in college choice for students of all ages and backgrounds. When it comes to tuition, community colleges have a clear advantage—a fact revealed in statistics from the 2003–2004 National Postsecondary Student Aid Study (NPSAS, 2004) which describe comparative costs at community colleges, public four-year colleges, and for-profit institutions.[61] In 2003–2004, annual tuition totaled $1,000 on average in community colleges compared to $4,200 and $7,300, respectively, at public four-year and for-profit institutions. On average, however, community college students received less in aid compared to public four-year colleges and for-profit institutions. After subtracting total aid from tuition, the net cost of attendance is roughly comparable among the institutions. Clearly, for-profits are successful in helping students remove financial barriers to education.

Financial aid can be divided into grants and loans. One out of two (53 percent) community college students received no aid according to 2005 NCES data compared to 31 percent at public four-year colleges and 11 percent at for-profit institutions.[62] Almost three-quarters (71 percent) of for-profit students receive either grants or grant and loan packages, compared to 57 percent for public four-year colleges and 43 percent for community colleges. The financial advantage enjoyed by for-profit students is amplified by data showing the value of financial aid for students receiving different types of awards. In 2005, students enrolled in for-profit institutions receiving any form of aid received an average of $8,800 compared to $3,200 for community college students.[63] For-profit students who receive both grant and loan funding receive an average of $10,600 compared to $6,900 for community college students.[64]

These data imply that community colleges have much to learn from for-profit institutions. Revenue at for-profits is almost entirely comprimised of tuition. However, student aid offsets a large portion of the cost of tuition and results in reduced out-of-pocket expenses for students. Indeed, Slaughter and Rhodes write that "for-profits envision themselves as able to run on Pell grants and loans alone."[65]

Low tuition partially explains why community college students receive less aid, but this obscures the fact that community colleges can and should develop better financial aid packages for students. There is no tuition floor below which students are ineligible for aid. Applying for federally sponsored financial aid is a complicated and daunting process. Student service units are generally responsible for helping students complete financial aid forms. However, all too many colleges are neither systematic nor customer-focused in carrying out this responsibility, and this results in a loss of opportunity for both the institution and the students it serves when costs beyond tuition are factored into the total cost of attendance.

Convenience

Community colleges have had an advantage in convenience over rivals since their inception. An overwhelming majority of citizens in most states are located within twenty-five miles of a community college campus.[66] This advantage is beginning to erode as a result of reinvestment in public four-year colleges and universities through capital funding, distance delivery, and facilities sharing. Public four-year institutions are building branch campuses to serve local communities, which were previously the domain of community colleges. The burgeoning for-profit industry has adopted a strategy of locating "campuses" at strip malls near major intersections. And, by removing all barriers to market penetration, distance education providers are changing all of the rules of convenience. Using sophisticated technology, these providers are able to reach students who cannot take classes on campus due to domestic responsibilities, disability, or a busy schedule. Furthermore, by equalizing cost and employing instructional modules that match student learning preferences, these providers are able to compete for students who would otherwise enroll at community colleges.

Value-Added

Competition on value-added differs depending on the target population. "Value" can take the form of real or perceived benefit through affiliation with an institution offering traditional prestige, unique experience, or superior outcomes. Over time, data has shown that the baccalaureate degree has more earning power and, hence, prestige than the associate degree. Additionally, although community colleges are becoming a preferred provider for legions of new students, they continue to struggle with public perception of their status as an extension of high school. Attributes identified as contributing to this perception are low cost, open admissions, and campuses that do not have the ambiance of a "real college." Exclusivity, the idea that buying a product earns admittance into an exclusive club, is a cornerstone of marketing strategy for four-year colleges and universities. Right or wrong, the perception that four-year institutions are at least moderately selective gives them an element of leverage over community colleges. This is reinforced by the "real college experience"—grassy knolls, residence halls, athletics, and social life that is seen as the province of four-year colleges. Interestingly, community colleges have discovered the value of campus ambience as part of their marketing equation and are beginning to compete on this dimension. Cy-Fair College's (Texas) campus master plan was designed to draw students and community residents into campus life through superior amenities, programs, and activities, and more and more community colleges are building residential facilities.

Community colleges have the advantage of providing a caring learning experience. Introductory lecture classes in public four-year institutions often number several hundred students, whereas class size in community colleges rarely surpasses thirty students. Many students who get lost in the shuffle at four-year colleges find comfort at a community college—a factor pointed out over and over by transfer students, returning alumni, reverse transfers, and adult learners. Altogether different is the learning experience at for-profit institutions. For-profits do not compete on the dimension of college "experience" since this would be perceived as frivolous for students who are most concerned with employment. Prestige at for-profits is associated with the labor market outcomes of their students.

CASE STUDY: CORPORATE FOR-PROFITS

Community colleges can learn much from the innovative practices of corporate for-profit institutions. The University of Phoenix and DeVry University are profiled as exemplars of cutting-edge strategy in educational delivery. Each employs a business model that distinguishes it from competitors and has a proven track record of success in delivering value to stakeholders. Both DeVry and Phoenix retain a lean cost structure while providing quality services by focusing on core competencies. These competencies are integrated student services, multimodal curriculum design and delivery, standardized curricula, outcomes-centered instruction, and value-added assessment.

Integrated Student Services

The following excerpt from the National Center for Postsecondary Improvement (NCPI) report provides a description of DeVry's approach to delivery of student services:

> Admissions, financial aid, assessment, advisement and registration are closely linked at DeVry, so that students remain under the same set of administrative practices for the first several terms. Students work with financial aid advisors to complete registration and financial aid forms online which smoothes the student entry experience. Academic advisors help students schedule classes, complete registration procedures and monitor their academic achievement for the first two terms, after which the student is assigned to a program area (major) advisor. By smoothing the entry experience for students, college officials hope to improve persistence and achievement.[67]

The corporate model for quality assurance is one of creating systematic processes that consistently deliver desired outcomes. The admissions process is seamlessly integrated with marketing. For example, if one visits the DeVry Web site (www.devry.edu) and fills out a brief form expressing interest in a course or program of study, it is likely that a phone call and/ or personalized e-mail will be received from an admissions officer within twenty-four hours. The University of Phoenix employs a similar practice.

Corporate for-profits employ an integrated approach in their job placement services as well. These services are important because the reputation of for-profits depends on providing customers with marketable skills and helping them get jobs. A report of the National Center for Postsecondary Improvement highlights DeVry's approach to career placement services:

> DeVry is proud of its career counseling and job placement services. Nationally, the college employs about 5 full-time counselors per campus whose job it is to help students find part-time employment while enrolled and full-time work after graduation . . . and alumni can continue to use the placement services after graduation. . . . TECH tracks the employment experience of its graduates. Indeed, data published on the college website they indicate that for graduates in 2000, 95 percent of those who looked for work found work in education-related fields within months of graduation . . . In contrast, admissions, counseling, and placement are far less integrated at community colleges. In most colleges, students usually have to go to different offices or people for financial aid, credit transfer, course selection, and career planning. Overall counseling at community colleges is notoriously uneven, with very low counselor to student ratios.[68]

The corporate approach to student services evidences a strong commitment to customer satisfaction that Brian Mueller, CEO of the University of Phoenix Online, describes as follows: "We benchmark ourselves against the best customer-service organizations in the world."[69] This statement provides insight into the market focus of corporate for-profit institutions. Traditional providers typically benchmark their performance against peer institutions. Rarely are organizations outside of education studied in terms of best practices and even more rarely are they consulted or visited as a model for organizational change and innovation.

Multimodal Curriculum Design and Delivery

The University of Phoenix has a simple framework for instructional delivery that is easily understood by customers. Three modes of learning are offered: face-to-face learning, online learning, and FlexNet—a combination of face-to-face and online learning. It offers forty-two unduplicated certificate/nondegree programs, two associate's degree programs, seventeen baccalaureate degree programs, forty-four master's degrees programs, and six doctoral programs—a total of 111 different programs in four areas of study: business, information technology, health, and education.[70] This is a comparatively small number of programs considering that the University of Phoenix is the largest university in the world with 163 campuses serving over 250,000 students.[71]

Standardized Curriculum

Instructional quality at the University of Phoenix is achieved through benchmarking the design of courses and curricula against industry standards. Phoenix recruits business and industry practitioners who hold at least a master's degree and have an average of ten or more years of market experience.[72] This model delivers value to students in the form of market-prime employment skills learned from instructors who are successful practitioners. Phoenix currently employs over 19,000 instructors of whom 1,500 are core faculty who provide instructional leadership and oversee academic quality.[73]

Phoenix highlights its proximity to industry as a competitive advantage. Instructors employed full-time in industry are positioned to inform the corporation when courses and curricula need to be updated to reflect industry changes. Courses are centrally designed by curriculum specialists who are in constant contact with employers to identify current and emerging needs. Standardization across courses and curricula is perceived to be the best way to ensure quality. With over 250,000 students, the economies of scale produced through a standardized curriculum yield important cost benefits to Phoenix and its stakeholders:

- The centrally designed curriculum ensures that a standardized, high-quality product is delivered at all campuses
- Uniform quality helps protect Phoenix's brand name
- Students receive the benefit of market-relevant courses and curricula
- Employers receive the benefit of workers with market-prime workforce skills

Standardization has great economic value in today's global economy. Think of the transition from small to large stores like Starbucks, Barnes & Noble, and Home Depot. When workers and travelers buy their morning coffee, they prefer a product with a brand name they can trust. When they are in an unfamiliar location, they can go to Barnes & Noble or Home Depot and know how the store is organized before walking inside.

The standardized Phoenix product has value for students, who know what they are getting, but more importantly for businesses who know whom they are hiring because of the value of the vocational credential that signifies the ability to perform a set of tasks. For a credential to gain positive economic returns, it must be reliable and relevant to the current needs of industry. Phoenix's close relationship with business and their practitioner-teacher model create such an advantage. The discrete number of programs Phoenix offers also creates a cache with employers that benefits learners. When employers hire a Phoenix graduate, they have a good idea of the skills that are in the new employee's portfolio. Now, consider how employers would perceive the skill set of a community college graduate, especially if the business and the college are located in different communities. In this case, the community college degree may not be backed by a differentiated brand name. This is reminiscent of the business traveler who orders a cappuccino at a local café and hopes for the best.

The analysis of proximity to industry and standardization has important implications for community colleges. Phoenix can develop new courses quickly. Community colleges are likely to move at a slower pace in new course and program development if credit is involved because of the number of approvals required—department approval, campus approval including the academic senate, board approval, and finally state external review.[74] Furthermore, community college courses are unlikely to be developed by an expert in curriculum design, and course delivery will not be standardized across full-time and part-time faculty. On many campuses the percentage of instructional hours taught by part-time faculty exceeds sixty percent, making it all but impossible to standardize instructional quality, which hurts brand name. New courses are often built on top of existing courses, rather than replacing them. The proliferation of programs and courses that are obsolete cuts into brand name because employers get less than what they are looking for when they hire a graduate.

Outcomes-Centered Instruction

Analysis of data in the Integrated Postsecondary Education Data System (IPEDS) reveals that students at for-profit institutions have higher rates of persistence and graduation than those at similar public institutions.[75] While critics may advocate that these institutions are diploma mills, for-profits are often accredited by the same agencies as public institutions. They use intensive retention strategies to improve student outcomes, including academic advisors whose job it is to ensure that students do not fall through the cracks in the first few semesters of enrollment.[76] They also use teaching strategies that work effectively with students who do best in a hands-on learning environment. Courses and curricula stress practical applications as opposed to theory, using experiments whenever possible.[77] For-profit students typically pursue a structured curriculum rather than having the freedom to choose courses—the idea being that a degree should represent a specific set of skills. The number of electives is relatively small in comparison to community colleges because students can get off track if they have to choose from a dizzying array of electives. Finally, courses are sequenced so that more theoretical, general education requirements are delayed. This creates two advantages: first, students are more likely to get "hooked" into a program if they take applied courses first and second, students needing developmental work before taking general education requirements can complete it while taking their introductory technical courses.[78]

Assessment as a Strategic Weapon

The University of Phoenix markets itself as an industry leader in assessment and institutional research. The Outcomes Assessments section of its Web site highlights its Academic Quality Management System (AQMS) and Adult Learning Outcomes Assessment Project.[79] AQMS focuses on assessment of student services and delivery of academic programs. It includes a Registration Survey, a Student End-of-Course Survey, a Faculty End-of-Course Survey, Comments to the Chair, and periodic assessments, such as alumni and employer surveys. The Adult Learning Outcomes Assessment Project is designed to assess student learning in the cognitive and affective domains through a Comprehensive Cognitive Outcomes Assessment, a Professional and Educational Values Assessment, a Communication Skills Inventory, an End-of-Program Assessment, and a the Critical Thinking Assessment.[80]

Many institutions view assessment as a compliance requirement and fail to use the results to good effect with programs and services. Research by the National Center for Postsecondary Improvement (NCPI) has shown that assessment is more likely to have a positive impact on institutional improvement if it is done for internal improvement purposes rather than for compliance purposes.[81] Assessment programs at DeVry, Phoenix, and other corporate for-profits extend beyond the requirements of accrediting agencies because these institutions rely on information about results as a platform for decisions on how to improve services. Additionally outcomes assessment is used to improve student outcomes and to demonstrate value to potential customers and stakeholders as exemplified in the NCPI report:

> An institution can be more responsive to student needs if it has good information about what those needs are. More so than at the comparison community colleges, DeVry monitors data on student progress to make curricular and programmatic decisions. During one of our interviews at DeVry, the entire wall of the meeting room was covered with graphs of student retention by week across the five terms of an associate's degree program. Because the administrators had identified a dip in retention during the term in which students traditionally had enrolled for Composition (second term), the sequence of the program was shifted so that students would take Composition third term when they had done some writing in technical courses and had developed a greater commitment to the program.[82]

ESCALATING CUSTOMER EXPECTATIONS

Students have more choices from a wider variety of providers than ever before, and the range of choice is expanding as new providers using innovative practices and more and better technologies enter the market. Each successive innovation raises the bar for providers by elevating customer expectations. According to Alfred:

> Whereas in prior years students would have been satisfied with expanded hours of service, they now expect services to be available 24/7 on the Internet. Whereas a comprehensive set of course offerings would have satisfied most learners five years ago, they now expect to be able to take courses anywhere, anyplace, and anytime to fit their schedule. They expect that a significant portion of their coursework will be taken electronically and that they will be able to take courses at several institutions and apply them to a "home" institution for the degree. Very few students enter college, progress through the curriculum in a linear fashion, and leave four years later with a degree. They swirl back and forth through multiple institutions and attendance modes, which puts pressure on colleges to implement common learn-

ing goals, standards, and competency assessments to determine student attainment.[83]

Students are arriving on campuses much better informed about what to expect and with significantly higher expectations of the college experience than earlier generations. Most carry cell phones and a growing number come with smaller and faster computers, Blackberries, smart cameras, and personal data assistants that put them a click away from instant communication and oceans of information. Others come with high expectations but limited academic and financial resources. Regardless of background or resources, they share one thing in common: they expect to engage in an experience that is meaningful when it happens and that is beneficial later on in terms of improved quality of life. Many factors underlie this expectation. Chief among them is the changing frame of reference for student experience with organizations in American society. Through growing exposure to best practices in a variety of organizations, they have widened their frame of reference for performance from a single organization to a host of organizations. Community colleges are no longer unique unto themselves. They are part of a far-reaching knowledge industry packed with players, products, and ploys.

LOOKING AHEAD

An understanding of forces and trends in the external environment is important because it helps leaders anticipate challenges that lie beyond the horizon for their institutions. To bring focus and meaning to the information in the preceding pages, we close with a synthesis of forces that will impact community colleges in the near- and long-term future.

The Knowledge Economy

Community colleges will need to think globally and act locally. The economy will continue to transition from an industrial economy to a knowledge economy and from a regional/national economy to a global economy. Community colleges will play a key role in the knowledge economy through programs crafting workforce skills that enhance the capacity of people, organizations, regions, and the nation to compete in a global marketplace. In the knowledge economy:

- Programs and services offered by community colleges will be central to the ability of the U.S. economy to compete on a world stage.

- Globalization and foreign competition will lead to large numbers of workers unemployed, barely subsisting, or holding multiple jobs to earn a reasonable wage. This market will have great potential for growth, but it will also place significant demands on colleges to design and deliver cost-effective programs.
- Businesses will look to community colleges to become the hub of a "supplier network" of schools, colleges, and for-profit providers working together to prepare workers with world-class skills.
- Colleges and universities will seek to open universal access to post-secondary education by establishing an electronic presence in countries throughout the world. Community colleges will become central players in this movement.
- Colleges and universities will be expected to make teaching materials and resources available to learners everywhere free of charge. Community colleges will find a niche in this emerging model of collaboration.
- Continuing elevation of knowledge and skills required for jobs in the knowledge economy will lead to lower economic returns on the associate degree. Community colleges will increase their baccalaureate offerings to compete in a knowledge economy.
- Global employment opportunities for community college students will significantly increase. Students will be expected to travel to and experience other countries or at least be prepared to do so.
- Foreign markets will become an important source of qualified faculty and staff. Community colleges will broaden their vision with regard to recruitment and build a culture that is capable of attracting and retaining diverse staff.
- Curriculum review and redesign will become increasingly important as proficiency in foreign languages and intercultural awareness become a requisite for education and work in a connected world.

Labor Market

Advancing technology and global competition will open up new industries and new jobs. Existing jobs will be reconfigured to meet changing knowledge and skill requirements, and new jobs will be created to support emerging industries. Jobs that once seemed to be a source of opportunity will disappear, and others that could not have been imagined five years ago will take their place as a gateway to opportunity in the "new economy." In a shifting labor market:

- Community colleges will need to continuously scan economic forecasts of emerging industries and move quickly to develop new programs and modify existing programs to address structural shifts in the economy.

- Advancing technology will lead to elevation in job skill requirements; community colleges will need to continuously evaluate courses and curricula to ensure that students are mastering state-of-the-art workforce skills.
- Community colleges will need to work closely with business and industry to address worker shortages in high-demand occupations; they will need to design and implement fast-track programs to develop a) skilled workers in rapidly growing occupations and b) "soft skills" and technical capabilities valued by employers.
- Community colleges will become the "hub" of a network of organizations (K–12 schools, colleges and universities, employers, community organizations, etc.) working together to prepare workers with skills that enable businesses to compete on a world stage.

Demographics

By 2050, the world population will have doubled in a century, and the United States will become a nation of minorities. The number of people fifty-five and older will outnumber those who are eighteen and under, and incremental resources will be needed to provide health care and services to an aging population. More age generations will be represented on college and university campuses. The definition and structure of the family will change as labor market shifts give rise to more multiple-worker families. More and more people will turn to postsecondary education for the skills needed to gain and hold a job in the knowledge economy. In a period of demographic transition:

- Enormous opportunities will be available to community colleges for programming in lifelong learning as adults live longer and better, baby boomers retire, and older workers enter second and third careers.
- Community colleges will have the opportunity to open new doors to private-sector giving through customized educational programs and services, which attract affluent seniors and engender awareness of, and enthusiasm toward, the community college ideal.
- Underserved populations will become increasingly visible as a human capital issue; community colleges will need to pay close attention to college attendance rates for different population groups and develop customized programs and services to attract underserved groups.

- The presence of increasingly diverse learners and multiple age groups on campus will need to be reflected in staffing, curricula and service delivery, and approaches to pedagogy.
- Students following generational norms will pose significant challenges to instructors and staff adhering to different norms.
- Demand will intensify for services customized to learner needs.

K–12 and Postsecondary Enrollment

The number of high school graduates will remain stable or decline. Large numbers of students will continue to drop out of high school before graduation, and a growing number of students will look for alternatives to the senior year. School districts seeking to improve retention to diploma completion will end compulsory schooling at tenth or eleventh grade and develop articulation agreements with regional colleges and universities to advance students into postsecondary education. A larger proportion of high school graduates will enroll in colleges and universities, and most will aspire to the baccalaureate degree. Half or more of the graduates will initially enroll in community colleges, and most will need remediation.

- Pressure will increase for access to postsecondary education.
- Learners will demand more flexible approaches to college entry and exit.
- The combined impact of growing high school drop-out rates, basic skills deficiencies, and declining standardized achievement test scores will spark policy initiatives to redesign K–12 education.
- Colleges will move to redefine educational boundaries with K–12 schools, particularly the senior-year experience and school-to-college transition.
- Lines between community colleges and four-year colleges will blur as students with baccalaureate aspirations bring pressure on community colleges to offer amenities and a learning experience similar in design to four-year residential colleges.

Technology

More learners will enter college with advanced experience and expectations for technology. New approaches to learning will evolve, and demand will increase for open access to postsecondary learning resources. Advancing technology will revolutionize the postsecondary education market by removing barriers to market entry of new competitors and making 24/7/365 access to learning and services a basic expectation of all learners.

- Student expectations for technology and e-learning will continue to grow.
- As courseware for learning becomes available free of charge on the Internet, textbooks will become a relic of the past.
- Increased reliance on technology vendors for technology services (information technology, distance education, enrollment management, etc.) will lead to a squeeze on community college profit margins.
- A larger portion of college operating budgets will be required for technology upgrading and acquisition.

Policymaking

Colleges and universities will move into an accountability era where government agencies—local, state, and federal—provide funding based on evidence of value added. Increased spending on education will be linked to increased accountability—a move that will force colleges to develop new assessment methodologies and to employ personnel with advanced skills in assessment.

- New accountability standards for colleges and universities will be developed and enforced by agencies of federal and state government as a condition for acquiring resources.
- Colleges will be expected to document and publish information about price, costs, and student learning outcomes using a reporting format that can be readily understood by the public.
- Community colleges will be drafted into the global war for economic competitiveness.
- Federal agencies will identify strategically important industries as part of a war for global supremacy and provide incentives to colleges for developing programs to produce skilled workers for these industries.

Competitors, Competition, and Collaboration

The market for postsecondary education will change dramatically with the entry of new providers playing by different rules. For-profit providers will challenge community colleges but only in specific program markets. The greatest threat will come from providers rewriting rules of access and cost by making educational materials available to the public free of charge on the Internet. More important than competition will be collaboration with partners in the delivery of education and transporting best practices from organizations outside of education into education.

- Community colleges will learn and adopt the best practices of for-profit providers and organizations outside of education as a means for building competitive advantage.
- Increasing economies of scale will lead to an oligopoly among distance education providers; community colleges that cannot match economies of scale with publicly traded for-profits will lose market share.
- Competition will broaden beyond institutional boundaries to include networks of collaborating organizations competing with one another for market share.
- Community colleges will adapt a "blue ocean strategy"—the identification of uncontested market space—to develop new markets for growth.

Escalating Customer Expectations

Learners will arrive on campuses much better informed about what to expect and with significantly higher expectations of the college experience. They will have more choices from a wider array of providers. Through exposure to the best practices of different types of organizations, they will no longer view colleges and universities as islands unto themselves. College services will be evaluated in relationship to equivalent services offered by multiple organizations. This evaluation will become the basis for determining service quality.

- The range of choice that students have for postsecondary education will expand as new competitors using innovative practices and more and better technology enter the market.
- Serial innovation in the design and delivery of education will raise the bar for service quality by elevating customer expectations.

CONCLUSION

Understanding forces at work in the external environment is important because it helps leaders envision the type of institution their colleges must become to thrive in the future. Knowledge of the present, however, is not a substitute for foresight into the future. It obscures the urgency of what lies ahead by limiting one's ability to see beyond the currently served market. A better starting point would be what Robert Galvin, the former chairman of Motorola, liked to term the "imaginable future." Imagining the future depends on many things: talented leaders and staff, a healthy culture, and a bias toward action. The people, resources, and capabilities inside the institution that determine its capacity to imagine and create the future are the topic of the next chapter.

NOTES

1. National Center on Education and the Economy, *Tough Choices, Tough Times,* Executive Summary (Washington, DC: National Center on Education and the Economy, 2007), 3–6.

2. National Center on Education and the Economy, *Tough Choices,* 3–6.

3. W. Norton Grubb and M. Lazerson, "Vocationalism in Higher Education: The Triumph of the Education Gospel," *Journal of Higher Education* 76, no. 1 (2005): 2–25.

4. F. Scharpf, "Negative Integration: States and the Loss of Boundary Control," in *The Welfare State Reader*, eds. C. Pierson and F. Castles, (Cambridge, UK: Polity Press, 2000).

5. Scharpf, "Negative Integration."

6. P. A. Hall and D. W. Soskice, *Varieties of Capitalism: The Institutional Foundations of Comparative Advantage* (New York: Oxford University Press, 2001).

7. T. Friedman, *The World is Flat: A Brief History of the Twenty-First Century* (New York: Farrar, Straus and Giroux, 2005).

8. Department for Education and Skills, *21st Century Skills, Realising Our Potential*, No. Cm 5810 (Norwich, UK: The Stationery Office, 2003).

9. United States National Commission on Excellence in Education, *A Nation at Risk: The Imperative for Educational Reform*, A Report to the Nation and the Secretary of Education (Washington, DC: U.S. Department of Education/Superintendent of Documents, U.S. Government Printing Office, 1983).

10. Organization for Economic Cooperation and Development, *What PISA Assesses*, http://www.pisa.oecd.org/pisa/skills.htm (retrieved February 2004).

11. National Center for Public Policy and Higher Education, *Measuring Up 2004: The National Report Card on Higher Education* (San Jose, CA: National Center for Public Policy and Higher Education, 2004).

12. U.S. Department of Education, *A Test of Leadership: Charting the Future of U.S. Higher Education* (Washington, DC: U.S. Department of Education, 2006).

13. D. Breneman, *Remediation in Higher Education: Its Extent and Cost* (Washington, DC: Brookings Institution, 1998).

14. E. El-Khawas, *Coordination, Consistency and Quality: Evolving U.S. Practices in Accreditation* (Paris: UNESCO, 2005).

15. L. Brainard and R. Litan, *Services Offshoring, American Jobs and the Global Economy* (Washington, DC: Brookings Institution, 2005).

16. McKinsey Global Institute, *The Emerging Global Labor Market* (San Francisco: McKinsey Global Institute, 2005).

17. D. E. Hecker, "Occupational Employment Projections to 2012," *Monthly Labor Review* (February 2004).

18. Apollo Alliance, "New Energy for America," *Christian Science Monitor* (January 2004).

19. Bureau of Labor Statistics, *Occupational Projections and Training Data, 2004–05 Edition,* http://www.bls.gov/emp/optd/ (retrieved October 20, 2005).

20. Bureau of Labor Statistics, *Occupational Projections, 2004–05 Edition.*

21. Bureau of Labor Statistics, *Occupational Projections and Training Data, 2006–07 Edition,* http://www.bls.gov/emp/optd/ (retrieved October 20, 2005).

22. Bureau of Labor Statistics, *Occupational Projections, 2006–07 Edition.*

23. Bureau of Labor Statistics, *Occupational Projections, 2006–07 Edition.*

24. Council on Competitiveness, *Innovate America* (Washington, DC: Council on Competitiveness, 2004).

25. H. Jorgenson, "Changing Public Perception in Wisconsin: Manufacturing a Good Life," *Community College Journal* (December 2005/January 2006), 53–55.

26. U.S. Census Bureau, 2004, *U.S. Interim Projections by Age, Sex, Race, and Hispanic Origin,* http://www.census.gov/ipc/www/usinterimproj/ (retrieved October 20, 2005).

27. U.S. Census Bureau, 2004, *U.S. Interim Projections.*

28. U.S. Census Bureau, 2004, *U.S. Interim Projections.*

29. National Center for Educational Statistics, 2003, *Projections of Education Statistics to 2013,* http://nces.ed.gov/programs/projections/ (retrieved October 20, 2005).

30. National Center for Educational Statistics, *Digest of Education Statistics, 2004* (Washington, DC: National Center for Education Statistics, 2005).

31. National Center for Educational Statistics, *Projections of Education Statistics to 2014,* http://nces.ed.gov/programs/projections/ (retrieved October 20, 2005).

32. National Center for Educational Statistics, *Projections of Education Statistics to 2014.*

33. W. C. Symonds, "Cash-Cow Universities: For-Profits Are Growing Fast and Making Money," *Business Week Online* (November 17, 2003).

34. R. Gallagher, "The Next 20 Years: How is Online Distance Learning Likely to Evolve?" (paper presented at the UCEA 88th Annual Conference, Chicago, IL, March 2003).

35. Massachusetts Institute of Technology, *MIT OpenCourseWare,* http://ocw.mit.edu/index.html (retrieved November 18, 2005).

36. S. Carlson, "Can Grand Theft Auto Inspire Professors?" *Chronicle of Higher Education* 49, no. 49 (2003): A31.

37. S. L. Howell, P. B. Williams, and N. K. Lindsay, "Thirty-Two Trends Affecting Distance Education: An Informed Foundation for Strategic Planning," *Online Journal Of Distance Learning Administration* 6, no. 3 (2003).

38. M. Prensky, "Digital Natives, Digital Immigrants," *On the Horizon* 9, no. 5 (2001).

39. M. Prensky, "Digital Natives."

40. S. Carlson, "The Net Generation Goes to College," *Chronicle of Higher Education* 52, no. 7 (2005).

41. M. Prensky, "Digital Natives."

42. J. C. Burke and H. P. Minassians, "Implications of State Performance Indicators for Community College Assessment," *New Directions For Community Colleges* 126 (2004): 53–64.

43. J. C. Burke and H. P. Minassians, "Implications of State Performance Indicators."

44. National Center for Public Policy and Higher Education, *Policy Alert: State Shortfalls Projected to Continue Despite Economic Gains* (San Jose, CA: National Center for Public Policy and Higher Education, 2006).

45. M. Mclendon and E. Ness, "The Politics of State Higher Education Governance Reform," *Peabody Journal of Education* 78, no. 4 (2003): 66–68.

46. R. Richardson, K. Bracco, P. Callan, and J. Finney, *Designing State Higher Education Systems for a New Century* (Washington, DC: American Council on Education/Oryx Press, 1999).

47. D. Osborne and T. Gaebler, *Reinventing Government: How the Entrepreneurial Spirit is Transforming the Public Sector* (Reading, MA: Addison-Wesley, 1992).

48. A. Dowd and J. Grant, "Equity and Efficiency of Community College Appropriations: The Role of Local Financing," *Review of Higher Education* 29, no. 2 (2006): 167–194.

49. A. Dowd and J. Grant, "Equity and Efficiency of Community College Appropriations," 167–194.

50. U.S. Department of Education, *A Test of Leadership: Charting the Future of U. S. Higher Education* (Washington, DC: U.S. Department of Education, 2006).

51. Education Commission of the States, *State Funding for Community Colleges: A 50-State Survey.* (Denver, CO: Center for Community College Policy, Education Commission of the States, 2000). National Center for Public Policy and Higher Education, *Policy Alert: State Shortfalls Projected to Continue Despite Economic Gains*, 2006 (see n. 44).

52. NASDAQ, *Summary Quote: Apollo Group, Inc.* (2005). http://quotes.nasdaq.com/asp/summaryquote (retrieved April 3, 2008).

53. University of Phoenix, University of Phoenix Website, http://phoenix.edu/ (retrieved November 25, 2007).

54. W. C. Symonds, "Cash-Cow Universities: For-Profits are Growing Fast and Making Money," 2003.

55. M. E. Porter, *Competitive Strategy* (New York: Free Press, 1980).

56. T. Bailey, N. Badway, and P. Gumport. *For-Profit Higher Education and Community Colleges* (Stanford, CA: National Center for Postsecondary Improvement, 2002).

57. National Center for Educational Statistics, *Digest of Educational Statistics, 2004*, 2005.

58. National Center for Educational Statistics, *Digest of Educational Statistics, 2004*, 2005.

59. A. Chung, *Who Are the Proprietary Students: An Analysis of NPSAS 1996 and NPSAS 2000* (Unpublished manuscript, Bloomington, IN, 2004).

60. A. Chung, *Who Are the Proprietary Students.*

61. National Center for Educational Statistics, *National Postsecondary Student Aid Study, 2004* (Washington, DC: National Center for Educational Statistics, 2005).

62. National Center for Educational Statistics, *Digest of Educational Statistics, 2004*, 2005.

63. National Center for Educational Statistics, *Digest of Educational Statistics, 2004*, 2005.

64. National Center for Educational Statistics, *Digest of Educational Statistics, 2004*, 2005.

65. S. Slaughter and G. Rhoades, "Markets in Higher Education: Students in the Seventies, Patents in the Eighties, Copyrights in the Nineties," in *American Higher Education in the Twenty-First Century: Social, Political, and Economic Challenges*, eds. P. Altbach, R. Berdahl, and P. Gumport (Baltimore: Johns Hopkins University Press, 2005).

66. A. Cohen and F. Brawer, *The American Community College*, 4th ed. (San Francisco: Jossey-Bass, 2003).

67. T. Bailey, N. Badway, and P. J. Gumport, *For-Profit Higher Education and Community Colleges*, 2002.

68. Bailey, Badway, and Gumport, *For-Profit Higher Education*.

69. W. C. Symonds, "Cash-Cow Universities: For-profits are Growing Fast and Making Money," 2003.

70. University of Phoenix, University of Phoenix Web site.

71. University of Phoenix, University of Phoenix Web site.

72. University of Phoenix, University of Phoenix Web site.

73. University of Phoenix, University of Phoenix Web site.

74. Bailey, Badway, and Gumport, *For-Profit Higher Education*.

75. T. Bailey, J. Jacobs, and T. Leinbach, *Community Colleges and the Equity Agenda: What the Record Shows*, 2003. (New York, NY: Community College Research Center/Columbia University).

76. Bailey, Badway, and Gumport, *For-Profit Higher Education*.

77. Bailey, Badway, and Gumport, *For-Profit Higher Education*.

78. Bailey, Badway, and Gumport, *For-Profit Higher Education*.

79. University of Phoenix. "Outcomes Assessment," http://www.phoenix.edu/about_us/media_relations/outcomes_assessment/ (retrieved November 18, 2005).

80. University of Phoenix, "Outcomes Assessment."

81. M. Peterson and C. Augustine, "External and Internal Influences on Institutional Approaches to Student Assessment: Accountability or Improvement?" *Research in Higher Education* 41, no. 4 (2000).

82. Bailey, Badway, and Gumport, *For-Profit Higher Education*.

83. R. Alfred, *Managing the Big Picture in Colleges and Universities: From Tactics to Strategy* (Westport, CT: Greenwood Publishing Group, 2005), 77.

3

Coming of Age

Although institutions facing different conditions undergo different patterns of development, there is a fundamental consistency to the development of community colleges that has branded them as a "movement." There have always been challenges. In the beginning it was establishing legitimacy because of values that set them apart from traditional rivals. Later it was coping with converging forces of growth, complexity, and resource austerity that threatened to upset the balance between demand and capacity. Obstacles are part of the life cycle of any successful organization, and community colleges are not an exception. To understand what they will become tomorrow, one needs to see them as the product of a progression between past and present that is without parallel in American higher education.

What community colleges will become is shaped by the interaction of forces in the external environment and their attributes as an organization. The focus of the previous chapter was the external dimension of this relationship, and in this chapter we focus on the internal dimension. We begin with a brief discussion of the growth and development of community colleges to set the table for analysis of their operating dynamics and capacity. Next, a framework is presented that portrays capacity as a product of interaction between three factors: external forces, tangible and intangible resources, and leadership. We use this framework throughout the chapter to describe the state of tangible and intangible resources and leadership in community colleges and their effect on capacity.

MATURATION OF AN INSTITUTION

Every organization has a natural development cycle. Generally, it involves a period of growth followed by deepening maturity, stability,

73

and then decline or renewal depending on whether a new cycle of growth can be launched.[1] Let's fast forward to the infrastructure of today's community colleges and then trace the pattern of growth that brought them to the place they occupy today.

Following their launch in the 1950s and 1960s, community colleges grew at a pace never before seen in American higher education. The number of colleges grew from 412 in 1960 to 1,058 in 1980 to 1,158 institutions in 2004.[2] Enrollment grew from 1.2 million students in 1965 to 4.5 million students in 1985 to more than 6 million students in 2004.[3] By 2005, more than one-third (37 percent) of undergraduate students attending Title IV institutions enrolled in two-year colleges. Money followed enrollment with public community colleges taking in almost $42 billion in revenues in 2005.[4] Virtually every tangible aspect of the institution—mission, programs, services, enrollment, staff, facilities, and money—grew between 1965 and 2005. Growth in intangible assets occurred as well but took a different form. Increasing size led to complexity and a scale of operations that changed the character of institutions. No longer were community colleges small start-up institutions fighting for legitimacy in a market dominated by four-year colleges and universities. Through a strategy of proximity, low cost, and convenience they attracted legions of new learners and morphed into fast-growing service organizations.

With growth and maturation came increasingly elaborate structures and systems to coordinate people and activities. Colleges continued to grow, but demand began to outstrip resources. People who in an earlier time had worked together to promote growth looked for ways to cope with growth. Internal silos grew and flourished, and cultures became fragmented as faculty and staff reduced their conception of the institution to the operating unit. These units took the place of the institution as the primary point of allegiance. One college president described this evolution as follows:

> One of the hallmarks of community colleges is that they're such nimble, responsive organizations. My sense, however, is that across the country they've matured and reached a new stage of development. They may not be as nimble and responsive as they were in the 70s and 80s when they were booming. Our college has a mature faculty and staff, so I'm looking at how to energize the organization to be able to do things it should be doing. How do we transform the organization to ensure that we're as high performing today as we were in the past?[5]

The challenge identified by this president is a challenge that all colleges face. The life cycle literature predicts that new organizational forms replace old ones in successful organizations. Will the same hold true for community colleges? Will they renew the spirit of innovation that made them so successful, or will they enter a period of decline and lose market share to competitors with novel ideas and deep pockets? To better understand the relationship between maturation and performance, we describe the dynamic of growth and expansion that has brought community colleges into the mainstream of American society.

Growth and Expansion

Expenditures and Costs

Historically, community colleges can be described by one word—growth. Growth in the number of colleges, in the number of students at each college, in the mission, in the types of programs and services offered, in revenue and expenditures, in facilities, and in staff. Nationally, community college expenditures have risen from just under $15 billion in 1977 to almost $30 billion in 2001 in constant dollars.[6] Expenditure per student has risen but not dramatically—a finding which points to the ability of mature institutions to produce increasing economies of scale by spreading cost over more students.[7] Lower expenditures per student fuel growth as out-of-pocket costs borne by students have risen more slowly at community colleges than at other institutions. Data from the American Association of Community Colleges and the National Center for Educational Statistics show that while tuition and fees at community colleges have more than doubled over the past thirty years, these increases pale in comparison to those at public and private four-year colleges and universities.[8]

Mission Expansion

When the first community colleges were conceived, over a century ago, most were focused on providing the first two years of a four-year college education. The idea of a comprehensive mission was introduced in 1947 by the Truman Commission on Higher Education, which encouraged the development of community colleges to meet a full spectrum of post-high-school education needs, including occupational and technical education. Over six decades since the Truman Report, an array of different functions have been added to the community college mission, including contract training, developmental education, continuing education and community service, K–12 dual enrollment, the community college baccalaureate, online services, and distance education. Research carried out by the Community College Research Center at Columbia University found mission expansion to be motivated, in part, by a quest for increased enrollment and revenue.[9] The contradiction to this finding is that the more public funding is cut, the more activities community colleges take on to make up the difference in funding.

Increasing Complexity

With increasing size, the organizational architecture of community colleges has become more complex. Mission sprawl has led to more programs, more staff, and increased specialization. These changes find form and expression in increasing breadth and depth of the organizational chart. To support more functions, colleges have distributed work processes among more staff, each performing more specialized tasks than workers before them. Increasing specialization has led to fragmentation as organizational subcultures have grown and proliferated among small numbers of staff working together to deliver a service. A new organization has emerged—one with multiple units pursuing highly specific operating objectives within the loosely coupled structure of a parent organization. The college that started as a handful of faculty and administrators serving several hundred students is now a multifaceted institution serving ten times the number of students through several hundred instructors deployed in multiple departments.

Communication and decision making in this new organization are different in form and function than their makeup in smaller organizations. An executive team tackling a problem in a small college will encounter a smaller number of obstacles to successful implementation compared to a team in a large college. In the larger college, players detached from the center of the institution, involved in different subcultures, or holding different aims may complicate communication and decision-making processes by reinterpreting them to fit the needs and perspectives of the work group. Staff in smaller institutions closer to an initiative's point of origin may have a better understanding of the need for it and, thereby, an easier time supporting it.

Most community colleges have transitioned from smaller-scale organizations to complex organizations. In an earlier day, staff could resolve problems through direct contact with leaders. Increasing size and complexity, however, have rendered direct solutions more difficult as policies, systems, and procedures have been created to coordinate the work of growing numbers of staff. Community colleges now rely heavily on networks and partnerships comprised of people and organizations outside of the college to get work done. Institutions are partnering with K–12 schools to dually enroll students and ladder school/college curricula; with business and industry employers to design and deliver customized programs for employees; with technology firms to design software for distance delivery; with government agencies to develop policies and programs that promote economic development; and with all of these organizations to develop programs and policies that equip youth with the skills needed to compete in a global economy.

Amid this background of increasing complexity, community college leaders are confronted with changing patterns of employee commitment, diminishing control over decision making and operations, and questions about what works and doesn't work in leadership. Is the college a "whole" institution or a sum of its parts? What approaches to leadership and management are effective in a multifaceted organization? How can leaders work to enhance performance in an institution staffed by personnel with multiple aims and different loyalties?

FRAMEWORK FOR INSTITUTIONAL CAPACITY

In 2003, a series of articles was published in the *Community College Journal* profiling a wolf at the door of community colleges.[10] The "wolf" was depicted as living *outside* and *inside* the college. The wolf outside took the form of external challenges—economic uncertainties, competitors, unfriendly legislation, and so on—that are perpetually knocking on a college's door. The wolf inside was described as manifesting itself in ways of doing business that were effective in the past but ineffective in the future. Difficult to see, this "wolf" is perpetually at work in the infrastructure of a college and has much to do with its capacity to perform in ways that meet, exceed, or fall short of expectations.

Capacity is made up of three building blocks that collectively determine how well a college performs: tangible resources, intangible resources, and leadership. Tangible resources are the material assets a college deploys to achieve goals—lines (positions), finances, facilities, equipment, and technology. Intangible resources are nonmaterial assets—culture and climate, processes and systems, communication, staff capabilities, tacit knowledge—that help or hinder a college's ability to achieve goals. The third part of the equation, leadership, is the human action of directing resources to achieve goals. These elements of capacity are the building blocks of institutional performance. Tangible and intangible resources are the raw material of performance, and leadership is the guidance system through which material is leveraged to produce a result—performance that is high or low, good or poor, encouraging or disappointing.

Figure 3.1 presents a framework that can be used to examine capacity in community colleges and the interplay of factors that contribute to it. External forces largely outside of a college's control influence *tangible resources* and, to a lesser extent, the *intangible resources* a college can use

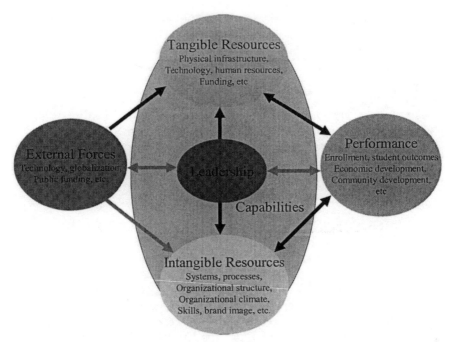

Figure 3.1   Framework for Institutional Capacity

to create value for its stakeholders. *Leaders* deploy these resources to generate a product that meets, exceeds, or falls short of stakeholder needs and expectations (*performance*). *Capacity* is the facility of a college to produce, perform, and deliver value to stakeholders. In its simplest form, it is an expression of a college's potential to achieve goals that meet or exceed stakeholder needs. A college with high capacity gets the most out of its resources by leveraging them into results that exceed performance expectations.

Leadership is posited in the framework as having a direct and indirect influence on performance. Leaders directly influence performance through the decisions they make. Indirectly, they enhance performance by managing tangible and intangible resources in ways that result in more and better value for stakeholders. Working with tangible resources, they enhance value by effectively deploying money, people, space, and technology. They add value through intangible resources by attracting and retaining top quality staff, managing staff and systems effectively, and promoting innovation and change. Leaders, of course, do not do this alone—they need help from others. For this reason, leadership is posited as an activity involving staff at all levels in the organization, not simply those at the top.

The capacity framework features a feedback loop between performance and tangible and intangible resources, which reveals an interesting dynamic of service organizations. Resources are simultaneously a precondition for improved performance and a product of improved performance. As performance improves, institutions become more attractive as settings for work. This phenomenon is readily observed in the hiring process when the volume and quality of applicant pools exceeds institutional expectations. It works the other way, too. Colleges experiencing a decline in reputation and visibility invariably become less attractive as work settings, thereby impacting the quality of staff they are able to attract and retain. The remainder of the chapter discusses the different components of capacity beginning with tangible resources.

TANGIBLE RESOURCES

Tangible resources—money, staff, facilities, and technology—are the first leg of the four-legged stool that is institutional capacity. While we indicated earlier that tangible resources are insufficient to leverage the capacity of a college in and of themselves because their effect is moderated by the actions of leaders, the overall importance of these resources cannot be minimized. For leaders and institutions, tangible resources drive much of what is possible in the way of development. They limit or expand an institution's potential and thereby determine the extent to which leveraging is possible.

Money

Clearly, financial resources are a constant area of concern for community colleges. State funding has steadily declined, local funding continues to depend on the health of regional economies and voter support, and private-sector fund-raising is in a nascent stage of development. A report released by the National Center for Educational Statistics in 2005 reveals the magnitude of the decline in public funding. In 2005, slightly over one-half (55 percent) of community college revenues came from public sources with states contributing 29.8 percent, local government 18 percent, and federal government .4 percent.[11] Only .6 percent came from gifts, 1 percent from investments, and 6 percent from other sources, such as selling noncash gifts and assets.[12] Colleges are increasing tuition and fees to offset the decline in public support, but in doing so risk turning away students most in need of assistance. In the face of diminished public support, most colleges have been forced to support growth through entre-

preneurial activities that leverage resources by reducing costs and generating new revenue.

Revenue

Up to the millennium, the distribution of revenue in community colleges
remained remarkably constant with state government the primary source
of revenue (roughly 45 percent of total revenue) followed by local government (19 percent) and tuition and fees (19 percent).[13] Altogether, these
sources accounted for 83 percent of the revenue taken in by community
colleges while gifts, grants, and endowment accounted for less than 5 percent. Interestingly, community college tuition and fees (adjusted for
inflation using constant 2005 dollars) more than doubled over three decades (1976–1977 to 2004–2005), but in so doing, remained proportional to
other sources of revenue.[14]

Community colleges are not as successful as four-year colleges and universities in garnering resources through private giving, grants, and
endowment. These sources hold considerable promise for the future, but
they account for less than 5 percent of community college revenue.[15]
When one considers the massive increase in charitable donations sparked
by the Gates Foundation, private giving by alumni and affluent benefac-
tors, and grant support by the Lumina Foundation to encourage adoption
of best practices, the possibilities are unlimited. Community colleges are
entering an age of personal and corporate philanthropy in which donors
no longer give principally to traditional institutions. Donors are seeking
evidence of value and impact for their money. This is most readily accomplished by institutions with an instrumental mission working in a
regional market.

Consider, for example, the case of a mid-Atlantic community college
that was a finalist for the MetLife award.[16] The selection committee
informed the president that it was impressed by the work being done by
the college, but insufficient student outcomes data was available to support its selection for an award. Until recently, this college lacked the
resources to establish an assessment office and did not have the capability
to produce outcomes data. This example provides an important lesson:
organizations and agencies that provide grants on a competitive basis will
not be swayed by heartwarming personal stories. They expect to have
access to longitudinal and cross-sectional outcomes data generated by
expert personnel as a basis for award determination.

Expenditures

While revenue provides an index of the capital that colleges have to pursue growth and opportunity, expenditures are an excellent index of their

capacity for growth. Generating revenue is one thing, but having the discretionary capacity to spend it is quite another. Fixed costs as a proportion of the operating budget have been rising in community colleges for more than a decade as public subsidies have declined and operating costs have increased. The net effect is a decline in purchasing power that affects every aspect of institutional operations.

Community college expenditures have more than doubled in constant dollars since 1980. Of note, however, is a rapid acceleration in expenditures beginning in 1997 and extending to 2005 compared to their growth in earlier periods.[17] For example, expenditures rose $5.5 billion between 1997 and 2001 and by an average of $2 to 2.5 billion in four-year growth periods between 1977 and 1997.[18] A number of factors account for this trend, including inflation, rising personnel costs, and start-up and replacement costs for technology. The inescapable bottom line, however, is that community colleges have become big businesses with infrastructure costs that are outstripping revenues.

Facilities

The quality, modernity, and expansiveness of facilities available to students have a lot to do with college choice and the capacity of a college to grow. More and more students are arriving on community college campuses expecting amenities they would receive at a residential four-year college. In the words of a community college president:

> I will not back down from building everything that a college campus should have, because I don't think community college students should be treated as second class citizens. I've seen that in states, where elected officials believe that universities require gymnasiums, fitness centers, and theatres, but community colleges just need classrooms. That gets me mad. People may not intend it, but the statement they are making is, "you're second class citizens and don't deserve the same amenities that other people are getting in higher education institutions."[19]

Data on facilities availability and usage are not available on a national scale for community colleges. Conversations with administrators, however, point to two trends shaping facilities planning on community college campuses: 1) the need for economy via joint-use facilities and 2) customization of facilities to meet changing learner needs. Financially strapped colleges seeking more space at lower cost are turning to joint-use facilities in which partners share construction and maintenance costs. The Community College of Denver (CCD) has created a joint-use campus with a regional state college and the state's premier research university.[20] CCD would not have been able to afford comprehensive facilities on its own, but the benefits of sharing facilities outweigh the benefits of sole ownership. In the words of CCD's former president:

> We share all academic facilities and space for the performing arts center and library . . . you know, virtually all space and there are gathering places as well for the students all over the campus . . . It is what we like to call the power of place because students see what is possible. On their first day, they are on a university campus and they see the next step . . . I think that is a very powerful experience for them and we use it.[21]

In addition to providing a means for expansion of space at reduced cost, joint-use facilities also encourage increased community support. They push a college out into the community and pull citizens onto campus as described by Diane Troyer of Cy-Fair College in Texas:

> We share a public library with the county which was built on our campus in the first phase of construction. Although the results of the library won't be felt for years, we have a steady stream of children on campus every single day, all weekend long—little kids and families, and teens coming to the library on campus and being a part of the college. What will happen 10 years from now or 15 years from now when these children are college ready? We hope that they will feel so comfortable here that enrolling will be something that they just expect to do. So, the library has totally merged the college and the community in ways that we might not have expected.[22]

A second trend in facilities design and usage for many colleges is customization of facilities to meet changing learner needs. College-age students are looking for amenities on community college campuses that separate them from the high school experience—a campus with green space, gathering space in all buildings, a full dining facility, a comprehensive schedule of social and cultural events, athletic and fitness facilities, and even residential facilities on or near campus. When queried about college plans, high school students indicate a growing interest in community colleges but also a desire to get away from home. They find the economy and convenience of community colleges appealing but want a "real college" experience—an experience that cannot be found on a commuter campus which feels like an extension of high school.

Facilities planning requires experience and foresight that looks beyond current student needs and interests. A president engaged in long-range facilities planning captured the essence of the problem:

> The future in terms of facilities will involve significant change. We're looking at flexible learning space as opposed to fixed classrooms and that's why master planning is so important to us. When we talk with design consultants, we

ask them to focus on blended courses and online courses and how they will impact facilities. As more learning takes place outside the classroom, we want to know the implications for long-term planning, particularly enrollment projections and the need for additional facilities.[23]

Human Resources

In today's fast-paced market, acquiring and retaining talented staff has never been more important. Just as sports teams aggressively recruit the best athletes, organizations in business, education, and health compete for the best talent. The skills required of savvy, technologically advanced administrators and staff will become ever more stringent. Organizations inside and outside of higher education will value these skills, and demand will exceed supply. The capabilities required for teaching technologically sophisticated students in varied learning environments will make learning-centered instructors with advanced technology skills a valued commodity. Again, demand will exceed supply. Successful colleges will be those that are most adept at attracting, developing, and retaining staff with skills, perspective, and experience sufficient to thrive in a fast-paced enterprise.[24]

Attracting and retaining top quality staff will be a primary responsibility of leaders, and it will require more than a casual approach. Leaders will need to systematically build and make transparent cultures of inclusion and engagement that provide staff with opportunities to make a difference. Decision making will need to become team focused and shared, rather than driven by a single person. Leadership will entail innovation and risk taking more than it will involve problem solving. It will also require a capacity to share ideas and information widely and with an acute sense of timing. This is a skill that has been mastered by professional service firms which have a unique capacity to generate and share ideas through wide dissemination or "rapid learning" technology. Rapid learning contributes to a culture in which the half-life of information becomes shorter—a circumstance that requires constant updating of staff. Building institutions in which staff work quickly and collectively with current information will be a significant challenge for leaders in the future.

Human Resource Infrastructure

The current condition of human resources in community colleges can best be described as urgent and moving toward a "tipping point." The number of staff has increased to meet the mission and resource requirements of a much larger organization, but one that is also vulnerable because its nucleus is largely part-time staff. Between fall 1991 and fall 2003, the total number of staff employed in community colleges increased 39 percent to 590,000 employees.[25] Of this number, roughly 52 percent of all head-count staff in fall 2003 were part-time—an increase of 5 percent over fall 1993.[26] When staff are parceled into work groups (faculty, nonfaculty professionals, technical and paraprofessionals, and clerical-secretarial), the number of faculty identified as part-time in fall 2003 was 68 percent of all head-count faculty—a significant increase from 58 percent in 1991.[27]

These data portray a condition of rising dependence on contingency staff to cope with dual conditions of escalating growth and diminishing resources. Part-time instructors are now the largest payroll group in community colleges by head count. Reliance on them is increasing, yet they are poorly paid and almost universally excluded from benefits. Colleges invest little in their development, but expect much. Though barely connected to the institution, they are the primary source of contact for many students.

A similar circumstance can be observed for clerical-secretarial staff. In 2003, this group constituted 14 percent of all head-count employees in community colleges.[28] Their work puts them in direct contact with students, and they provide essential office support for administrative operations, yet they are among the lowest paid and least recognized staff in many institutions. They are subordinate to faculty and administrators in voice and influence and, when pressed to describe their work, express frustration at their status as "bit players." What keeps them going is a strong attachment to their work group. When asked why they choose to continue their employment, answers commonly given are affiliation with the work group, a desire to help students, job security, and liberal benefits.[29] This neglected group views itself as the glue that holds the institution together despite the efforts of faculty and administrators.

Beyond the number and qualifications of staff is the issue of diversity. National data are available only for age and race of community college faculty. Community college faculty are older and more diverse today compared to their composition in the early 1990s. Full-time faculty were almost evenly split between those who are fifty and older and those under fifty compared to 56 percent who were under fifty in 1991.[30] The percentage of faculty of minority origin has steadily increased since 1992 (14 percent) to a level of 20 percent in 2003.[31] Viewed in the larger scheme of things, there is ample room for improvement in diversity in all personnel groups in community colleges. The vast majority of faculty and staff are white, yet by 2050 the United States will be a nation of minorities.

Technology

Technology is another resource whose importance cannot be overstated. College operations are increasingly conducted using advanced software.

Furthermore, younger students—the digital natives of the world—expect high-quality, automated services that they can access via the Internet. Community college leaders and staff are becoming increasingly adept with newer technologies but do not yet possess the skills and capabilities of digital natives. The real question with technology, however, is not one of personal skills and technology use, but the capacity of institutions to invest in it.

Data collected through annual surveys of technology investment in community colleges reveal substantial growth. Between 2002 and 2005, centralized IT funding increased from $3.2 million to a mean level of $3.6 million per college and mean IT funding per FTE student increased from $540 to $670.[32] On the administrative side, almost 100 percent of community colleges had invested in student information, financial information, library, and course management systems by 2005.[33] On the academic side, the percentage of classrooms equipped with various technologies increased in virtually every category between 2002 and 2005 except television. In 2005, over 90 percent of community college classrooms were equipped with wired Internet technology followed by LCD projectors (58 percent), computers (54 percent), wireless Internet (40 percent), and television (37 percent).[34]

Technology investment can be intimidating because of up-front fixed costs, lead time required for implementation, and the real risk that technology will be obsolete before it is fully implemented. A key is to invest strategically, with a constant focus on institution-wide goals. Listen to the words of a president describing the state of technology on campus:

> I don't look at technology as a drain. It's a resource and it's a necessary resource, just like electricity. You can't operate the buildings without electricity, and I look at technology in that sense. Technology needs to be tied to your mission and your institutional goals. It is very easy to get caught up in the glamour of the technology itself. To give you an example, a sister institution is promoting the whole college as completely wireless. So you wonder whether wireless is necessary because of the need to keep up. Is an investment needed to make the whole college campus wireless, or does it make more sense to have some areas on campus wireless? What makes the greatest sense in terms of the use of resources?[35]

An example will illustrate this point. Enterprise Resource Planning (ERP) systems integrate all data and processes of an organization into a unified system. A college we worked with recently had an antiquated ERP system that could not perform many basic operations, especially those related to storing and utilizing student data. The counseling department convinced the college to pay a consultant to design a system to store and utilize student data for use by counselors. The project ended up costing a million dollars and took two years to complete. During this time the college decided that it needed to migrate to a more modern ERP—one that easily performs the functions that the college paid the consultant to design, thereby making the consulting fee a wasted expense. The lesson learned is that colleges should invest time and resources up front to make sure they are making sound technology decisions.

An important question on any campus is whether technology for a given purpose should be bought, developed in-house, or outsourced. An advantage of outsourcing is that a college will typically lease hardware and software and therefore need not worry about technology obsolescence. Investment in online courses and blended course delivery is becoming increasingly important, but what makes the most sense— designing and delivering courses in-house, accessing courses through a network, or outsourcing course design and delivery to a third-party vendor? The up-front costs and economies of scale for online education courses are significant. Some colleges have realized benefits by investing early in the game. Others, particularly colleges that are just beginning to invest in online education, may be better off working with third-party vendors or in networks.

INTANGIBLE RESOURCES

Intangible resources are the second leg of the four-legged stool that supports institutional capacity. These resources cannot be easily quantified, and they constitute the informal, subjective, emotive, and process-oriented elements of an organization. They take many shapes and forms depending on how one defines them but generally fall into six categories:

- *People:* the nature of the workforce in a college, including competencies, work experience and skills, tacit knowledge, needs and expectations, perceptions, diversity, and satisfaction
- *Culture:* the values and beliefs that are shared by most of the people in an institution
- *Organizational Architecture:* the administrative structure of an institution that defines its basic units of authority and accountability and its approach to decision making and communication
- *Time:* a continuum comprised of events that succeed one another
- *Systems, Policies, and Processes:* elements of a framework denoting a course of action to achieve a specific goal or purpose
- *Reputation:* attributes of an institution as seen by its stakeholders

People

Interviews with executives and interaction with faculty and staff as part of campus-based projects reveal that human resources are viewed as the most important determinant of success in community colleges. This corresponds to much of the corporate literature which stipulates that what truly makes good companies great is their ability to attract and retain the right people—staff with highly developed competencies who are excited about what they are doing and the environment they are working in.[36] But, how do colleges attract the right people and get the most out of them? Conversations with community college leaders reveal a simple formula: create a distinctive culture, hire the right people, strive for consistency, let your staff lead, and celebrate achievement.

Create a Distinctive Culture

A distinctive culture is made up of signature experiences that are visible and unique, that create value for a college, and that serve as a constant reminder of what the institution values and what it stands for. These experiences are created by everyday routines that are difficult for other institutions to mimic because they develop internally and reflect the ethos of leaders and staff.[37] Colleges with distinctive cultures excel at expressing what makes them unique. They know what they are and what they want to be. They understand their current and prospective staff, and they vividly demonstrate what they are with stories of actual practices and events in contrast to vision statements and core values that appear on placards and the college Web site. By defining and communicating who they are in clear and memorable ways, colleges with visible and distinctive cultures empower prospective staff to make well-informed employment decisions.[38] As a consequence, these colleges hire people who readily and enthusiastically fit in, thereby cultivating a more motivated staff.

The seeds of a healthy culture exist in most colleges. The challenge is to find them and extend them to the needs of prospective staff. Consider the remarkable transformation of Central Piedmont Community College (CPCC) in North Carolina from a single-campus operation to a flourishing multicampus system in the short space of ten years. CPCC's leaders credit the change to a work environment that values connectivity, action, and commitment.[39] Faculty and staff continuously deliver high-quality results with limited resources—a signature experience that is part of CPCC's culture communicated through stories, anecdotes, and the everyday behavior of people.

Early in its development, CPCC developed a deep connection with the citizens of Charlotte. Name recognition was high, and the college branded itself as an institution delivering quality educational experiences to students of all backgrounds. Through the efforts of high-performing faculty, CPCC took on the ambience of a dependable organization—one that would move in step with the community and would be there for its constituents. The community side of the equation changed, however, with explosive growth in the 1990s that transformed Charlotte from a small city into a flourishing metroplex.[40] Charlotte grew beyond the single-campus structure of CPCC and required an educational delivery system capable of operating on a larger playing field. The mismatch between educational need and capacity posed a "sink or swim" circumstance for CPCC—either significantly expand the delivery system or give up market share to competitors. The can-do attitude of leaders and staff and their commitment to serving Charlotte's needs resulted in a dramatic expansion to a six-campus system placing full-service facilities in proximity to regional citizens. This is a central element of the "signature experience" at CPCC, and it sends a clear message about its culture to prospective employees.

Hire the Right People

Nurturing talent begins with setting clear expectations for the job and hiring the right people. One president put it this way:

> The big thing is to be careful with the people you hire for each and every position, because they're going to be the culture. They're going to be the deciding factor in whether you end up with the culture you hope to get or you don't. You can't have a culture that people aren't a part of. This is especially true when hiring for full-time positions because it is difficult to fire even the worst employees and they have an impact on others.[41]

There are a number of factors involved in hiring that can help or hurt a college in the hunt for talent. Beyond the obvious, such as supply of candidates, college reputation, and ability to pay, are more discrete factors; for example, attributes of the workplace, perceived fit with culture, and the hiring process itself. Successful colleges hire on the basis of fit with the institutional mission and culture. They also use rigorous screening processes, including screening by a search committee, multifaceted interviews, teaching and management demonstrations, and comprehensive reference checks. Finally, they engage new hires in an extended orientation process that carries through the first year of employment and beyond to ensure assimilation into the culture.

Strive for Consistency

To attract and retain talent, distinctive attributes of a college's work environment must be buttressed by processes that deliver consistent messages to staff. One of the most common causes of disengagement is staff perception that some elements of the work experience aren't as they were described in the hiring process. It is not uncommon in conversations with recent hires to hear the lament, "This is not what I expected or wanted." Resolving disappointment at this point in affiliation is not going to be easy because disparity between expectation and experience is something that takes time to reconcile.

Several years ago, a college we were working with discovered a problem in morale with recent hires that it thought was due to an ineffective orientation process. A closer look revealed that the orientation process was not the problem; it accurately reflected the top-down, highly structured nature of the institution. The problem was occurring much earlier, during recruitment, when the institution promised prospective staff a flexible work environment with opportunities for growth and innovation. To create consistency between expectation and experience, this college faced a choice of changing its pitch to job candidates or changing the work experience. The easier choice, of course, was to change the recruiting pitch—an adjustment the college made in its literature and recruiting practices.

Let Staff Lead

People are more apt to become invested in a college if they feel that they have a voice in decisions that give direction to the institution. The best strategy for retaining quality staff is to let them lead in areas that make a difference in their work. The experience with change of many colleges is a telling example of the price that leaders pay for failing to let staff lead. In research carried out with fifteen community colleges in 2004, we found that most of them were experiencing difficulty in managing change.[42] Conversations with representative staff groups in each institution revealed that although change did happen, the experience was often unpleasant because personnel who would be expected to implement change were often not consulted in its design. Disengaged staff are costly for any institution. They are its "face" for prospective students and staff who get a "read" on the institution through their actions and demeanor. The difference between success and failure in attracting and retaining talented staff can often be traced back to employee engagement.

Celebrate Achievement

Hiring people that fit the culture, striving for consistency, and providing leadership opportunities will go a long way in attracting and retaining talent. However, it is important to recognize the contributions of staff and to remind them that they are having an impact on one another and on the lives of students. For many, it is not about money or benefits—it is about feeling valued as a member of a community.

In the corporate world, optimizing the productivity and creativity of staff is viewed as critical to long-term competitive success. Among the more common methods for renewing and reinvigorating employees is the redesign of performance appraisal systems to provide feedback and allocate rewards based on performance. Recognition processes that highlight and reward employees and teams for extraordinary performance are also used. Investing in these methods creates an organization that can anticipate and respond to changing business conditions through the initiative of committed employees.

Culture

Culture can most easily be understood as values and beliefs that are shared by most people in an organization. In the voluminous literature on this topic, Schein's work has done much to influence the thinking of practitioners about culture and its relationship to performance. Schein describes culture as defined by six properties: 1) shared basic assumptions that 2) develop over time within a given group as it 3) learns to cope with changes in the external environment and internal organizational dynamics that 4) have worked well enough to be considered valid, and, therefore 5) can be taught to new members of the group as the 6) correct way to perceive, think, and feel about the organization.[43] Staff inside community colleges interpret Schein's properties much more simply: culture is *how we do things around here* and *what we expect around here*. If everyone feels strongly about the importance of a behavior, there is little latitude for deviation, and departures from the norm are dealt with swiftly.[44] For instance, if most staff feel strongly that a smoke-free campus is essential, anyone who attempts to smoke in or near a building is likely to be sanctioned. If, however, agreement is less widespread and staff hold mixed feelings about the issue, there will be a soft norm about smoking, deviations will be more commonplace, and the culture itself will do little to hold the group together.

Working with community colleges, we have had the opportunity to observe leaders and staff in a variety of cultures, some functional and others dysfunctional. Common themes have emerged from our observations irrespective of time, place, and the condition of culture:

- *Culture is important.* Leaders spend a lot of time managing culture because it shapes the attitudes that staff bring to work, how they interact with one another, and how they act with students.

- *Culture is complex.* Most definitions of culture describe it as "assumptions and beliefs shared by members of an organization." The reality is, however, that with increasing size and complexity, community colleges have become loosely coupled organizations with multiple cultures. Many of today's colleges are "many institutions in one"—an aggregate of subcultures (divisions, departments, and hierarchies) that espouse different values and work differently depending on their charter in the institution.
- *Culture is difficult to change.* Organizational culture is notoriously difficult to change. Core values that are internalized by staff drive how people perceive issues and shape norms for behavior. These values induce conformity that, in turn, fuels resistance to actions which do not fit prevailing values.
- *Leaders are the stewards of culture.* Despite the intractability of organizational culture, leaders are constantly in a position to shape and influence culture. They are closely watched, and their behavior and actions reinforce or introduce shifts in culture. Behavior that is consistent with cultural norms reinforces while that which is contradictory signals a shift.
- *Employee turnover is an opportunity and a threat to culture.* Individuals have an impact on organizational culture. Leaders that guide an institution through significant obstacles may become part of an organizational saga, lasting long after their departure.[45] Successful leaders view hiring and acclimation as critical events in the life of a college because each new hire is an opportunity to enrich or change the culture.

Organizational Architecture

Architecture refers to the way in which an organization divides administrative tasks between divisions, departments, and positions to achieve important goals.[46] It could be argued that it is a tangible resource because it contains structural properties that are commonly represented on an organizational chart. It also has intangible aspects in the form of authority, power, and influence used by leaders to give direction to an institution—where it goes, what it does, and how it works. It is the intangible aspect of architecture that is of interest to us in the discussion that follows.

Theoretical Perspectives

Three schools of thought have evolved over time in organizational theory that are helpful in describing the impact and importance of architecture.

They are the *rational perspective*, the *natural perspective*, and the *open systems perspective*. According to proponents of the rational perspective, an organization is an entity that has a formal structure (a hierarchy) in which each member seeks to pursue the specific goals of the organization.[47] Theorists favoring the natural perspective see things differently: leaders and staff are motivated by their own self-interest rather than the goals of the organization; goals are problematic because organizations pursue multiple, conflicting goals; and the overarching goal is survival of the organization itself.[48] The open systems perspective swings full circle from the emphasis on organization in the rational perspective and people in the natural perspective to an emphasis on the environment. It acknowledges the impact of the external environment on organizations because of their need for resources and conditions in the environment that affect the flow of resources.[49]

Layering and Complexity

This backdrop provides a framework for analysis of organizational architecture in community colleges. Our colleges are no longer simple organizations in which staff perform prescribed tasks in pursuit of organizational goals. They have become complex organizations—some would say "bureaucracies"—that have evolved to address uncertain conditions and logistical complexities. Bureaucracies are well suited to deal with stable routine tasks and become a basis for organizational efficiency. When rapid change is necessary, however, the efficiencies of bureaucracy are more difficult to realize, and alternative approaches to organizing are needed to accomplish institutional goals. In community colleges this has taken the form of developing layers in the organization that are closer to the external environment (e.g., workforce development institutes, corporate services, continuing education departments, etc.) that provide a buffer, so that core functions can continue their work unimpeded.

Layering, while designed to ease the harmful effects of bureaucracy, has increased complexity. For example, on many campuses continuing education is an entirely separate division from academic affairs. It has its own administrators, its own information system, and its own infrastructure, but its purpose is the same as academic affairs—delivering instruction to learners. There are countless examples of layering in community colleges ranging from foundations to reduce financial dependence on public funding, to administrative divisions that house the office of development, to marketing experts who play a critical role in image building, and to lobbyists who work with local and state policymakers. Interestingly, layering does not seem to lead to productivity gains until it is reflected in changes in operating systems and processes. For example, the movement toward a one-stop design for student services holds considerable promise for improving processing times for students as well as customer satisfaction, but its full effect is generally not felt until institutional systems, processes, and technology are brought up to speed with changes in structure.

Our experience with organizational architecture in community colleges has taught us that the way people are deployed and their function in the organization has a lot to do with performance. By "deployment" we mean the latitude people have to make decisions that get work done and move the institution forward in pursuit of its goals. In the past, leaders have relied on structural change like reorganization, realignment, and rightsizing to improve staff and organizational performance. Changing the structure, however, does not necessarily change the people or improve their performance, as leaders have all too often discovered. A host of factors are involved in performance enhancement. Hammer identifies five characteristics that are essential for an organizational structure to work in today's landscape.[50] The structure must provide staff with an *opportunity to learn and grow*, or they will lose interest and disengage from the institution. Staff must have appropriate *skills and knowledge* if they are to perform effectively. *Owners* need to be in place throughout the organization with responsibility for ensuring that people deliver results, or staff will lose sight of their contribution to the goals of the organization. The institution must align its *infrastructure*—systems, processes, and technology—with the formal structure in order to perform effectively. Finally, the institution must develop and use the right *metrics* to assess performance if the structure is to deliver the best results.

Time

A fundamental way in which work life in any organization is different from the past is the time frame in which it is conducted. Today, speed and simultaneous tasking are essential for getting things done. Information life cycles are getting shorter, deadlines are getting tighter, and students and staff expect almost instantaneous attention to their needs. The need to bring together and harmonize widely different stakeholders, to coordinate and manage work groups with different portfolios, and to maintain networks of collaborating organizations has made time a valuable resource.

Put yourself in the shoes of a president about to begin a workday. Here is a likely sequence of events for the day:

- 5:00 to 6:00 a.m.—Scan news on the Internet and e-reports on a handheld PDA.

- 7:00 a.m.—Arrive on campus to scan college e-mail and review information and reports that are background material for scheduled meetings.
- 8:00 a.m.—Breakfast meeting with faculty and staff representatives on the College Governance Council; check Blackberry and return urgent messages during the meeting.
- 9:00 to 9:30 a.m.—Draft comments for opening remarks that will be delivered at a Chamber of Commerce dinner on campus that evening; return e-mail and phone calls from the office.
- 9:30 to 10:00 a.m.—Participate in an audio conference on the impact of community colleges on the regional economy sponsored by the State Community College Board.
- 10:00 a.m. to noon—Weekly meeting with the executive team; scan Blackberry at intervals during the meeting, and use cell phone to gather information about a discussion item.
- Noon to 1:15 pm.—Attend off-campus luncheon meeting with local business leaders.
- 1:30 to 1:45 pm.—Return to college and provide welcoming remarks to regional K–12 guidance counselors who are holding a workshop on campus.
- 2:00 to 3:00 p.m.—Meet with Strategic Planning Steering Committee; scan Blackberry at intervals throughout the meeting and reply to important messages.
- 3:00 to 3:30 p.m.—Conference call with regional community college presidents on technology requirements for e-college consortium.
- 3:30 to 3:45 p.m.—Meet with administrative assistant to coordinate meeting schedule for the week.
- 3:45 to 4:30 p.m.—Meet with vice president of administrative services on the college budget.
- 4:30 p.m.—Attend a reception for graduating nursing students.
- 5:00 p.m.—Participate in a telephone interview with a local newspaper reporter regarding a new program that will be offered by the college.
- 5:30 p.m.—Check e-mail, return phone calls, and review remarks to be delivered at dinner meeting.
- 6:00 to 7:30 p.m.—Attend reception prior to dinner meeting and deliver remarks at close of dinner.
- 8:00 p.m.—Return home and quickly scan e-memos, phone messages, and e-mails.

The lives of leaders and staff are heavily impacted by technology and a constant flow of information—both requested and disbursed—from a variety of sources. Multitasking is necessary to keep up with unrelenting demands for time, information, and action. Even "downtime" is spent acquiring information as a prelude to action. For leaders and staff working in the fast lane, time is a precious resource. It provides the opportunity to disengage from operations and work with the big picture.

Systems, Policies, and Processes

As community colleges have grown from small to large-scale organizations, systems and policies have been created to get things done. Some would liken policies to "rules" and decry the impersonal nature of work in today's colleges compared to an earlier time when communication was face-to-face and decisions could be made through informal conversation. Our experience with faculty and staff in community colleges reveals mixed feelings about policies and systems. They are an inconvenience, but a necessary evil. On the one hand, rules are missing where needed, and procedures have not been developed to bring consistency to the work performed by different units. On the other hand, there are too many rules, and staff express frustration at outdated policies and procedures which constrain their work.

High-performing colleges have found ways to make policies and systems work as a lever for improving performance. Institutions engaged in process management like Illinois Central College, Northern Essex Community College (Massachusetts), and Owens Community College (Ohio) have created a culture of collaboration in which staff are continually engaged in improving processes (and, by extension, policies and systems) to better meet the needs of the people they serve. These colleges know that faculty and staff working in silos detached from the center of the institution are a breeding ground for inefficiency and duplication. In the process of becoming entrenched, departments and staff develop comfortable ways of doing business that convenience them but often inconvenience other units. This phenomenon is known as "process ownership," and it can be observed on every community college campus. Dealing with process ownership is tricky, but there are steps that colleges can take to make policies, systems, and processes work more effectively.

Foster a Supportive Environment

In order to develop high-performance policies, systems, and processes, leaders must develop organizational capabilities in four areas: leadership, culture, expertise, and governance. Change efforts are doomed in circumstances in which the executive team is not visibly committed to system and process improvement.[51] Redesigning systems and processes requires extensive change that can lead to resistance and failure without the backing of senior leaders. Only institutions whose cultures value personal accountability and a willingness to change will find it possible to move forward with process-focused change initiatives. And, for these initiatives to be successful, leaders must have meaningful ways of involving staff in decisions that affect their work.

Invest in Communication

An effective communication system is vital to the success of most change initiatives and essential in process redesign. Poor communication is costly in terms of staff time and commitment. In larger institutions its consequences are especially severe as the need for effective communication increases exponentially as more individuals are added to the change process. The converse is also true—as people are removed or excluded from communication, the effect is to detach them from the change process and limit its likelihood of success.

Colleges that have experienced success with internal communication have maintained a commitment to accepted forums of communication, such as faculty senates, all-college meetings, and convocations. In these forums, ideas are vetted college-wide, and adjustments are made based on staff feedback. Slower, more frequently used modes of communication are augmented by modes that are quicker and less costly in terms of staff time. This is important because from the moment they arrive on campus, staff are blitzed with information coming from multiple angles. To direct attention to important information, some colleges are moving to "quick capture" systems in which information is provided to staff in easy display formats at convenient locations (kiosks, video boards, storyboards, etc.) where it cannot be missed. Furthermore, multiple venues are being used to communicate the same information so it is continually being reinforced. A community college president new to a college and seeking to gain the attention of staff described the approach to communication she used to plant seeds for college-wide organizational restructuring as follows:

> I immediately put in place a month long, college wide vetting of a restructuring proposal. I personally not only attended forums on each campus, but had an all college meeting where I presented the whole proposal, had it videotaped, and put it on our "daily posts." The first thing you see when you open up your computer every morning is the daily post. We put the videotape out so nobody in the college would have any reason to feel that they'd not heard about this, and that's a big part of my approach to anything that involves change.[52]

Networks and Partnerships

Perhaps the most significant and least understood intangible resource that community colleges work with is the network of organizations that partner with them to deliver educational services. Partnerships have become a sine qua non for most colleges, and they are a prominent part of high-performing colleges. The value of partnerships can be most easily understood through the experience of colleges that use them to create competitive advantage.

Build Competency through Partnering

In case studies and interviews with community college leaders, we have found that innovative colleges focus very little attention on competition. This finding is consistent with recent corporate research indicating that organizations perform better if they focus their energy on making a good product rather than on beating the competition. The video game industry provides an interesting example. Microsoft (Xbox) and Sony (PS3) focused their energy on competition with one another and essentially compromised their product. The Nintendo Wii—which everyone had discounted—became a surprise success, despite inferior specifications. Flying under the radar, Nintendo focused on creating a product that gave great value to customers, rather than competing with Xbox or PS3 on specifications.

Similarly, we have found that entrepreneurial colleges do not worry about high-flying competitors like the University of Phoenix or DeVry. The best way to overcome competitors is to create greater value for your customers by creating and sustaining superior networks. In the words of a president:

> I think the way to approach competition is to enhance what we already do well and that is to craft partnerships and linkages that make sure our institution is on everybody's radar screen relative to what we can do—the beginning of a four-year degree, the training component of local business, or occupational connection with a business. We will continue to work hard at not being a threat to anyone, but to being everybody's best partner.[53]

Imagine a law enforcement program in which a college co-constructed and shares facilities with a local law enforcement agency. The agency is given a voice in curriculum design to ensure that courses are relevant to the profession. The college employs full-time law-enforcement professionals as adjunct professors. The president of the institution that developed this program gives voice to the synergy of such a partnership:

They [the local police officers] love teaching. . . . It really adds something to their lives, that they can come back and share what they do with the people that want to come through that pathway. And students love someone who's just come off the shift, teaching them about . . . undercover, or self defense, or whatever. I mean, you don't want a theoretician teaching in those areas. You want a practitioner. That's how partnerships work and why they're so successful.[54]

Take Care of Business

Community college leaders, especially those without local funding, know that financial stability depends on enrollment growth. However, growing enrollment depends on targeting specific types of students and building programs that cater to their needs. Partnerships can be pivotal in targeting services to new populations. Dual enrollment programs with high schools bring in students and increase the number of students attending community colleges following high school graduation. Developing expansive articulation agreements with regional four-year colleges and universities increases student flow as does the creation of on-campus facilities like university centers. Partnerships with area businesses in the form of facilities sharing, equipment donation, curriculum design, and so forth expand the pipeline as do partnerships with government agencies and technology providers.

Leverage Prestige

Recent network theory research has found that institutions can enhance their reputation by creating partnerships with prestigious organizations. We have found ample evidence of this phenomenon in our research on community colleges. A college in Florida, for example, was the only college in the state to establish a transfer agreement with a prestigious engineering school. "That got people's attention in the community more than anything we've ever done," said the president. "When I would talk about that example people said 'What—students can go to your college and then go to engineering school?' Students are being denied access to this school across the world, but they can access it through our program."[55]

Partnerships come with strings. Faculty from the engineering school referenced above were allowed to serve on search committees for math and science instructors at the community college and to make curriculum recommendations. "We had the president of the engineering college on our advisory council and now he's retiring and is going to be a foundation board member."[56] This is a good example of a win-win prestigious partnership. The visibility gained through the partnership was an effective marketing tool while the extension of the partnership into the inner workings of courses and curricula enabled the college to improve the quality of its offerings.

Nurture and Sustain Relationships

Like anything involving trust, partnerships are hard to build, require work to maintain, and are easy to destroy. College presidents with successful partnerships spend significant time nurturing these relationships. A president commented on his efforts to grow and maintain partnerships:

> You really have to work on it. It's all about relationships with people. We wouldn't have partnerships with our universities if the presidents of those institutions and I didn't have strong personal relationships and know each other as friends and not look at each other as competitors. There are communities where colleges don't even talk to each other, and so it's all about the personal relationships. You need to cultivate friends—if you don't, the partnerships can unravel pretty quickly.[57]

Reputation

Presidents of high-performing colleges indicate that reputation is an important resource for an institution. There are many ways to establish a reputation, but high-performing colleges do it through metrics that benchmark performance in a particular area and making sure that key stakeholders are aware of the results. Stakeholders acknowledge superior performance by providing more resources, thereby enriching program and service offerings and attracting more learners—a circumstance which fuels growth and adds to the aura of success. A college president explained the power of reputation this way:

> When I first came to the college, it was on the verge of closure due to corruption and scandal. We worked hard to put the college on a better footing with important stakeholders and it has paid off. Our reputation has improved to the point that this has become the most prestigious county board you can be on. When I first took office enrollment was a little under 3,000. This fall it was 6,707. Next fall we'll certainly be breaking 7,000 students. Credit hours have gone up as much or more. We have higher than the national average retention rate for community colleges. Only 9 percent of our students pay full tuition—70 percent plus are on some kind of financial aid or scholarship. So this is a prestigious thing for this county, coming from where we were.[58]

LEADERSHIP

Capacity is a function of an institution's facility to leverage tangible and intangible resources into value for stakeholders. Leveraging—enhancing performance through the effective use of resources—is only as good as the people who are using the resources. Executives are the primary decision makers about resources in institutions with a traditional top-down administrative structure. In our view, however, leaders operate at multiple levels in an institution. They are executive officers and deans, department chairs, middle administrators, unit heads, faculty, and support staff—virtually anyone in a position to make a decision about and deploy resources. We can see the action of leaders in a decision made by a president to recommend a new program to the board for approval, a decision by a department chair to add a new course, a decision by a director or coordinator to streamline a process, and a decision by a service unit head to realign staff roles within a work team. We can also see the action of leaders in faculty who engage in curriculum reform and support staff who develop new approaches to serving students without the urging of superiors.

Leadership is the third leg of the four-legged stool that is institutional capacity. It is a complex phenomenon that takes different shapes and hues as contextual forces change inside and outside of an organization. For example, people expect different things from leaders in different periods of organizational development. When community colleges were started, leaders were expected to perform goal setting and managerial roles that are part of a new enterprise. As they grew in size and stature, skills in planning and managing growth became more important. Today, community colleges are at the cusp of a movement toward shared governance in which staff will be expected to make decisions on their own in contrast to seeking directives from leaders. In an ideal sense, they will reach the zenith of their development as complex organizations when staff in every part of the organization realize and exercise the full potential of their capacity for leadership.

Irrespective of where an organization is in its development, leaders who are effective are adept at leveraging resources. Learning about the behavioral attributes that make them effective is instructive because it provides insights into the role that leadership plays in building organizational capacity. Over the next several pages, we focus on the attributes of leaders who have a proven record of success in elevating institutional performance through leveraging. These attributes are gleaned from the ideas of leading scholars in organizational leadership and management, interviews, and case study observations involving community college presidents and executive officers. Particularly useful in the world of scholarship were the works of Deborah Ancona, Thomas Malone, Wanda Orlikowski, and Peter Senge (*In Praise of the Incomplete Leader*) and Karl Weick and Katherine Sutcliffe (*Managing the Unexpected: Assuring High Performance in an Age of Complexity*).[59] Useful in the world of practice were the ideas of leaders in abundant institutions; that is, institutions marked by plentiful resources leveraged through the efforts of leaders.

Leadership Is about Visioning

Let's start with the obvious—an effective leader must be able to create a picture of what a college should look like as a platform for change and development. Visioning involves creating a compelling image of the future—a portrait of what a college could be and, more important, what it should be. An effective vision is far more than a statement on paper. It is a dynamic process of articulating what people want for the institution. It provides a sense of meaning for their work and unites them in commitment to a common purpose.

Leaders who are skilled in visioning are able to get staff excited about their conception of the future while inviting them to sharpen the image.[60] They use stories and metaphors to paint a vivid picture of what the vision is and what it will accomplish, even if they don't have a clear plan for getting there. They work to embody the core values and ideas contained in the vision. The president and executive team at Tulsa Community College provide a good example. Tulsa's president—a twenty-year career administrator at the college—is committed to core values of inclusiveness and staff engagement.[61] Upon his selection as president in 2004, he moved to build a more inclusive culture by opening communication channels and expanding staff involvement in goal setting and decision making. Administrators, faculty, and staff achieved common ground in planning and decision making through an institution-wide training program in strategic thinking—a protocol designed to sharpen analytical capabilities by increasing awareness of trends and forces in the external environment. Facilitators trained in strategic thinking worked with small groups of faculty and staff throughout the institution. Their agenda was to cultivate interest in strategic thinking and to encourage faculty and staff to use it in their work. Inclusion and engagement were no longer abstract ideas in a vision statement; they became an important part of the culture in which staff carried out their work.

Leadership Is about Inventiveness

To transform a vision of the future from an idea to a reality, leaders need to devise processes to make it real. Even the most compelling vision will lose its power if it floats unconnected above the everyday reality of organizational life. Inventing is what leaders do to relate a vision to what people are actually doing.[62] It moves a vision from the abstract world of ideas to the concrete world of implementation.

Effective leaders recognize and understand the world of operations and the comfort that staff draw from involvement in routine activities. They know that a new vision will be essentially meaningless unless new ways of organizing and interacting are found that stretch people and help them overcome previously insurmountable obstacles. Lorain County Community College (LCCC) in Ohio provides an excellent illustration of the inventive capability of leaders in visioning a college to a new future.[63] Twice over a ten-year period (1996 and 2006), Lorain has embarked on a community-wide visioning program to frame a new vision for the college. In 1996, structured conversations with campus and community groups led to the creation of a vision and strategic priorities that positioned Lorain to become a hub for community development. In this capacity, LCCC moved to define and energize redevelopment of the county through strategic priorities that included raising technological competencies of the community, developing the whole person, advancing creative learning opportunities, stimulating workforce and economic development, and promoting community collaboration and growth.

These priorities created a new horizon for the county and the college and challenged leaders to design new ways of doing business. To transform the vision of community development into an operational reality, LCCC's leaders created a sixth priority—building the college's infrastructure. The portfolios and position titles of senior administrators and job descriptions of key staff were changed to place an emphasis on identifying and pursuing opportunities with the community. Senior administrators were empowered to reach out and work directly with community organizations and conduct much of their work outside of institutional boundaries. In partnership with community leaders, they identified areas for development, who to work with, resource requirements, and desired outcomes. Coupled with this commitment to community development, Lorain's infrastructure enabled it to work with a network of collaborating organizations that leveraged each other's performance to new heights. What makes the inventiveness of Lorain's leaders so unique is that it has led to the creation of a new relationship between college personnel, and the community. In this relationship, the structure of the network that Lorain has created is more important than its own administrative structure.

Leadership Is about Smart Choices

The burgeoning needs of stakeholders in an increasingly complex environment can easily distract leaders and divert their attention from important challenges and opportunities. Effective leaders have the capacity to concentrate on issues that make a difference for the institution. They are able to cull important challenges from among many problems requiring attention. The skill of an executive in picking the "right" challenges and acting on them adds an important dimension to our understanding of leadership in community colleges. It involves the wise investment of time—a scarce resource—to realize maximum return on investment.

When Maurice Hickey became president of Clinton Community College (New York) in 2005, he encountered a college in disarray.[64] The college was situated in a community struggling to maintain its balance. The regional economy was in a tailspin following the loss of a military base and major industries, unemployment and substance addiction rates were rising, high schools were reporting a sharp increase in the number of dropouts, and workers and families were leaving the area to find a better future elsewhere. Inside the college, a series of presidents had come and gone after short stays, the leadership team was off balance, academic and administrative units were working in silos, internal competition for resources was fierce, and acrimony prevailed in relationships among faculty and staff. As Hickey took stock of the many and varied challenges facing the college, the question that came immediately to mind was: Where do I begin?

Lacking an easy answer, but knowing that choices would have to be made because of limited resources, Hickey initiated a fast-track strategic planning process. Over a six-month period, information was gathered through structured conversations with elected officials and community organizations, employers, K–12 schools, and influential citizens. Faculty and staff met in small group sessions facilitated by consultants to describe their perceptions of college capacity, performance, and areas for improvement. Published documents and reports describing regional trends and projections were acquired from planning agencies and reviewed for themes and implications. Information from these sources was merged and synthesized in a comprehensive report describing different scenarios for college development and priorities associated with each. The report was distributed electronically to all full-time staff for review and consideration prior to a retreat in which alternative paths for development would be weighed and decisions made regarding priorities. This process culminated in the selection of eight priorities that would guide Clinton into the future:

- Build *community* through a shared vision of the future, a respect for the importance of the past, and open and honest communication.
- Pursue a strategy of targeted growth by determining optimum size, pursuing opportunities for collaboration, and developing innovative systems for student recruitment.
- Become an active player in regional economic development through partnerships with business and industry and local government.

- Build educational bridges to K–12 and four-year colleges and universities by serving as the hub of a seamless continuum for student transition between K–12 education, postsecondary education, and work.
- Position the college as a community resource and as a hub for community development.
- Build on the existing quality of learning at the college and make it the hallmark of Clinton Community College.
- Cultivate a holistic approach to student success by developing curriculum "ladders" and a "success academy" to raise student expectations and bring completion within reach of all students.
- Place a renewed emphasis on, and aggressively address, the learning needs of adults in the service region.[65]

Interestingly, the choices made by Clinton's faculty and staff were consistent with the values and preferences of its new president. Among many alternatives the college could pursue, the "smart" choice boiled down to building harmonious working relationships inside and bridges to partners outside for the purpose of leveraging resources.

Leadership Is about Balancing Ideas and Execution

Colleges frequently get stuck in an "either-or" trap—either manage for today by focusing on operations or invest in the future by focusing on strategy. Savvy leaders take a dual approach by surrounding themselves with talented staff who excel in operational and strategic disciplines. While insisting on efficiency and strong performance in current operations, they also invest wisely in what it will take to be an innovator in the future.

Consider Anne Arundel Community College (Maryland) which has grown from just shy of 12,000 credit students and 450 full-time staff in 1998 to more than 23,000 credit students and 750 full-time staff today.[66] Developing and nurturing the college's unique learning-centered culture has been one of President Martha Smith's biggest challenges; it is also one of her biggest successes. Smith has made it clear that consciously and consistently executing tactics central to Anne Arundel's strategy as a learning-centered institution is of paramount concern. Faculty and staff are expected to rigorously analyze their courses, programs, and services and to justify their plans and performance on the basis of the value they deliver to learners. At the same time, they are expected to create initiatives to serve future generations of learners by looking ahead and identifying trends in learner needs and expectations. The emphasis is on managing high performance through value delivered to learners *today* as well as *tomorrow*.[67]

Leadership Is about Sensemaking

The term "sensemaking" was coined by organizational psychologist Karl Weick, and it refers to the "way people interpret situations to make sense of the world around them."[68] Effective leaders are constantly striving to understand the contexts they are operating in. How will new technologies reshape the industry of education? How will the entry of new competitors affect market share? What effect will globalization have on public expectations for education?

Weick likened the process of sensemaking to cartography.[69] What we map depends on where we look, what factors we choose to focus on, and what aspects of the terrain we decide to depict. The key for leaders is to determine what would be a useful map given particular goals and how to draw a map that accurately represents the context the college is operating in. Executives who possess this capability know how to capture the complexities of their environment and explain them to others in simple terms.[70] They acquire information from multiple sources, involve others in sensemaking activities, check with staff who have contrary perspectives, use early observations to frame small initiatives to test their ideas, and open themselves to new possibilities.[71]

The sensemaking literature emphasizes the importance of first impressions. People often latch on to the first plausible interpretation of a situation or event that they encounter. They develop opinions that reinforce previous actions and selectively ignore evidence to the contrary. In the words of a president: "Perception is reality. Even if what someone thinks is not accurate or true, if enough people believe it, it becomes reality."[72]

College leaders are the ultimate sensemakers of a college, but they cannot focus exclusively on people and activities inside the institution and expect to be effective. Sensemaking also has to do with the way in which a college is seen by stakeholders in the external environment. Leaders bear responsibility for managing image and constituency impressions. The ultimate test of their ability to lead is perhaps their ability to interpret the meaning and importance of the institution to stakeholders with rapidly shifting needs and expectations.

Leadership Is about Relating

Leaders are expected to foster trust, optimism, and harmonious relationships among employee groups, more often than not, working in silos. For leaders who have difficulty relating to others, especially those who don't see the institution as they do, these efforts can reap feelings of anger, cynicism, and conflict. Building trust is a requirement of effective leadership—a lesson that the president of a multicampus community college in the Southeast learned during his first year in office:

I came here with a clear agenda and pushed it as hard as I could. I talked about my vision for the college with faculty and staff, pushed for new programs and services that put students and the community at the center of everything we do, and reached out to the community. I worked long hours to put this agenda in place and, although we've made some progress, there were a lot of unhappy people around here. I learned that you can push all you want, but if they don't like you, your agenda isn't going anywhere.[73]

Leaders generate support for initiatives through earnest and meaningful interaction with people. Holding a genuine interest in what instructors and staff do, listening with the intention of understanding their thoughts and feelings, promoting and supporting what they do, and celebrating success are key elements of engagement. A president described her approach to engagement with faculty and staff as follows:

I meet with all groups. I have an open door. There is a notorious half-hour interview with the president for every new full-time employee we would like to hire . . . and it's nothing more than "tell me about yourself." There hasn't been one individual with whom I haven't forged a connection at a personal level . . . so the next time I see that person, I know something about them that reinforces the connection.[74]

Effective leaders know the difference between inquiry and advocacy. They distinguish their observations from opinions and judgments and explain their reasoning without aggression or defensiveness. Leaders with strong relational skills exhibit a healthy balance between inquiring and advocating: they actively try to understand others' views but are able to clearly convey their own.[75] In strategic planning projects with community colleges, we've seen countless relationships undermined because leaders disproportionately emphasized advocating over inquiring. Even though leaders and managers pay lip service to the importance of mutual understanding and shared commitment to a course of action, all too often their real focus is on getting their way or reinforcing their point rather than strengthening the connection. Relational leaders cultivate a network of confidants who can help achieve a wide range of goals.[76] They turn to a number of people for help in thinking through difficult problems or support in key initiatives. They understand that time spent building and maintaining connections is time spent investing in their capacity to lead. In today's complex organizational environments, no one person can have all of the answers or know all the right questions to ask. It is important, therefore, for leaders to be able to tap into a network of people who can fill in the gaps.

Leadership Is about Inclusiveness

At the heart of any successful college is something that can best be called an "inclusion factor"—a critical building block in high performance. Although inclusion, like culture, is an elusive concept, it is something that leaders can shape, rather than simply allow to evolve on its own. Over the course of our work with community colleges, we have identified five activities that effective leaders use to engage people and foster a spirit of inclusion: 1) they employ institution-wide vetting procedures to establish goals and priorities, 2) they encourage dialogue about change by making themselves accessible to staff through formal and informal channels of communication, 3) they involve staff in the design and execution of change, 4) they routinely move around the institution and interact comfortably with staff in their work setting, and 5) they encourage people to share ideas and opinions.

A commonly voiced belief among leaders of institutions undergoing change is that growth and complexity pose a serious obstacle to staff involvement in the strategic life of the organization. The basis for this belief is real given the operational realities of staff burdened with increasing responsibility and dwindling resources. Effective leaders do not let complexity get in the way of inclusion. They work to turn large organizations into small ones by flattening the administrative organization and breaking down walls and boundaries. Academic and administrative divisions operate as usual, but whenever possible they organize around cross-functional project teams that are capable of rapid response to customer and market needs.

Illinois Central College (ICC) adopted Six Sigma in spring 2003 as a way of building a culture of inclusion and collaboration toward the goal of enhancing organizational performance.[77] Developed in 1987 by Motorola, Six Sigma is a process-improvement methodology used by organizations to improve performance by comparing results to customer/constituent expectations. ICC got underway with it by selecting and training staff in Six Sigma methodology to work full-time with teams charged with identifying and solving institutional problems and improving business processes. The teams are cross-functional in composition and employ a methodology known as DMAIC—Define, Measure, Analyze, Improve, and Control—to identify and solve problems. Currently more than half of the full-time faculty and staff at ICC are working on teams engaged in improving processes, such as advisement, reporting of time for payroll purposes, processing of financial aid, and reporting of student performance (grades).[78] The college has delivered an introductory three-hour course on Six Sigma to more than five hundred employees, and twenty-one employees are on the way to becoming team leaders through participation in advanced training.

By engaging faculty and staff in collective problem solving using an accepted and widely practiced industry technique, Illinois Central has directly tackled the problem of inclusion. It is faculty and staff working directly with customers and constituents who make strategic and operational decisions and determine the resources needed to execute decisions.

Leadership Is about Creating and Managing Change

Malcolm Gladwell's book *The Tipping Point* (2004) describes leadership as involving "tipping points" that impel organizations toward change.[79] Ideas and behavior in organizations sometimes take the form of an epidemic. Think for a moment about the evolution of communication between people through a Blackberry. One person in a work group buys a Blackberry and begins to use it. Others buy the Blackberry and within days the entire group is using it. It becomes customary and "routinized" as a form of communication. Even those who held out and resisted it have to purchase and use a Blackberry because everyone else is using it. Successful leaders know that change can happen quickly or slowly, but that until a tipping point is reached—a critical mass of subscribers—change will not happen. One community college leader described her philosophy for starting a new initiative as follows: "You need a critical point at which there are enough people seeing the vision to buy into it. If you can't get to that point, it's gonna be a long, slow journey."[80]

New initiatives need to experience early success if subsequent, related initiatives are to have any chance. An interview with a vice president for continuing education at an urban community college disclosed the journey taken by an initiative to integrate academic affairs and continuing education by laddering credit and noncredit courses. After considerable thought, she decided that the best path toward achieving integration was to create a for-credit EMT (emergency medical technician) program borrowing off the success and reputation of the noncredit program. The successful creation of the credit EMT program, however, required a tipping point:

> The tide turned when we convinced the president to give the chairperson a [funding] line for a paramedic director, who would work with the EMT director. The department then had a say in the hiring of the paramedic director, and all of a sudden it was sensing ownership.[81]

Successful leaders also monitor change initiatives closely:

> You'd like to believe that you're only doing policy when you're a vice president or a dean. That's not the case. You're rolling up your sleeves and bring-

ing your expertise in certain areas where you can give it. . . . This model was
so new and so experimental, that I didn't dare risk handing it off to someone
else—even to another senior person. You're tampering with the quality of the
program and the last thing you want to have happen is to have it fail.[82]

Leadership Is about Simplicity

Conversations with leaders of high-performing organizations reveal a
commitment to simplicity that is central to effective leadership. This commitment is expressed in two ways: 1) don't overload the system and 2)
help people understand what is going on by keeping processes simple.
System overloading occurs when an organization takes on too much at
one time resulting in failed initiatives that diminish credibility. A conversation with the president of a large midwestern community college
underscored the value of timing initiatives for success: "You don't want
to get too many initiatives going at the same time. We are trying to make
up for lost time and are approaching the point where we've got a lot
going on and an organization that can only handle so much at one time."[83]

Simplicity is more easily described than accomplished. Its importance
can be understood through the actions of leaders who are bombarded
daily by an ocean of technology-generated data. Effective leaders make
the institution's business model as simple and transparent as possible, by
determining what information is required to measure performance. They
emphasize a simple model and a small number of carefully selected measures which serve to imprint a scorecard mind-set in staff, and connect
their work to the goals of the institution.

The effectiveness assessment system in use at Anne Arundel Community College (AACC) provides a good example of the importance of simplicity in process design and implementation.[84] Anne Arundel's leaders
know that a simplified assessment process comprising a small number of
performance indicators central to the learning-centered mission of AACC
will deliver better results than one comprising multiple indicators. A key
indicator the executive team uses to track institutional performance is student satisfaction with instruction. Generated by survey, satisfaction
scores indicate student perceptions of the quality of instruction and its
effect on learning. Anne Arundel's leaders use the scores to understand
how instructor variations relate to satisfaction. In an internal study, staff
found that instructors who used principles of active learning received the
highest satisfaction scores while instructors using more passive
approaches to learning received lower scores. The college's leaders make
sure that instructors are aware of the importance of this number to high
performance. Effective leaders understand that simplicity is a virtue.

They do not get caught up in thinking that a process must be sophisticated or complex to be good.

Leadership Is about Identifying and Multiplying Talent

Colleges operating in a knowledge economy have little hope of achieving high performance unless top administrators lead the charge to acquire, develop, and retain the best talent. Effective leaders are compulsive talent scouts. They are personally involved in the search for quality staff, both inside and outside of the organization—and they work to develop talent.

Colleges and universities have been slow to adopt the idea of transforming institutional culture through strategic hiring and development of staff. Consider the example provided by hypothetical High Performing Community College to illustrate how a commitment to finding, growing, and retaining talent can work to transform a culture and elevate performance:

> High Performing is an out-of-the-box institution known and recognized for its capacity for continuous innovation. Unlike most colleges which focus on matching or exceeding competitors' salaries and working conditions in their approach to hiring, High Performing has chosen to attract talent by emphasizing attributes of its culture that set it part from competitors. Its leaders know that different types of people excel in different organizations and that High Performing's culture is not for everyone. So they have developed a "signature experience" that explicitly communicates what makes the institution unique.

Imagine your institution in competition with High Performing for a talented candidate to fill a new administrative position in business operations. In her interview at your college, the candidate hears about the mission and programs of the institution, the responsibilities and expectations associated with the job, the salary and benefits she will receive, the background and quality of colleagues, and the quality of life in the service region. In her conversation with leaders at High Performing Community College, she learns about the values of the organization and important aspects of its culture. She will be immediately immersed in a three-month orientation program in which top managers, including the president, oversee the learning process. In the first month, she will work with a cross-functional team on a fast-paced creative project designed to streamline business operations. In the second month she will be assigned to a smaller "breakthrough team" charged with creating a new model for an important business function. In the third month, she will be expected to demonstrate her capacity for personal initiative by driving an existing project to completion or initiating a new project. Upon completion of the program, she will receive detailed feedback on her performance by colleagues, superiors, and executive officers.

High Performing's signature immersion experience serves as one of the institution's primary engines for innovation.[85] The experience also serves as a proving ground for its next generation of leaders: the personnel who work on cross-functional and breakthrough teams as well as the new hires themselves. Most important, the immersion experience at High Performing provides a compelling illustration of life in the institution. A candidate who prefers a static, well-defined work environment will almost certainly decline after hearing details of the immersion process. But a candidate who likes intense challenges and can tolerate ambiguity will probably jump right in. This capacity for choice would not be possible at institutions following traditional hiring procedures because candidates would not know enough about the institution to make an informed decision.

Leadership Is about Knowing How to Create and Use Networks

Typically, community college administrators rise through the ranks as a result of capable performance on operational aspects of jobs like instructor, coordinator, director, or dean. When challenged to move beyond their technical expertise and address strategic issues, many administrators do not immediately grasp the fact that relational skills will be needed to address the issue. Nor do they understand that interactions with a diverse array of stakeholders are at the heart of problem solving in their new leadership role.

Effective leaders use distinct but interdependent forms of networking—*operational, personal,* and *strategic*—to pursue and achieve institutional goals.[86] One network comprising key faculty and staff inside the institution helps them get important operational tasks done; a second comprising kindred spirits outside of the institution helps in their personal development; and a third comprising lateral relationships with leaders in organizations outside of education helps open their eyes to new strategic directions and the stakeholders they will need to enlist. While leaders differ in the way they operate with each network, it is the strategic network that appears to make the biggest difference in their ability to leverage institutional performance. One president we studied forged relationships with executives in industries outside of education— real estate, logistics, plastics, retail, health care, information technology, and so on—and systematically exposed himself to cutting-edge practices in customer service that he never would have learned inside the college.[87] Hearing about their problems and techniques enabled him to view his own from a different perspective and helped define principles that he could "operationalize" inside his institution. The key was his ability to build outside-in links for maximum learning.

Leadership Is about Establishing and Sustaining a Sense of Urgency

Any college that drives forward while looking backward through the rear view mirror will, sooner or later, run into a brick wall. Making the brick wall apparent to staff while there is still time to turn and avoid a crash is one of the great tests of leadership. Effective leaders know that a successful change effort begins with an uncompromising look at an institution's circumstances, its resources, and its performance. A problem is identified, possible solutions are determined, and the implications of inaction are communicated broadly. This first step is essential because just getting a change initiative underway requires the understanding and cooperation of a lot of people. Without a sense of urgency, staff won't pitch in and the initiative will stall.

As obvious as a sense of urgency is to the achievement of change, many leaders have difficulty in moving a change initiative through to successful completion. Effective leaders have the innate ability to move people out of their comfort zones not only in periods of transformation, but in circumstances where staff need to step up to help the institution achieve important priorities. They are patient, know how to realistically assess the extent to which people are motivated to change, and know that urgency cannot be maintained at a continuous high level without risk to the institution. These leaders are engineers of motivation.

The words of a president when asked about the ability of his college to stave off competition for students and resources ring true for leaders in some colleges today: "We have a vested interest in advancing our share of the market as we see it today."[88] This leader had a stake in the present that was larger than his stake in the future, and it stymied innovation. This is why colleges are creating leadership academies and futures institutes that are charged with identifying and pursuing new opportunities. Leaders who are looking ahead know it is their responsibility to create an alluring vista of the future—an *opportunity horizon*—that presents a compelling alternative to reliving yesterday's successes. In the words of Hamel and Prahalad:

> To give up the bird in hand, an organization must see a dozen birds in the bush. The future must become as real as the present and the past. Senior management must help the organization build an intellectually compelling and emotionally enticing view of the future.[89]

Leadership Is about Integrity and Commitment

Successful leaders cultivate managerial styles that fit the needs of the institution but also fit their own beliefs and personality. They are authentic in word and deed and draw people to them by staying true to their beliefs and principles, which others find attractive and engaging. In the words of a vice president commenting on the leadership style of her president:

> We (the executive team) have never seen him lose his temper. The only sign of anger or irritation is a fixed jaw and tightly closed mouth, and even then we are not sure of how upset he is. . . . I feel like I can talk with him about almost anything involving my career and he will understand and want to help. . . . He is so deeply respected that no one wants to disappoint him. This makes all of us want to work harder to make things right.[90]

Implicit in this vice president's words is the leveraging power of a leader who, through belief and behavior, is able to inspire staff to higher levels of performance. Leaders with integrity stay true to themselves and impel others to follow. They understand how personal character can—positively or negatively—affect credibility and the performance of the institution. Authentic leaders know that awareness of self and others is critical to success. They commit people to work and the institution by opening—and leaving open—a door of opportunity for personal and organizational development. Individuals are not penalized for mistakes—they are encouraged to learn from them and to move forward. Faculty and staff are not judged as high or low performers, but as a resource for institutional betterment. And, most importantly, people are assessed in relationship to themselves, not others. They are rewarded for their own growth and development, not for meeting an artificial performance standard.

Leadership Is about Balancing Extrinsic and Intrinsic Motivation

Because leaders need to sustain high levels of energy and motivation and keep their lives in balance, it is critically important for them to understand what drives them. Effective leaders stand out because they are driven as much, if not more, by intrinsic motivation than extrinsic motivation. Although reluctant to admit it, some leaders are propelled to achieve by measuring their success against external parameters. They enjoy the recognition and status that comes with heading a large institution, having a large salary and perks, or membership in an exclusive consortium or project. Leaders driven by intrinsic motivation, on the other hand, derive

satisfaction from their sense of the meaning of their life.[91] Examples
include personal growth, helping colleagues and staff develop, and making a difference through their work.

Effective leaders avoid getting caught up in social, peer, and community relationships that compromise their work by setting artificial standards. Intrinsically motivated leaders seek congruence between personal
values and work. Ursula Schwerin, president of New York City Community College from 1978–1988, said, "I am motivated by doing a good job
at whatever I am doing, but I prefer to gauge my success through the
feelings that people—faculty, staff, and students—have about this college."[92] Or as Roy Church, president of Lorain County Community College put it, "I have stayed here because I am committed to the
revitalization of Lorain County, its people, and its institutions."[93] Church
is an enormously successful leader who has turned away attractive offers
in order to pursue the goal of invigorating the county through the
resources of Lorain County Community College.

PERFORMANCE

Performance is the fourth and final leg of the four-legged stool that is
capacity. Viewed from the standpoint of resource dependence, it is determined by the tangible resources a college has to pursue goals in concert
with internal and external stakeholders. Viewed in another way, however,
performance is an expression of leaders' ability to leverage tangible and
intangible resources into value for important stakeholders. In a world of
limited resources colleges can only maximize performance by getting the
most out of their resources. It is the role and responsibility of leaders to
make this happen.

In institutions with long-serving staff holding fixed beliefs about how
things should be done, performance is often improved one partnership at
a time, one permanent hire at a time, one process at a time, and one initiative at a time. Solutions that focus on specific components of performance
in isolation understate the degree to which performance depends on a
host of factors that must come together to achieve success. For example,
if enhancing regional economic development is a performance goal, a college can leverage the value of existing programs by taking several steps:
developing industry partnerships; using industry professionals to help
design curricula which adds relevance to programs and courses and
increases their market value; and hiring faculty with professional experience to increase the legitimacy of programs with prospective students.
These steps take existing resources and leverage them into more. The
result is improvement in two performance goals: local businesses benefit

through the supply of qualified workers and students benefit through access to higher paying jobs.

Improved performance is part of a feedback loop that eventually leads to more resources—the true measure of leveraging. To illustrate, improvement in transfer, retention, and graduation rates leads to improved reputation, which carries a host of benefits that includes higher enrollment, enhanced public and private support, and increased visibility. With increased visibility comes enhancement in the talent pool of applicants. The cumulative result is that everything goes up, creating a rubric of "high performance" in which multiple aspects of performance feed one another. This leads us to believe that although community colleges are especially vulnerable to the external environment because of their mission and charter, they also have a unique capability to shape the environment because of their capacity to leverage resources.

CONCLUSION

A significant amount of information has been presented in this chapter about institutional capacity. To make the task of absorption easier for the reader, we have summarized key points below. The takeaway is that an informed understanding of institutional capacity is critical to the concept of abundance—the topic of the next chapter and the foundation for analysis of alternative scenarios for community college development.

Maturation of an Institution

Organizations have a natural development cycle beginning with growth followed by deepening maturity, stability, and then decline or renewal. Between 1965 and 2004, community colleges tripled in number and grew by 500 percent in enrollment. Virtually every tangible aspect of the institution has experienced explosive growth over four decades, beginning with mission and extending to programs, services, and resources. To enable and support growth, community colleges have become complex organizations with expansive requirements for money, staff, technology, and facilities:

- Between 1977 and 2001, total college expenditures rose from $15 billion to $30 billion in constant 2001 dollars.
- Between 1991 and 2003, the number of full-time staff increased from 435,000 to 590,000 employees.
- In four years (2002–2005) mean IT funding per FTE student in community colleges increased from $540 to $670.

The prototypical college that started in 1965 with a handful of administrators and instructors serving 1,200 students is now a multifaceted institution serving 12,000 students through 1,200 full-time and part-time staff deployed in sixty academic departments and thirty service units.

Institutional Capacity

Institutional capacity is the potential of a college for achieving stated goals and meeting constituency needs and expectations through the interplay of four factors: external forces, tangible and intangible resources, leadership, and performance.

- *External forces* determine the *tangible resources* and, to a lesser extent, the *intangible resources* a college can use to create value for stakeholders.
- *Leaders* deploy tangible and intangible resources to generate a product that meets, exceeds, or falls short of stakeholder needs and expectations (*performance*).
- *Capacity* is a product of the interplay of these factors; it is an expression of a college's potential to leverage tangible and intangible resources into value for stakeholders.

Tangible Resources

Tangible resources in the form of money, staff, facilities, and technology are the first leg of a four-legged stool that is capacity. They drive much of what is possible in institutional development, but they are insufficient to leverage institutional capacity because their effect is moderated by the behavior and actions of leaders.

Money

- Public support is declining, local support depends on the health of regional economies, and private giving has not been sufficient to offset the loss of public support.
- Tuition and fees have more than doubled over three decades (1976–1977 to 2004–2005) but have remained roughly proportional to other sources of revenue.
- Community college expenditures have increased to support growth—more than doubling in constant dollars between 1997 and 2001 and growing by an average of $2 to 2.5 billion in four-year growth periods between 1977 and 1997.

Staff

- The number of staff in community colleges has swelled dramatically to support growth, but human resource deployment in most colleges is rapidly approaching a "tipping point."
- Between 1991 and 2003, the total number of staff in community colleges increased 39 percent to a level of 590,000 employees; over half of this number (52 percent) were part-time employees in 2003.
- Part-time faculty represented 68 percent of all head count faculty in 2003 (up from 58 percent in 1991) and taught more than 60 percent of instructional hours on most campuses.
- Faculty and staff in community colleges are aging and lag significantly behind the general population in diversity.

Technology

- Viewed in terms of funding, volume, and dedicated staff, technology investment in community colleges is substantial and growing.
- Centralized technology funding grew to a mean of $3.6 million per college in 2005 compared to $3.2 million in 2002; the number of dedicated IT staff increased from a mean slightly below 25 per institution to 29 per institution.
- Technology will consume a significantly larger portion of operating budgets in the future as colleges strive to remain abreast of changing student needs and competitor practices.

Intangible Resources

Intangible resources are the second leg of a four-legged stool that is institutional capacity. In contrast to tangible resources that can be quantified on a balance sheet, intangible resources (people, culture, tacit knowledge, systems, and time) make up emotive and subjective elements of the institution.

People

People—the nature of a workforce in a college, including competencies, experience, and skills—are the foremost intangible resource in community colleges.

Culture

- With increasing size and complexity, many of today's colleges have become loosely coupled institutions with multiple cultures; differentiation is the distinguishing feature of culture in community colleges.

- Successful colleges create and sustain a distinctive culture—one that contains elements of a "signature experience" that attracts talented staff and works to retain them.
- Hiring decisions in successful colleges are viewed as an opportunity for culture change or affirmation.
- Colleges with positive cultures find ways to overcome obstacles through the leveraging behavior of leaders and staff.

Organizational Architecture

- The administrative organization in community colleges is layered and complex; layering—the grafting of units closer to the external environment than to the organization—works against efficiency.
- The administrative structure in high-performing colleges embraces five characteristics that fuel success: 1) people have the opportunity to learn and grow, 2) staff have appropriate skills and knowledge, 3) owners are present throughout the organization to ensure that people deliver quality results, 4) elements of infrastructure like process, systems, and policies are aligned with structure, and 5) appropriate metrics are used to measure performance.

Time

- The time frame in which work is conducted is fundamentally different in organizations today from what it was in the past; information life cycles are getting shorter, deadlines are getting tighter, and people expect almost instantaneous attention to their needs.
- *Time* has become synonymous with opportunity in the lives of leaders and staff who are heavily impacted by technology and a constant flow of information.

Systems, Policies, and Processes

- Systems, policies, and processes are viewed as a double-edged sword in community colleges—staff decry the lack of processes to bring consistency to work in a differentiated organization but express frustration with too many rules and outdated systems and processes.
- High-performing colleges engage in continuous improvement of processes and systems using industry techniques, such as Six Sigma and CQI; staff in these institutions become part of a culture of collab-

oration which fosters a supportive environment for innovation and change.

Networks and Partnerships

- Networks of partnering organizations are vital for success in a fast-paced turbulent market as a means for creating opportunity and controlling costs.
- Entrepreneurial colleges focus very little attention on competitors—they focus on creating value for customers by creating and sustaining superior partnerships.

Reputation

- Leaders of high-performing colleges indicate that reputation is a priceless resource; it is established by measuring performance in an arena that is important to stakeholders and in a venue that is compelling to them.

Leadership

Leadership is the third leg of the four-legged stool that is institutional capacity. The skill of leaders in deploying tangible and intangible resources in pursuit of goals contributes in important ways to institutional performance.

- Community colleges will reach the zenith of their development as complex organizations when staff throughout the organization exercise their potential for leadership.
- Leaders who are effective possess discernible attributes that enable them to leverage resources in pursuit of goals; among these attributes are capabilities for:
  - Visioning and inventiveness
  - Making smart choices
  - Balancing ideas and execution
  - Sensemaking
  - Relating and engaging
  - Creating and managing change
  - Simplifying
  - Identifying and multiplying talent
  - Creating and using networks
  - Maintaining a sense of urgency

   ◦ Modeling integrity and commitment
   ◦ Balancing extrinsic and intrinsic motivation

Performance

Performance is the fourth and final leg of the four-legged stool that is institutional capacity. It is a product of interaction between tangible and intangible resources and leader behavior that results in outcomes that meet, exceed, or fall short of stakeholder needs.

- Performance influences, and is influenced by, the tangible and intangible resources a college is able to deploy.
- Performance is an expression of leaders' ability to leverage tangible and intangible resources.

Awareness of capacity—the potential of a college to achieve stated goals and meet constituency needs through the resources it can deploy—is an important step in securing the future. A college that lives strictly within its current resources and fails to broaden or *stretch* the resources it can deploy in pursuit of opportunity will be left behind by fast-moving competitors. This is where the leveraging instincts and capabilities of leaders come in—it is the attribute of leadership that determines whether a college will realize, exceed, or fall short of its potential.

NOTES

1. J. Kotter, *Leading Change* (Boston: Harvard Business School Press, 1996).

2. American Association of Community Colleges (AACC), *National Profile of Community Colleges: Trends and Statistics,* 4th ed. (Washington, DC: Community College Press, 2005).

3. AACC, *National Profile of Community Colleges.*

4. AACC, *National Profile of Community Colleges.*

5. Interview, community college president, April 25, 2006.

6. National Center for Educational Statistics, *Digest of Education Statistics, 2004* (Washington, DC: National Center for Education Statistics, 2005).

7. AACC, *National Profile of Community Colleges*; National Center for Educational Statistics, *Digest of Education Statistics, 2005*, Report #882, 2006. (Washington, DC: National Center for Education Statistics, 2005.)

8. AACC, *National Profile of Community Colleges;* National Center for Educational Statistics, *Digest of Education Statistics, 2005.*

9. T. Bailey and V. Smith-Morest, *The Organizational Efficiency of Multiple Missions for Community Colleges* (New York: Community College Research Center, Teachers College, Columbia University, 2004).

10. R. Alfred, "The Wolf at the Door: Where Colleges Could Fail," *Community College Journal*, April/May, 2003 (Washington, DC: American Association of Community Colleges), 16–24; R. Alfred, "Outsmarting the Wolf: Critical Pathways to Performance," *Community College Journal*, June/July, 2003 (Washington, DC: American Association of Community Colleges), 17–23.

11. National Center for Educational Statistics, *Digest of Education Statistics,* 2004.

12. National Center for Educational Statistics, *Digest of Education Statistics,* 2004.

13. National Center for Educational Statistics, *Digest of Education Statistics,* 2005.

14. National Center for Educational Statistics, *Digest of Education Statistics,* 2005.

15. National Center for Educational Statistics, *Digest of Education Statistics,* 2005.

16. This illustration is drawn from our strategic planning experience with a college that entered the MetLife competition between 2004 and 2008.

17. National Center for Educational Statistics, *Digest of Educational Statistics, 1996,* Report #794; National Center for Educational Statistics, *Digest of Education Statistics, 2001,* Report #881; National Center for Educational Statistics, *Digest of Education Statistics, 2005,* Report #882.

18. National Center for Educational Statistics, *Digest of Educational Statistics, 1996,* Report #794; National Center for Educational Statistics, *Digest of Education Statistics, 2001,* Report #881; National Center for Educational Statistics, *Digest of Education Statistics, 2005,* Report #882.

19. Interview, community college president, April 24, 2006.

20. Interview with Christine Johnson, former president of Community College of Denver, on April 12, 2006.

21. Interview with Christine Johnson, April 12, 2006.

22. Interview with Diane Troyer, former president of Cy-Fair College, on November 20, 2006.

23. Interview, community college president, April 25, 2006.

24. D. Ulrich, *Human Resource Champions* (Boston: Harvard Business School Press, 1997).

25. National Center for Educational Statistics, *Digest of Education Statistics, 1996;* National Center for Educational Statistics, *Digest of Education Statistics, 2005.*

26. National Center for Educational Statistics, *Digest of Education Statistics, 1996;* National Center for Educational Statistics, *Digest of Education Statistics, 2005.*

27. National Center for Educational Statistics, *Digest of Education Statistics, 1996;* National Center for Educational Statistics, *Digest of Education Statistics, 2005.*

28. National Center for Educational Statistics, *Digest of Education Statistics, 1996;* National Center for Educational Statistics, *Digest of Education Statistics, 2005.*

29. This illustration of staff perceptions of work life is drawn from our strategic planning experience with a midwestern community college in 2002.

30. National Center for Educational Statistics, *Digest of Education Statistics, 2001;* National Center for Educational Statistics, *Digest of Education Statistics, 2002,* Report #883.

31. National Center for Educational Statistics, *Digest of Education Statistics, 2005.*

32. B. Hawkins, L. Rudy, and R. Nicolich, *Educause Core Data Service Fiscal Year 2004 Summary Report* (Washington, DC: Educause, 2005).

33. Hawkins, Rudy, and Nicholich, *Educause Core Data Service Fiscal Year 2004.*

34. B. Hawkins and J. Rudy, *Educause Core Data Service Fiscal Year 2005 Summary Report* (Washington, DC: Educause, 2006).

35. Interview, community college president, April 25, 2006.

36. J. Collins, *Good to Great* (New York: Harper Collins, 2001).

37. T. Erickson and L. Gratton, "What It Means to Work Here," *Harvard Business Review* (March 2007): 104–112.

38. Erickson and Gratton, "What It Means to Work Here," 104–112.

39. This case illustration of organizational change and development is adapted from our strategic planning experience with Central Piedmont Community College in 1994–1995.

40. Case illustration with Central Piedmont Community College in 1994–1995.

41. Interview, community college president, April 24, 2006.

42. Center for Community College Development, "Assessment of Strategic Capabilities in Horizon Network Colleges," *Strategic Horizon Network,* February 2005.

43. E. Schein, *Organizational Culture and Leadership* (San Francisco: Jossey-Bass, 1985).

44. K. Weick and K. Sutcliffe, *Managing the Unexpected: Assuring High Performance in an Age of Complexity* (San Francisco: Jossey-Bass, 2001).

45. B. Clark, "The Organizational Saga in Higher Education," *Administrative Science Quarterly* 17, no. 2 (June, 1972): 178–184.

46. R. Alfred, "Governance in Strategic Context," in *Governance in the Community College: New Directions for Community Colleges,* eds. S. Kater and R. Cloud, no. 141 (Spring 2008): 79–89.

47. R. Scott, *Organizations: Rational, Natural, and Open Systems* (Upper Saddle River, NJ: Prentice Hall, 2003).

48. C. Perrow, *Complex Organizations: A Critical Essay* (New York: Random House, 1986).

49. M. Peterson, *Models of Colleges and Universities as Organizations: An Evolutionary Perspective* (Ann Arbor: Center For the Study of Higher and Postsecondary Education, University of Michigan, 2005).

50. M. Hammer, "The Process Audit," *Harvard Business Review* (Boston: Harvard Business School Press, April 2007).

51. Hammer, "The Process Audit."

52. Interview, community college president, April 24, 2006.

53. Interview, community college president, April 24, 2006.

54. Interview, community college president, April 24, 2006.

55. Interview, community college president, April 24, 2006.

56. Interview, community college president, April 24, 2006.

57. Interview, community college president, April 25, 2006.

58. Interview, community college president, October 13, 2006.

59. D. Ancona, T. Malone, W. Orlikowski, and P. Senge, "In Praise of the Incomplete Leader," *Harvard Business Review* (Boston: Harvard Business School Press, February 2007), Reprint # R0702F; K. Weick and K. Sutcliffe, *Managing the Unexpected.*

60. Ancona, Malone, Orlikowsky, and Senge, "In Praise of the Incomplete Leader."

61. Interview, community college president, April 25, 2006.

62. Ancona, Malone, Orlikowsky, and Senge, "In Praise of the Incomplete Leader."

63. Lorain County Community College, *Lorain County Community College Web site*, http://lorainccc.edu (retrieved July 15, 2007).

64. This case illustration of executive leadership in a period of organizational change is drawn from our strategic planning experience with Clinton Community College (New York) in 2005–2006.

65. Clinton Community College, Strategic Plan, *Shaping Our Future*, April 2006.

66. Community College, *Anne Arundel Community College Web site*, http://aacc.edu (retrieved August 2, 2007).

67. Interview, community college vice president for learning, July 12, 2007.

68. K. Weick. "Sensemaking as an Organizational Dimension of Global Change, in *Organizational Dimensions of Global Change,* eds. D. L. Cooperrider and J. E. Dutton, 39–56 (Thousand Oaks, California: Sage, 1999).

69. Weick, "Sensemaking," 39–56.

70. Ancona, Malone, Orlikowski, and Senge, "In Praise of the Incomplete Leader."

71. Ancona, Malone, Orlikowski, and Senge, "In Praise of the Incomplete Leader."

72. Interview, community college president, October 13, 2006.

73. This description of leader effectiveness was drawn from a series of conversations with the president of a southeastern community college during a strategic planning project in 1994–1995.

74. Interview, community college president, April 24, 2006.

75. Ancona, Malone, Orlikowski, and Senge, "In Praise of the Incomplete Leader."

76. Ancona, Malone, Orlikowski, and Senge, "In Praise of the Incomplete Leader."

77. Illinois Central College, *Illinois Central College Web site*, http://icc.edu (retrieved August 10, 2007).

78. Illinois Central College, *Illinois Central College Web site.*

79. M. Gladwell, *The Tipping Point: How Little Things Can Make a Big Difference* (Boston: Little Brown, 2000).

80. Interview, community college president, October 23, 2006.

81. Interview, community college president, October 23, 2006.

82. Interview, community college president, October 23, 2006.

83. Interview, community college president, April 25, 2006.

84. Interview, community college vice president for learning, July 12, 2007.

85. Jackson and Gratton, "What It Means to Work Here," 104–112.

86. H. Ibarra and M. Hunter, "How Leaders Create and Use Networks," *Harvard Business Review* (Boston: Harvard Business School Press, January 2007).

87. This approach to learning and executive development was identified through a series of on-campus conversations with a community college executive team on February 18, 2007.

88. This outlook on competition was expressed by a community college president to the senior author as part of a casual off-campus conversation on April 14, 2007.

89. Hamel and Prahalad, *Competing for the Future*, 71 (see chap. 1, n. 2).

90. This sentiment was expressed by a community college vice president during a focus group meeting with an executive team in February 2007.

91. Ibarra and Hunter, "How Leaders Create and Use Networks."

92. This viewpoint on leader satisfaction was obtained by the senior author in 1979 in discussion with Ursula Schwerin during his tenure as dean of finance, planning, and management at New York City Community College.

93. Interview, community college president, February 18, 2007.

Part II

SCENARIOS FOR DEVELOPMENT

4

Alternative Scenarios

The confluence of forces, conditions, and circumstances described in chapters 2 and 3 point to a future for community colleges marked by constant change and upheaval. Consider the array of forces facing institutions and leaders at any point in time. Externally, they will need to navigate forces of globalization, volatility in economic markets, demographic transition, shifting values, labor force transitions, changing federal and state funding priorities, advancing technology, the privatization of public services, intensifying competition, the changing regulatory environment, escalating customer expectations, the emergence of worldwide learning communities, and more. These forces are interwoven, and they are exacerbated by eroding boundaries separating domestic and foreign markets and a shifting balance of power among nations in what is now a global economy.

Internally, leaders will need to become adept at doing more with less. They will need to generate new sources of revenue to support growth; increase the capacity and productivity of full-time staff; win the war for talent with fast-moving rivals; build cultures that embrace innovation and change; and create networks that enable institutions to pursue opportunity. They will be challenged to develop new organizational designs to get in front of change, and they will need to think differently about competition. Organizations that were once looked upon as rivals will simultaneously become competitors and collaborators, and the definition of "fair play" will change as new players with new ideas enter the market. Changing relationships and alliances in a world in which boundaries have little meaning will require leaders and staff to have a strategic awareness they have never had before.

LEVERAGING

Leveraging will become increasingly important if community colleges are to successfully navigate these forces of change. Leveraging refers to an organization's capacity to achieve superior performance by optimally using its resources. As a concept, it is derived from the mechanical advantage gained in lifting heavy objects through the action of a lever. Pate describes leveraging as a process of "magnification, without practical limit, of an organization's output realized from a given amount of input."[1] There is "no limit to the amount of output that leverage can provide"—its benefits are limited only by the imagination of those wielding the tool.[2] When leveraging occurs, "the output realized with a given resource increases with little or no increase in the effort or amount of time required to do so."[3] In other words, leveraging is a self-perpetuating phenomenon that builds upon itself and, over time, enables resources to be amplified.

For community college leaders who want to grow their institutions with limited resources, an obvious choice will be to leverage current resources. This can be done in a number of ways—using money more effectively, motivating people to work harder and faster, getting more and better results through technology, and so forth. The advantage of leveraging is that it does not require incremental resources to be effective. It requires incremental effort from people—a controllable resource. Leveraging therefore is not about the resources that an institution needs or wants, but what it can do for itself through the resources it has. The following illustrates the magnifying effect of leveraging:

Resource	Elementary	Leveraged
People	performing work	delivering superior results
Culture	coping with change	embracing change
Leaders	managing and directing	motivating, facilitating, enabling
Money	allocated and expended	effectively used
Technology	investment	cost/benefit
Space	fixed commodity	fluid resource
Time	allotment	value

The positive effects of leveraging are clearly evident in the chart. Its uplifting quality is realized in words, such as "facilitating," "enabling," "embracing," and "motivating." Its basis is that of *abundance* (creating more) rather than *deficit* (coping with less), and its focus is on valuing strength and achievement (positive deviance) in contrast to solving problems (negative deviance).[4] This brings us to a new field of study in the business world called Positive Organizational Scholarship (POS) in which leveraging and abundance are central elements. POS is centered on a relationship between the human condition in organizations and superior performance.[5] Its end point is abundance, and its starting point leveraging—how to move people and organizations from ordinary to extraordinary. POS is fundamental to our conceptualization of alternative futures for community colleges because its overarching aims—a capacity to leverage and the attainment of abundance—help to explain the way institutions navigate forces inside and outside of their boundaries that impact performance.

THE CONCEPT OF ABUNDANCE

An irony associated with organizations is that although understanding and correcting problems is essential to their survival, too much emphasis on problem solving may deflect attention away from positive aspects of their performance. In community colleges this irony can be observed in the behavior of leaders and staff in institutions that have fallen on hard times. Cynicism is apt to prevail and there is a tendency to focus on what the institution is doing wrong instead of what it is doing right. Negative experience somehow seems to occupy a more prominent place in our memory and to have a stronger effect on our emotions and cognition than positive experience. This tendency is not without reason: it is an oversight to ignore a positive event, but potentially an invitation to trouble to ignore a negative event.[6] This can be likened to a "survival instinct," and it helps to explain why leaders and staff are more likely to pay attention to negative aspects of organizational life than those that are positive. It also helps to explain why a focus on leveraging and abundance will be so important to community colleges in the future.

By focusing explicitly on the positive side of organizations, leveraging and abundance broaden the view of performance to include aspects of people, resources, and outcomes that are often overlooked. A good illustration is provided by Feldman and Khademain in their examination of "empowerment and cascading vitality" in organizations evolving from virtuous behavior of leaders.[7] Actions that leaders take to empower staff work to improve relationships between individuals, organizations, and communities and lead to improved performance. For example, employee involvement can lead to increased meaningfulness in work through its effect on job design, which, in turn, results in more motivated employees. In other words, positive activities or events at the individual level (employee involvement) can lead to favorable outcomes at the organizational level (job design), which in turn can create positive outcomes for the individual (meaningfulness).[8]

Leveraging and its ultimate outcome, abundance, have amplifying effects because of their association with three consequences for people and organizations: positive feelings, constructive relationships, and facilitating behavior.[9] Numerous authors have reported that exposure to positive behaviors produces positive feelings in individuals, which, in turn, lead to a replication of positive behavior and, subsequently, to an elevation in organizational performance.[10] When staff observe helping behavior, experience gratitude, or witness authenticity in leaders, a sense of elevation occurs leading to improved cognitive functioning, better decision making, and more effective interpersonal relationships.[11] As the level of satisfaction rises, the entire organization is positively influenced leading to elevated performance. When communication and cooperation among staff improve, customers receive better service, and the organization operates more efficiently and effectively, all of which reciprocally contribute to the enjoyment of work and a greater sense of pride in the organization.

Leveraging also has a buffering effect on people and organizations by shielding them from the negative effects of trauma or stress.[12] Seligman and Csikszentmihalyi describe the important role that positive feelings play in buffering individuals and groups against dysfunction and illness.[13] Feelings of hope, optimism, faith, and belonging act as agents of prevention against psychological distress, dysfunctional behavior, and illness. Fredrickson, Mancuso, Branigan, and Tugade found that cardiovascular, emotional, and intellectual systems in individuals recover more rapidly and completely when they experience positive effect.[14] At the group and organizational levels, positive effects through leveraging enhance the ability to absorb threat and bounce back from adversity.[15] Hence, the positive effect produced through leveraging strengthens organizations by increasing their capacity to respond assertively to forces and conditions inside and outside of their boundaries.

An effective way to illustrate the concept of abundance and its relationship to leveraging is to locate it on a continuum as shown in table 4.1. Derived from the work of Cameron, Dutton, and Quinn, this continuum depicts abundance as a condition or state of being that is positively skewed from a normal or healthy condition.[16] Health is defined as "wellness," and negative and positive deviance refer to aberrations from healthy functioning, with marginal functioning on one end and superior functioning on the other end.

At an *individual* level, abundance can be understood as a condition of psychological and physical illness on the left and healthy functioning in the middle (that is, the absence of illness). On the right side is positive deviance, which may be likened to a high level of physical fitness or superior health.[17] At the *organizational* level, the figure portrays conditions

Table 4.1. Model of Abundance

	Negative Deviance	Normal	Positive Deviance LEVERAGING
Individual			
Physiological	Illness	Wellness	Superior Health
Psychological	Illness	Wellness	Vitality
Organizational			
Goal	Survival	Equilibrium	High Performance
Focus of Leaders	Stability	Efficiency	Leveraging
Mode	Manage Crisis	Identify Problems	Create Ideal Future
Adaptation	Coping	Navigating	Flourishing
Risk	Aversive	Selective	Embracing
Change	Decremental	Incremental	Boundless
Effectiveness	Ineffective	Effective	Excellent
Result	Erosion	Stasis	Optimization
Attractiveness	Unattractive	Attractive	Compelling
	Deficit Gap	*Abundance Gap*	

ranging from survival, coping, and ineffective performance on the left to effective, efficient, and incremental performance in the middle. On the right side is extraordinary organizational performance captured in words like "excellent," "flourishing," and "optimization."[18] The extreme right and left points on the continuum are qualitatively distinct from the center point. They do not represent more or less of any of the attributes of healthy or normal functioning.

As mentioned earlier, most organizational and management research has been conducted on phenomena associated with negative deviance and normal functioning. More attention has been paid to solving problems, surmounting obstacles, competing with rivals, achieving effectiveness and efficiency, and closing deficit gaps than identifying the leveraging and flourishing aspects of organizations or closing abundance gaps. This is especially true in community colleges where problem solving and closing deficit gaps consume a great deal of administrators' time. It is also part and parcel of a tendency of leaders and staff to focus on keeping institutions in equilibrium in contrast to leveraging them to superior performance. Leveraging involves hard work and its end point, abundance, is difficult to envision and quantify. As a result, most institutions direct their energy and resources to the middle of the continuum as we shall see in the applied research findings discussed in the next section.

COMMUNITY COLLEGES AND ABUNDANCE

Understanding and correcting problems and keeping institutions on track in achieving stated priorities is important, but an exclusive focus on "what is" may deter community colleges from pursuing "what could be." As predictable relationships take hold between operations and results, confidence grows, and leaders and staff narrow their outlook to the familiar. In the words of a long-serving senior administrator who will remain anonymous, "If we continue to do the things that have made us successful, we will be successful in the future."

This worldview is not uncommon in community colleges. Research carried out with thirteen colleges in 2004 revealed a tendency on the part of leaders and staff to gear strategic capabilities to important features of the operating environment.[19] The more turbulent the environment, the greater the emphasis on strategic capabilities, whereas the more predictable the environment, the greater the emphasis on operations. Each of the thirteen colleges was effectively serving stakeholders in service regions with adequate resources and predictable patterns of competition. When staff were asked to assess the strategic capabilities of their colleagues, they were able to identify deficits but not to understand their relationship to performance. In other words, when institutions are performing to expectation, there is a tendency to be satisfied with the skills that are in place and not to worry about those needed to take performance to a higher level.

In the next few pages, we present the results of our research on strategic capability and draw upon key findings to develop an abundance model for community colleges. The research is significant because it reveals the difference between ordinary and extraordinary performance and the potential of institutions to achieve a state of abundance; that is, to achieve superior performance by leveraging their resources to a level beyond reasonable expectation. People are central to abundance. Talented leaders and staff working effectively together contribute in positive ways to performance whereas unhappy or unproductive staff detract from performance. Therefore, by determining the extent to which staff view themselves as possessing capabilities that enable the institution to work at or beyond its potential, it is possible to ascertain abundance.

Research on Strategic Capabilities

Focus groups comprised of homogeneously grouped personnel were used to gather information about perceptions of strategic capability from 1,300 full-time personnel in thirteen colleges.[20] Capability was examined in four categories of performance: awareness of the external environment, knowing the value created for stakeholders, awareness of strategic capabilities, and ability to design and manage change effectively.

Awareness of the External Environment:

- Knowledge about trends, forces, and opportunities in the external environment
- Awareness of competitors, who they are, what they are doing, what they are apt to do
- Comprehension of the impact of external forces on the college
- Familiarity with innovative practices in organizations outside of this college

Knowing the Value Created for Stakeholders:

- Knowledge of the goals and outcomes that students seek through enrollment
- Awareness of student and stakeholder wants, needs, and expectations
- Knowledge of the value the college creates for students and stakeholders

Awareness of Strategic Capabilities:

- Awareness of the difference between strategy and tactics
- Informed understanding of the college's culture
- Knowledge of the inner workings of college systems and processes
- Awareness of the way in which decisions are made in the college

Ability to Design and Manage Change Effectively:

- Effectiveness in mapping out a plan for change working with and through staff
- Capability for executing change and making it work

An index of strategic capability for each performance category was created by averaging participant responses to multiple items into a composite score and placing it on a continuum. In this way, it was possible to determine the difference between current and desired levels of capability and each institution's potential for abundance. The narrower the gap between actual and desired levels of capability, the closer a college would be to achieving a state of abundance.

Awareness of the External Environment

As portrayed in figure 4.1, outside the ranks of the executive team, faculty and staff in the thirteen colleges did not see themselves as fully aware of *trends and forces in the external environment*.[21] Most subscribed to a belief that staff working in academic departments and administrative units had specialized knowledge and related to the environment on the basis of this knowledge, but not in a holistic way. Additionally, most staff reported a lack of knowledge about the capabilities of other units—an indication of the extent to which walls and boundaries between units obstruct communication and the flow of information. Self-initiative was acknowledged as important in staying on top of information related to the environment, but most indicated that initiative was stymied by the constant press of operations. Nonstop growth and the likelihood of more growth led many to believe that the "institution is without serious threats" and "my job is safe." Extensive information about the environment was thereby perceived as unnecessary.

Competitors were seen as a force at work in each service region but not as an immediate problem for the college. What was known about competitors tended to be limited to easily observed information through marketing, advertising, media, and the Internet. The feelings of many about

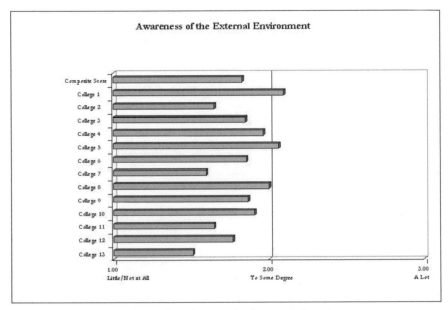

Figure 4.1 Awareness of Trends and Forces in the External Environment

competition were summed up by expressions such as "I know they're out there" or "If I can see them, I know who they are and what they are doing." The vast majority of respondents indicated a lack of awareness of what information to gather about competitors or how to go about getting it. For most, competition was something that was the responsibility of individual departments and units or something that the institution should be more concerned about in the future.

Professional staff felt that colleagues were able to *comprehend the impact of external forces and competitors* but limited their thinking to the area in which they worked. Support staff were viewed as enmeshed in operations and as ceding responsibility for strategic management to administrators. There was a tendency on the part of all staff to limit their vision to events and circumstances inside the institution. Colleagues were viewed as being unfamiliar with innovative practices in other organizations and as lacking time to explore best practices. When respondents were queried about their experience with innovative practices in organizations outside of education (airlines, hotels, hospitals, etc.), most responded by indicating that they could appreciate service that was effectively rendered. There was limited evidence of active thought given to the utility and portability of these practices to their own institutions.

Awareness of Value Created for Stakeholders

As disclosed in figure 4.2, a focus on *creating value for stakeholders* was seen by respondents as an area of strength in all colleges.[22] Professional and classified staff perceived themselves as reaching out to understand and serve students and as advocating a service philosophy that put students at the center of everything the institution does. While a broad array of information was collected from students, respondents indicated that minimal efforts were made to mine this data to gain a better understanding of factors related to student motivation, satisfaction, and success. The primary focus of data analysis was on meeting external reporting requirements and on internal needs for data that could be used to make year-to-year comparisons. Rarely were steps taken to gather information that would permit deep analysis of student needs, interests, expectations, and the quality of their experience in college.

Respondents indicated an adequate (or better) understanding of the role that *experience* plays in student and stakeholder satisfaction. Faculty and staff reported that they were interested in "their students," knew a lot about them, and maintained good rapport with them in and out of class. When pushed to think about "experience" in a different way—that of engagement in an inherently personal way instead of the exposure to different aspects of campus life—faculty and staff were more guarded in

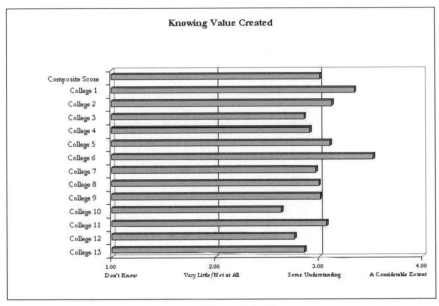

Figure 4.2   Awareness of Value Created for Stakeholders

their assessment. Engagement was viewed as an interesting concept, but one that was difficult to comprehend and "operationalize." Further, experience was not something that was orchestrated in a systematic way by instructors in classrooms and staff in service transactions. It was not understood in conceptual or practical terms nor was it something integrated into institutional behavior. It is interesting to note that although faculty and staff in all colleges viewed themselves as devoting considerable energy to meeting student expectations, knowledge was lacking about the extent to which they exceeded them.

Assessment of Strategic Capabilities

Self-assessment of *strategic capability*—a proficiency in strategic aspects of management such as strategy, planning, and organizational dynamics— yielded an interesting pattern of results as shown in figure 4.3.[23] Respondents indicated a basic awareness of the difference between strategy and tactics, but their primary focus was on operations. There was a tendency to assign general meaning to concepts such as "strategy" and "tactics" and to report optimistic views of the extent to which colleagues used them meaningfully. There was little, if any, evidence of understanding or commitment to *strategic thinking*. Most found the concept to be interesting, but it was seen as novel and requiring time to grasp.

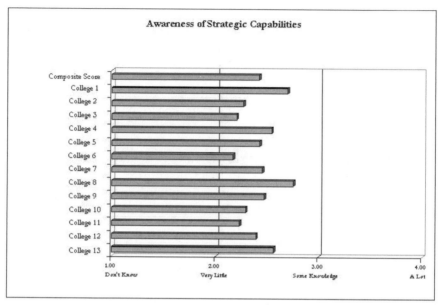

Figure 4.3 Assessment of Strategic Capabilites

Although many colleges have moved to gather information about culture and climate in recent years through surveys and other data collection techniques, faculty and staff indicated that they had limited knowledge and understanding of institutional culture. Perceptions varied regarding different aspects of culture, but most felt that empirical evidence about culture was either missing or inadequate. There was evidence of significant interest in the topic and actions that can be taken to enhance culture and climate. Much of this interest appeared to be related to concerns about the effects of increasing size, complexity, and resource reduction on culture. "We are growing larger and more impersonal." "People are working under stressful conditions because we are being asked to do more with less." "Large numbers of part-time faculty are being hired, and this has changed the culture of the institution." "When we were a small institution, I knew everyone—I can no longer say that." These are the voices of faculty and staff interested in culture because the institution they came to five, ten, fifteen, or twenty years ago is different from the institution they are working in today. They want to grow and change with the new institution, but first they have to understand it.

These voices also pointed to something else that must be recognized as a serious challenge in community colleges—the deep and continuing problem of communication. Embedded in our consulting experience is something we call the "communication rant"—a diatribe that is encountered within the first thirty minutes of interaction with most organized groups on campus. This diatribe generally takes the form of a simple statement: "We have serious problems with communication on this campus." Growth and complexity are a major part of the problem. More significant as contributors, however, are conceptual and definitional problems faculty and staff have with communication implicit in questions such as: "What do we mean by 'communication'?" "What is 'effective' communication?" "Under what conditions is communication effective or ineffective?" "Who is responsible for making sure that communication is effective?" "What has to change in this college to make communication better?"

A different picture emerged when faculty and staff were queried about their knowledge of the inner workings of systems and processes. In some institutions, capability in process management was significantly enhanced through initiatives carried out on an institution-wide basis with selected processes and staff. In others, processes and systems were described as in serious "disrepair" and in need of attention. Staff were either 1) tied up in operations and too busy to take time to break down and redesign processes; 2) process owners who for reasons of convenience and comfort declined to participate in process improvement; and/or 3) creatures of habit who preferred traditional ways of doing things. In colleges where inroads had been made in process redesign, leaders and staff indicated that process management skills had not penetrated parts of the institution. Further, when consideration shifted to the larger world of systems, there was a sense that staff had difficulty getting their arms around the makeup and composition of a "system," thereby hampering their ability to improve capability in this area.

Finally, respondents indicated limited awareness of organizational dynamics and the way decisions are made. They knew the "who" in decision making but felt that the "why" and "how" were not readily apparent. The attribution of decisions to people rather than to need and circumstance were perceived to cloud the decision-making process. For example, while an executive team may fully understand the rationale and circumstances surrounding a decision, this level of understanding did not extend to others in the institution. All of the colleges were larger and significantly more complex institutions than they were ten years before. Multiple approaches to decision making were in place in most institutions which, when compared and contrasted with earlier decision making models, tended to blur the why and how in decision making. Additionally, closely knit executive teams had developed over time in most of the colleges—a circumstance that unknowingly worked to disconnect staff from the dynamics of decision making.

Ability to Design and Manage Change Effectively

Discussions with faculty and staff about change yielded an interesting pattern of results in the participating colleges. As illustrated in figure 4.4, change was a way of life and administrators were perceived as pushing change all or most of the time.[24] Staff viewed themselves as working hard to move with and adjust to the reality of change, but buy-in lagged behind initiative because too many change initiatives were underway at one time. Typical comments included "We are not effective at designing and managing change." "Too much change is being attempted and just as we figure out what we need to do in one area of change, another initiative gets underway." "People are bogged down with the process of change and have difficulty seeing the outcome." Overall, respondents indicated that there is a lot of talk about the need to change, but that it is carried out in a manner that is rushed, noninclusive, and ineffective.

Along with communication, designing and managing change was viewed as an "Achilles' heel" for community colleges. It was perceived to be an area in which significant change would need to happen to bring colleges to a superior level of performance. Colleges were viewed as successful in carrying out change because market conditions gave them no other option—it was change or face the prospect of decline. Left in the

Figure 4.4   Assessment of Ability to Design and Manage Change

wake of poorly designed change processes, however, were dissatisfied personnel who could negatively impact institutional performance in service transactions with students.

KEY THEMES

A number of themes can be extracted from these findings that have utility for looking at community college development from a perspective of abundance.

In colleges moving toward abundance:

1. *Internal cohesion is a driving force underlying enhanced performance.* Human factors and leveraging are the keys to improved performance. Two actions, in particular, are important: a) push decision making as far down in the organization as possible by enhancing the strategic capabilities of staff and b) meaningfully and consistently involve staff in direction-setting and decision-making activities. As staff become more involved in strategic aspects of management, resources are leveraged through improved efficiency and productivity, enhanced commitment to work, ownership over results, and a deeper connection to the institution. Leaders and staff become bound by a common purpose, and the resulting sense of cohesion creates positive emotions that lead to positive outcomes for the institution which, in turn, further elevate the emotions of staff.

2. *Success is the adversary of leveraging and high performance.* Lurking inside every organization are forces that undercut performance by limiting the capacity of people to think beyond convention. In part, these forces are the all-too-familiar product of prior success: feelings of self-satisfaction, immunity from threats, inertia for change, and other emotions which are part of feeling advantaged. The lack of awareness of forces and conditions in the external environment among staff in the thirteen colleges could be construed as evidence of softening and a lack of urgency that comes with continuous success. Research has shown that leaders are less likely to make optimal decisions during and after prolonged periods of success.[25] The flush that comes with continuing success combined with the inhibiting effect of declining resources impels leaders and staff to turn inward and tweak the system to produce even greater gains. This is most readily accomplished by resolving problems that stand in the way of efficiency, with the end result that resources are protected, but they are not leveraged and performance is incrementally improved, but it is not amplified.

3. *The outlook and performance of staff is enhanced by a focus on strategy.* When problem solving becomes the primary focus of managers, operational efficiency takes on greater importance as a means for eliminating problems that impact performance. This tendency was evident in three phenomena disclosed by respondents that narrowed their perceptual field to the operating unit: a) distancing and insulation from colleagues in other parts of the institution, b) minimal working knowledge of people, activities, and outcomes in other units, and c) limited exposure to strategic aspects of management, such as planning and decision making. With progressive distancing from the center of the institution, staff intensified their operational focus, thereby creating enclaves and fragmenting the institution into parts—literally creating organizations within an organization. Interestingly, once staff were exposed to strategic aspects of management, their focus began to shift back to the whole institution and its position in relationship to other organizations. Awareness of market forces and competitor behavior became more important as did consideration of actions that would need to be taken to improve institutional performance.

4. *The administrative structure of the institution is tightly coupled, enabling staff to work collaboratively toward achievement of important goals.* In high-performing colleges, work is carried out in operating units tightly bound by an overarching purpose. There is a deep understanding of the business of the institution and commitment to the goals it is pursuing. Often a single theme serves as the driving purpose for what everyone is doing, and they do not depart from this theme. At Lorain County Community College in Ohio, for example, the theme is "The New Decade Challenge," and its operating goals are expressed in a plan delineating enrollment growth targets, increased productivity, and revenue enhancements aimed at enabling Lorain to creatively grow its way out of financial challenges.[26] Administrative units pursue these goals within the framework of a holistic organization. It is a given that units will help one another, and collaboration among and between units is high.

5. *Wellness—the absence of major problems—is not an acceptable standard for performance.* Colleges that emphasize organizational strengths and achievement in contrast to deficits set the bar high for performance. Normative performance (the absence of problems) is seen as insufficient, and "stretch"—the positive gap between resources and aspirations—becomes the standard for performance. Leaders and staff are united by high expectations and the creativity they use in getting the most out of resources. Superior performance is the product of stretch when a college develops a capacity for resource leveraging and possesses a galvanizing ambition. It does not mean that big risks are taken,

but that performance targets are stretched and tools of leveraging are used to achieve the target. Institutions operating from a deficit perspective tend to equate change with risk. Opportunities are missed or selectively pursued because they cannot be seen or limited resources discourage pursuit. In this way, faculty and staff foreclose the potential for leveraging by falling prey to the limits of their own imagination. In abundant institutions, the operating climate is exactly the opposite—faculty and staff are committed to achieving extraordinary results regardless of conditions.

6. *Challenges and threats are seen as opportunities.* Challenges and threats are acknowledged and approached as potential opportunities. The behavior of leaders and staff is oriented to what could be, not what is, and opportunities are found where others encounter problems. Constraints to exceptional performance are overcome by foresight about the future that provides the energy for envisioning and pursuing opportunities. Leaders and staff believe that opportunities are created by challenging accepted ways of doing things, redrawing boundaries, and setting heightened performance expectations.

7. *Competitors and competition are irrelevant.* Colleges moving toward abundance are never satisfied—they compete against neither competitors nor against their own past performance. Benchmarking is shunned in favor of performing beyond seemingly impossible goals. The start and end point for an abundant institution is to understand its own genetic code—the way leaders and staff perceive their industry, their institutions, and their roles.[27] In high-performing institutions, leaders and staff are encoded to think differently about competition. They make industry and competitor conventions explicit, understand how a focus on convention could imperil an institution's performance by diminishing expectation and limiting foresight, delve deeply into the future, establish systems for leveraging resources, and work collectively to meet or exceed ambitious performance goals.

8. *Leaders are in place throughout the institution.* In all too many institutions, a rigid sense of hierarchy kills initiative and creativity. High-performing institutions are lean-staffed administratively with fewer layers between leaders and staff. Reducing layers of management does not necessarily reduce the dysfunctional consequences of hierarchical behavior. Hierarchical behavior voids active dialogue between leaders and staff on critical issues. It uses authority and power to make decisions rather than inclusion and meaningful input. In institutions moving toward abundance, leaders are in place throughout the organization. This happens through the efforts of leaders to include staff in decision making within an operating context marked by a

shared sense of direction. In this way, leadership involves an obligation and an opportunity to contribute to a specific end.

MODELING ABUNDANCE

When we critically examine community colleges and how they organize and operate in an environment of fast-paced change, we are struck by a stark reality: colleges operating in similar circumstances are capable of achieving different results—that is, of performing differently. Conversely, colleges operating in different circumstances can produce the same results—that is, they perform similarly even though their operating environments are entirely different. Community colleges vary in performance because of differentiation in their ability to use resources, the quality of their leadership, and the capabilities of their staff. Performance, therefore, a variable state that colleges achieve to a greater or lesser degree by virtue of their capabilities.

If we equate performance with abundance and use themes extracted from research to identify attributes of abundance, it is possible to construct a model of abundance for community colleges as shown in table 4.2. Variation in the extent to which colleges possess attributes of abundance is depicted in the horizontal axis by classifying community colleges into three positions—*challenge, choice,* and *abundance*. Colleges in the position of *challenge* are characterized as being in a state of organizational decline or negatively skewed from normal or healthy functioning. Their focus is almost exclusively on deficit reduction to alleviate problems caused by austere resources, ineffective leadership, and marginal performance. Community colleges in the position of *choice* are characterized as functioning normally. They have choices regarding their direction and priorities because they have access to resources, their leadership is stable or strong, and they perform at a level that meets expectations. Finally, colleges in a position of *abundance* are characterized as being in a state of superior health or positively skewed from normal functioning. They have been able to create exceptional resources through leveraging, their leaders are highly effective, and their performance is extraordinary.

Attributes of abundance on which colleges can be compared and contrasted are depicted in the center of the model under captions such as "Institutional Outlook," "Cohesion" "Resources," and so forth. These attributes are derived from our research, and the abundance literature and their utility lies in their capacity to differentiate colleges on specific dimensions of abundance based on the level at which they are functioning—negatively skewed from normal, normal, or positively skewed from normal. When a college is functioning below normal on most attributes,

Table 4.2. Community College Abundance Model

Challenge	*Choice*	*Abundance*
Managerial Emphasis		
Solving Problems	Building capacity and internal capability	Building upon strengths and valuing assets
Cohesion		
Void between top leaders and staff	Segmental relationship between leaders and staff	Leaders and staff work in teams bound by common purpose
Resources		
Resources consumed by fixed costs	Resources adequate or limited resources leveraged	Exceptional resources through leveraging
Resource Perspective		
Excessive emphasis on tangible resources	Emphasis on tangible and intangible resources	Primary emphasis on intangible resources
Organizational Architecture		
Fragmentation, silos, and insularity	Interactive silos and outreach between units	Holistic organization emphasizing unity
Operational Focus		
Ownership over processes	Improving efficiency in processes and systems	Process and system innovation
Risk		
Risk aversive	Selective approach to risk and change	Embrace and reward risk and change
Collaboration		
College is unattractive to potential partners	Growing network of partners	College is the hub of an expansive network
Competative Focus		
Coping with rivals	Competing with rivals and winning	Collaborating with rivals for mutual gain
Performance Objective		
Survival	Growth, efficiency, and resource acquisition	Stretch and leveraging
Leadership		
Absent or ineffective leadership	Punctuated leadership (segments of the institution)	Leaders throughout the organization
Attractiveness		
Difficulty in attracting/retaining quality staff	Selective capacity to attract/retain quality staff (depends on unit)	Capable of attracting quality staff throughout institution

it would be considered a *college of challenge* whereas a *college of choice* would be functioning at a level of normalcy, and a *college of abundance* would be functioning above normal on most attributes.

ALTERNATIVE SCENARIOS FOR DEVELOPMENT

The abundance framework is useful for determining why some colleges operate with a steady efficiency, others thrive, and some struggle even though they may be matched on important characteristics. Abundance is not simply a matter of location or resources since many colleges are nicely situated on both but have not achieved abundance. It is more than a matter of people and commitment because if staff do not have the resources they need to operate, abundance will be difficult to achieve. Finally, while a talented president and effective leaders figure prominently into abundance, they cannot, in and of themselves, guarantee its achievement. As an organizational state, abundance is a product of many factors coming together at the same time to leverage performance.

Although community colleges continue to grow in size and importance, most cannot be described as having achieved a state of abundance. Formidable obstacles confront them. Escalating service demands, scarce resources, entrenched staff, resistance to change—all slow the advance to abundance. These obstacles have forced colleges to focus on growth as a means for increasing revenue, but there is a downside and it has to do with performance. Growth is not a substitute for high performance. When leaders and staff concentrate on operational efficiency (instead of valuing assets), tangible resources (in contrast to intangible resources), growth and efficiency (instead of stretch and leveraging), and competing with rivals (rather than collaborating with them), prolblem solving prevails and abundance is squandered. We believe, therefore, that most community colleges can be fairly described as colleges of choice as depicted in figure 4.5.

The actions that enable a college to move toward abundance are long term and not accomplished through quick fixes. Resource leveraging requires a high level of partnering, network building, and outreach. The development of human capabilities depends on the extent to which a college is able to develop existing talent, find new talent, and commit members to a shared vision of the future. Effective leadership is a transitory state that can change with the entry or exit of key personnel. Making sure the right mix of leaders is in place to move an institution forward is a continuing pursuit that requires constant vigilance. All of these actions are important for abundance, and all of them are premised on continuing and intentional efforts to improve the position of the institution.

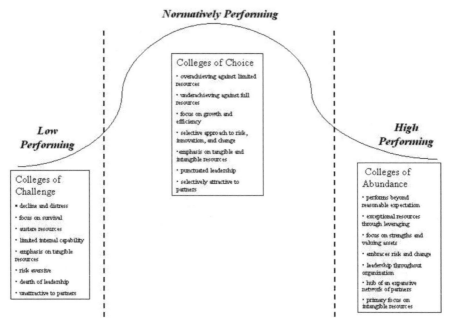

Figure 4.5   Distribution of Colleges by Type

Analysis of data gathered through our research with thirteen community colleges in 2004, strategic planning projects carried out with ten community colleges between 2002 and 2008, and interviews conducted with twenty CEOs in 2006–2007 disclosed five categories of attributes that determine the extent to which a college is abundant. These categories are:

- Appreciation of the importance of the individual
- Awareness of the internal environment
- Quality and pervasiveness of leadership
- Awareness and responsiveness to the external environment
- Level of strategic activity

Appreciation of the importance of the individual refers to factors such as the emphasis of leaders on intangible resources, their interest in the needs and capabilities of staff, the extent to which individual achievement is recognized, the level of support for professional development, the presence of well-established hiring practices, and the ability to develop a shared vision. *Awareness of the internal environment* includes factors such as the level of organizational cohesiveness and trust (culture and climate), leader and staff knowledge of organizational dynamics, and commitment to innovation and change. *Quality and pervasiveness of leadership* refers to the degree to which leaders are distributed through the organization, employee empowerment, and the commitment of leaders to positive and ethical leadership. *Awareness and responsiveness to the external environment* includes factors such as leader and staff awareness of environmental forces, stakeholder needs, and competitor practices. *Level of strategic activity*, the most obvious indicator of leveraging, refers to the ability of leaders to articulate and engender commitment to stretch goals, the temporal orientation of the organization (past, present, or future), and degree to which leveraging is understood.

Each category includes attributes that mark the extent to which a college is abundant. The larger the number of attributes on which a college is represented and the higher its scores on these attributes, the greater the likelihood it will be identified as a *college of abundance*. Conversely, the smaller the number of attributes on which a college is represented and the lower its scores, the more likely it will be identified as a *college of challenge*. For example, a college with a history of ineffective leaders will experience more difficulty in leveraging resources than a college with high-quality leaders at the executive level and spread through the organization. While not a guarantee that the organization with high-quality leadership will reach abundance, the opportunity to do so will, at least, be greater.

CONCLUSION

An informed understanding of abundance and the attributes that give it legs makes an important contribution to community college development by stretching the vision of leaders and staff to a level of functioning that lies beyond current performance. It is difficult to aspire to something that cannot be seen or understood. So the action of constructing a model and identifying attributes that can be used to determine the extent to which a college is more or less abundant is essential to understanding its current performance and its future prospects.

The relationship between institutional characteristics and abundance is the topic of discussion in the next three chapters, which focus on development paths followed by three very different institutions: colleges of challenge, colleges of choice, and colleges of abundance.

NOTES

1. R. D. Pate, *Leverage: A Key to Success and Wealth* (Rocky Mount, NC: VP Publishing, LLC, 2004), 5.

2. Pate, *Leverage*, 6.

3. Pate, *Leverage*, 9.

4. K. Cameron, "Organizational Virtuousness and Performance," in *Positive Organizational Scholarship: Foundations of a New Discipline*, eds. K. Cameron, J. Dutton, and R. Quinn, 48–65 (San Francisco: Berrett-Koehler, 2003).

5. Cameron, "Organizational Virtuousness and Performance," 1–8.

6. K. Cameron, A. Caza, and D. Bright, *Positive Deviance, Organizational Virtuousness, and Performance* (Working Paper, University of Michigan Business School, 2002).

7. M. Feldman and A. Khademian, "Empowerment and Cascading Vitality," in *Positive Organizational Scholarship: Foundations of a New Discipline*, eds. K. Cameron, J. Dutton, and R. Quinn, 343–358 (San Francisco: Berrett-Koehler, 2003).

8. Feldman and Khademian, "Empowerment and Cascading Vitality," 358.

9. Cameron, Caza, and Bright, *Positive Deviance*, 2002.

10. B. Staw, L. Sandelands, and J. Dutton, "Threat-Rigidity Effects in Organizational Behavior: A Multilevel Analysis," *Administrative Science Quarterly*, 26 (December, 1981): 501–524; S. Fineman, "Emotion and Organizing," in *The Handbook of Organizational Studies*, eds. S. Clegg, C. Hardy, and W. Nord, 543–564 (London: Sage, 1996); B. Fredrickson, "The Role of Positive Emotions in Positive Psychology: The Broaden-and-Build Theory of Positive Emotions," *American Psychologist*, 56 (March, 2001): 218–226; M. Seligman, *Authentic Happiness* (New York: Free Press, 2002).

11. Cameron, "Organizational Virtuousness and Performance," 48–65.

12. K. Weick, K. Sutcliffe, and D. Obstfeld, "Organizing for High Reliability: Processes of Collective Mindfulness," *Research in Organizational Behavior*, 21 (April, 1999): 81–123.

13. M. Seligman and M. Csikszentmihalyi, "Positive Psychology: An Introduction, *American Psychologist*, 55 (January, 2000): 5–14.

14. B. Fredrickson, R. Mancuso, C. Branigan, and M. Tugade, "The Undoing Effect of Positive Emotions," *Motivation and Emotion*, 24 (December, 2000): 237–258.

15. J. Dutton, P. Frost, M. Worline, J. Lilius, and J. Kanov, "Leading in Times of Trauma," *Harvard Business Review* (January, 2002): 54–61.

16. Cameron, Dutton, and Quinn, "Foundations of Positive Organizational Scholarship." (see chap. 1, n. 10).

17. Cameron, Dutton, and Quinn, "Foundations of Positive Organizational Scholarship."

18. Cameron, Dutton, and Quinn, "Foundations of Positive Organizational Scholarship."

19. Center for Community College Development, *Assessment of Strategic Capabilities of Horizon Network Colleges* (Research Report, Strategic Horizon Network, February 2005).

20. Center for Community College Development, *Assessment of Strategic Capabilities*.

21. Center for Community College Development, *Assessment of Strategic Capabilities*.

22. Center for Community College Development, *Assessment of Strategic Capabilities*.

23. Center for Community College Development, *Assessment of Strategic Capabilities*.

24. Center for Community College Development, *Assessment of Strategic Capabilities*.

25. R. Charan and J. Useem, "Why Companies Fail," *Fortune*, May 22, 2002, 50–58.

26. Lorain County Community College, *Lorain County Community College Web site*, http://lorainccc.edu (retrieved August 2, 2007).

27. Hamel and Prahalad, *Competing for the Future*, 49–56 (see chap. 1, n. 2).

5

Colleges of Challenge

Failing organizations are usually over-managed and under-led.

Warren Bennis

Colleges of challenge are institutions that are easily discerned as in trouble. Their options are few, their resources are limited, and leaders within them face significant obstacles in getting things done. Survival is the highest priority in these institutions as reflected in cultures of self-preserving behavior. They are besieged by stakeholders who want a piece of the institution whether it be a favor, an opportunity, or a benefit. They inhabit a veritable "no-man's land" in which organizational identity is more often determined by what is going wrong than what is right with the institution. The goal is stability, not vitality.

We begin our examination of colleges of challenge with a description of three attributes drawn from the abundance model—austere resources, organizational incapacity, and ineffective leadership—that typify these institutions. Next, we present findings from conversations with community college leaders that describe the operating dynamics of these institutions. The chapter closes with an analysis of where colleges of challenge fit within the abundance framework.

RESOURCES, INCAPACITY, AND LEADERSHIP

Resource Austerity

Colleges occupying or moving toward a position of challenge are commonly found in states in which public colleges and universities have been

151

asked to do more with less. Resource austerity is not new to community colleges—most of our colleges have experienced cutbacks due to economic hard times or mandated state appropriations for K–12 education, health care, corrections, and infrastructure. What is different for colleges of challenge is that they are locked in a debilitating cycle of decline that occurs when services are reduced to offset lost revenue which, in turn, negatively impacts enrollment and necessitates further reductions to bring spending into line with revenue. Lost revenue is only one part of the problem for these colleges. Administrative bloat, underenrolled programs, inefficient processes and systems, and expensive collective bargaining agreements limit opportunities for growth by leaving operating units bereft of discretionary income.

The oft-chosen path out of crisis is the "quick fix"—programs, services, and delivery systems that promise an infusion of new resources without a lot of work. These resources end up costing more than the benefits they generate if institutions fail to develop the self-sufficiency necessary for long-term survival. Budget shortfalls morph into protracted decline as resources are used to implement new services, but oversight is lacking to ensure their long-term survival. There is nothing worse than having something new and promising go bad in an organization that desperately needs help. Promising initiatives squandered by inept leaders serve as a continuing reminder of the futility of an institution's efforts and the severity of its circumstances.

Colleges of challenge do not have the resources, the leadership, or the talent to achieve important goals. Missed opportunities and squandered resources reinforce what survivors already know—gains are slow to achieve and easy to lose in a badly managed institution. These institutions will not go out of business—most are publicly funded entities—but they muddle along, and they drag survivors with them. Recognizing that the road is long and littered with obstacles, survivors avoid risk by putting their energy into operational tasks. Indeed, an all-too-familiar outcome of decline is the tendency to become ultraconservative—maintain the status quo and squash anything that could disrupt the flow of business, including innovation and creativity.[1]

Facing insurmountable obstacles, leaders and staff retreat to the safety of the small group and take direction from group norms. In so doing they narrow their focus to operations and fail to grasp the importance of information about external forces that could serve as a lever for opening new markets and revenue streams. Strategic concepts like market share, penetration rates, competitive advantage, value, and innovation are overlooked or regarded as secondary in importance to operational problems. Ironically, the very behaviors that could help to reverse the cycle of decline—focusing externally, creating partnerships, and identifying opportunities—are the behaviors that are least valued by colleges in crisis. The reason is simple: it is difficult for leaders and staff to see the connection between effort and results when the focus moves from operational to strategic. Time spent on activities outside of operations is perceived as wasted.

Organizational Incapacity

The ongoing development of resources is important in any organization as a means for enhancing strengths and creating advantage.[2] Tangible resources are finite, but intangible resources—people, processes, and culture—have an enormous impact on institutional development. By promoting or hampering change, people make a difference in what institutions can and can't do. They are a strategic asset in healthy organizations and a drain in unhealthy organizations. At their best, they are intellectual capital, and at their worst they are "costs"—something to be increased or decreased based on ability to pay.

In colleges of challenge, an atmosphere of mistrust discourages people from sharing knowledge essential for the good of the institution. Effort and resources tend to be centered on the needs of a core team at the top—a circumstance that works to create "mind-set enclaves" that exclude staff from decision making. Administrative architecture is essential in any organization for healthy functioning, but in colleges of challenge it is a whirlpool that pulls everyone into its swirl. When leaders do not encourage or value input from staff in decisions that determine institutional direction, a void develops that precludes the effective use of talent. These voids are rampant in colleges of challenge, and their effect is to drain the institution of talent as qualified staff look elsewhere for meaningful work. The intellectual exodus that occurs when people feel a loss of connection with the institution is aptly described in *The Cesspool Syndrome*:

> In contrast to a successful organization, in which cream rises to the top, organizations falling victim to decline often suffer from the "cesspool syndrome," wherein, figuratively speaking, dreck floats to the top. In declining organizations, the early departure of qualified employees will inhibit recovery and, if unchecked, can accelerate decline. Those who have talent and credentials move on and the least qualified individuals are left to chart the road to recovery. The all-too-predictable outcome is a stinky and costly mess.[3]

The cultures that evolve in colleges of challenge have an indelible impact on those who remain. They encourage allegiance to established norms and perpetuate practices that are counterproductive to organizational development. By encouraging personnel to resist initiatives that contradict group norms, they place institutions in a precarious position during periods of transition. Failed initiatives add fuel to the fire in organizations caught in a downward spiral. They demoralize staff and diminish the capacity of institutions to change.

Leadership

While it is difficult for colleges with limited capital to leverage resources, they do have control over who leads the institution. Leadership in low-performing organizations is all too often expected to be the answer to everything. A new president will cull out dead wood, bring in the right people, locate new resources, make the right decisions, and put the institution on a trajectory toward recovery and health. The president, however, is only one wave in an ocean of people who have developed mechanisms to cope with uncertainty and disappointment. The wasted years that come from setbacks and the numerous challenges facing the institution imperil leadership in colleges of challenge. Upon arrival on campus, a newly appointed president quickly discovers that the people, resources, and intellectual energy needed to regenerate the institution have been lost or squandered. Thus, the question about leadership in colleges of challenge becomes this: can leaders put resources in place and raise the sights of staff to a level sufficient to improve the institution's performance, or will challenges overcome them and hamper progress?

Leaders come and go in colleges of challenge. Most are incapable of generating a deep sense of what the college is or, more importantly, what it could become with the staff who are responsible for making a vision happen. There are exceptions. Northern Essex Community College in Massachusetts overcame serious obstacles to development under the skilled leadership of a new president, and Hudson County Community College in New Jersey regenerated itself through the leadership of a president who established a working partnership with county government that led to improved operating and capital resources. Craven Community College in North Carolina regenerated itself through the efforts of a president who raised the bar for performance and stretched the college beyond the limits of its resources.

It is hard to attract talented staff to undercapitalized colleges—a circumstance that compounds the task of leaders trying to promote change. To escape the gravitational pull of the past, leaders will need to convince staff that change is possible and that they are capable of being part of the process. Staff will not walk away from the past unless they have hope for the future. A key role of leaders in colleges of challenge, therefore, is to envision and bring to life a scenario for the future that is so urgent it cannot be ignored; for example, a precipitous decline in enrollment culminating in budget reductions that would impact people by separating them from jobs and income. The urgency thus engendered would provide an incentive for staff to change their approach to work and to begin the task of thinking and doing differently.

Leadership in colleges of challenge is all too often considered the province of a person or group at the top of the organization. In healthy organizations, leaders exist and actively lead throughout the organization. Professional subcultures govern daily operations as well as institutional direction.[4] Support staff assume responsibility for processes, systems, and decisions, and participatory management is the norm. In colleges of challenge the opposite is true: leaders work more on the basis of authority, and engagement is restricted to a few. How do leaders foster inclusion in an institution lacking a precedent for involvement? How do they get enough people to recognize the need to do things differently before it is too late? Perhaps the problem in colleges of challenge is a perpetual belief among staff that it is already too late or, worse yet, that the bottom will not fall out. After all, community colleges are publicly funded institutions and are critically important to the vitality of communities. There will always be a tomorrow.

IN THE EYES AND WORDS OF LEADERS

It is one thing to rely on theory and literature to describe colleges of challenge, but words are not a substitute for experience and observation. What follows is a description of colleges of challenge through qualitative information gathered from leaders in interviews, on-campus visitations, and informal conversations. These leaders have significant working knowledge of low-performing institutions through administrative positions they have occupied within them or exposure to them in the role of consultant or evaluator.

Five themes emerged from our conversations with leaders regarding colleges of challenge:

- Marginalization of people and organizational capacity
- Preoccupation with the internal environment
- Ineffective leadership
- Limited connectivity with the external environment
- Minimal engagement in strategic activity

Marginalization of People and Organizational Capacity

Ethics and Trust

Due to highly politicized environments, poor leadership, and protectionist mentalities, individuals and groups within colleges of challenge tend to be heavily invested in their own interests. There is limited concern for goals of the organization—a worldview captured in the words of a president reflecting on his first year in office after taking over a college embroiled in politics and infighting:

> There was corruption. [In the culinary program, for example, there was gratuitous entertaining of politicians.] The food budget in culinary was over $100,000 a year—it was an astonishing thing. There were numerous contracts for services not being performed, leases on property were being used for personal reasons, and sympathy sick-outs were used to protect departments. When individuals are seeking to protect their own interests, there is no commitment beyond the group or unit level and a college cannot move forward.[5]

> Another president indicated that early in his tenure he was approached by a rogue board member interested in starting a radio program without bringing the idea before the full board.

> The board had not even talked about it and the trustee who had come forward with the proposal was saying things like we could start a program in radio broadcast and we could use the broadcast students to do the on-air. We've got all these students taking marketing classes and they could sell advertising and the state is going to pay for half of the acquisition costs. Now, I had been in office for all of two days. I had no clue what she was telling me was right.[6]

Colleges of challenge routinely contend with individuals seeking to advance their own agendas by any means available. The time and energy of executive officers is drained by behavior that exceeds ethical boundaries. Decision making by fiat—a mandated course of action that staff must follow—is often the only way out. Listen to the words of a president who took a tough stance in his first year on the job after hiring into a maverick organization:

> We had a decentralized student services model when I came here. That was interesting. Counselors were allowed to determine whether they were going to work a 9-, 10- or 12-month contract. They were allowed to take vacation when they wanted in the summer. The counselors were assigned by the building they were in. One counselor might have a load of less than 100 students and another might have a load of over 1,000. It didn't make any sense. So one of the first things I did was to non-renew all of the counselors. They were given a choice: you can have your appointment back immediately with a 12- month contract or you can leave the institution. You may not keep your job on a 9- or 10-month contract and you must work from July 15th to semester opening . . . We also had a four-day summer schedule when I came here—a lot of colleges do. I abolished that for my first two or three years

here. I made everybody work five days in the summer until the enrollments came up and I was very visible at enrollment time.[7]

Issues regarding trust underlie lack of commitment in colleges of challenge, and self-serving behavior and actions are commonly observed. Their effect is to push people away from the center of the institution into safe harbors. The immediate work group becomes the basis for survival, and trust does not extend beyond it. In some cases, problems with trust are so extreme that they extend beyond institutional borders into the community. Such was the case with a president navigating through a breach of trust involving the board of trustees and college staff over county sponsorship:

> One of the things that the County board was being told by the college board of trustees was that college staff didn't support County sponsorship because they thought the County was going to demand staffing cuts in order to balance the budget, and that people were going to lose their jobs. They painted this horrible picture of what County sponsorship was going to do.[8]

In reality, faculty and staff *did* support County sponsorship, and members of the board were protecting their own interests. When relationships among internal stakeholders sour, new initiatives cannot take root. Building trust is a difficult process in any institution, but in colleges of challenge it is especially difficult. Staff who have lost the bond of trust are reluctant to put their stock in leaders, even if they are new to the organization. The road to trust is positive behavior repeated over time with an unrelenting consistency—a difficult task even in the best of circumstances.

> I have this theory—very unscientific—that you can be the perfect president coming into an institution and do and say everything right and it will still take a minimum of a year and a half for trust to develop. People have to see a consistent pattern of behavior before they believe that you will do what you say.[9]

Human Capacity

Staff are an institution's key resource—a belief commonly voiced by leaders of healthy institutions. Seasoned leaders understand the importance of attracting and retaining talented staff, but this a luxury beyond the reach of colleges of challenge. Stability is a performance goal in organizations embroiled in controversy and self-protecting behavior.[10] The results that people deliver, not the people themselves, are the primary focus of the institution. Operations take on increasing importance, and leaders' attention centers on what can be controlled. Further complicating the picture are full-time/part-time staffing ratios that place enormous demands on permanent staff. While community colleges typically have a 2:1 ratio of part-time to full-time faculty, colleges of challenge routinely lack resources to maintain this level. An allocation upward of 70 percent of college expenditures for salaries and benefits is not uncommon in these colleges, leaving them with little choice but to increase the percentage of part-time faculty to make ends meet.

Colleges of challenge are not attractive destinations for talented staff. Austere resources and climate problems easily distinguish them from healthier destinations. Without the ability to bring in qualified staff from outside, leaders must rely on internal resources to get things done. This adds consderable stress to the job of the president. Professional development (PD) budgets are often inadequate to bring staff up to speed, and PD is among the first things to go when money gets tight. One president, when queried about priorities in budget reductions, responded by indicating: "Well, what goes first are professional development dollars, professional travel dollars, and things of that nature."[11] This is a common practice for most colleges in times of financial difficulty, but time and circumstance do not drive decision making in colleges of challenge. These colleges lack the capacity to offer PD opportunities irrespective of what is going on inside or outside of the college. The implications of this incapacity are both direct and indirect: it sends a clear message to employees about what is important, and it diminishes the capability of the organization to respond to new challenges.

Caught in a trap of marginal resources and limited talent, colleges of challenge limit their focus to getting work done in the here and now. The future is beyond the sightline of leaders and the allure of the quick fix—bringing in new people to change something or make it better—is almost overwhelming. Unfortunately, small pools of applicants turn up for many positions. Attracting top-notch applicants is difficult because broken colleges cannot provide the environment, salary and benefits, or opportunities that high-caliber applicants expect and demand. And beyond the position listing is a hiring process that may be flawed by neglect, politics, or manipulation. In describing the interrelationships of employees at his college, one president recalled that:

> My director of human resources' mother was the chairman of the board. The chairman of the board's brother also worked for the college as a custodian. We also had a position called a director of advancement management. The position occupant's mother and mother-in-law were both on the board. Another member's daughter was the secretary of the allied health division. Just before I got here, the director of marketing and public relations had retired and her sister was on the board. So nepotism was alive and well.[12]

With their protectionist modes of behavior, low level of trust and commitment, incapacity to support professional development, and inability to attract talent, the human and organizational capacity of colleges of challenge is, at best, compromised.

Preoccupation with the Internal Environment

Organizational Myopia

With an inward focus on resources and operations, faculty and staff in colleges of challenge are not disposed to looking at the environment outside the institution. The context for their work is academic departments and administrative units. What happens outside is the province of someone else—most often senior administrators. Morale is elevated in operating units but remains low in relationship to the institution as a whole. One president noted that a residual effect of low morale in distressed colleges is a need for interventions that perform an integrating and sensemaking function. She indicated that a focus on mission provides direction for an organization as well as an opportunity for leaders and staff to make sense of the environment.

The price of myopia is vulnerability to change inside and outside the institution. Colleges of challenge do not have the architecture and systems to help personnel anticipate and react to change. Faculty and staff hunkered down in departments cannot envision it nor can they understand how it will benefit them. The upshot is that work groups resist change because it is a threat to established ways of doing things. Even when prime opportunities present themselves, staff are reluctant to take advantage of them. Witness the frustration of a senior administrator describing a new program that would have helped her college move forward if staff had been willing to embrace change:

> We desperately wanted to create a weekend nursing program. We knew that there would be students banging on the door. We wanted to start out with nurse's aids and build up to LPN and RN, and the nursing faculty just said "no." We can't find the hospitals for the clinicals and we can't find the faculty. They had 25 "no's" for every possible scenario. I had to walk away from that one.[13]

Leaders in colleges of challenge find inertia to be their most vexing challenge. They seek ways to work around recalcitrant staff—reassigning work, reorganizing units, bringing in consultants, and eliminating positions if necessary. Resistance takes many forms ranging from overt behavior to covert attitudes, but feelings buried deep in the minds of staff are problematic for leaders. Overt resistance is out in the open and can be addressed through dialogue and action while covert resistance cannot easily be seen. The result is a discrepancy between the need of leaders for change and the beliefs of staff that mitigate against change. Discrepancies between change initiatives and cultural values have a predictable result— culture almost always wins.[14]

Campus Climate

Rousseau defines climate as the beliefs and perceptions individuals hold in relationship to an organization.[15] Staff in distressed institutions are, not surprisingly, negative and emotionally charged. Presidents in these institutions describe them as populated by staff holding feelings of frustration, anger, and distrust. Another term that surfaced with some frequency in interviews with presidents was that of corruption. Corruption was not limited to people in positions of power but included faculty and staff and vendors contracting with colleges. One president explained the depth of corruption in his college as follows:

> The scandals were so serious here that the choice of president had to be an outsider. They had one president who had a 17-year contract. I can't even explain it, but it came with a 2–3 year severance package. It was an interesting thing. I was told that there was legislation passed afterwards to ban this sort of thing, but there are a lot of scandals like it. So I was appointed in August and took office in September. It was so bad that the chairman of the board told me that it was imperative that even though I wasn't installed to be physically present. I flew in two days after the board meeting and I remember coming to the campus at 6:30 A.M. and beginning to walk the campus. Between August and September the FBI subpoenaed great numbers of the college's records for potential irregularities, and, to be honest, they were so complex I didn't even understand them. The board that appointed me was relatively new—they hadn't been in office for most of the scandal. The state had an observer at all board meetings. Our accrediting body contacted me two weeks after I took office to arrange a site visit. I was able to persuade them to give me three months. We were operating out of one checkbook and did not even know what our reserves were.[16]

While climate is defined as the beliefs and perceptions individuals hold of an organization, culture is a product of shared values, beliefs, and expectations that develop from social interactions among people within the organization.[17] In colleges of challenge, self-protection and avoidance of risk are values that guide behavior. One president, newly arrived at a college that was struggling, described the culture this way: "It was "fractured—broken into units . . . it was 'us' versus 'them' instead of just 'us.'"[18] Conflict, fragmentation, and in-group behavior are terms that describe the downside of culture in colleges of challenge. The upside is hope for the future in the form of skilled leaders who stay the course until better times are achieved.

Organizational Drift

Organizational drift—a tendency to lose sight of organizational goals—is an unfortunate by-product of cultural fragmentation in colleges of challenge. In high-performing colleges, organizational vision and goals are the primary focus of work by faculty and staff. In low-performing institutions there is a greater emphasis on the instrumental function of work—performing operations as part of a job, but not as a calling to higher service. This amounts to a means/ends disjuncture with the means (performing operations) displacing the ends (achieving goals) and becoming ends in themselves. In healthy settings, goals are at the center of what people do; in dysfunctional settings, established routines are at the center. One president described the loss of focus on goals this way:

> Even in the face of extreme financial strain, a million dollar deficit, and flat enrollment for nearly a decade, I had to push the college to focus on goals related to students. We were not reaching inner city students, yet serving these students was one of our strategic priorities. Opening the door to opportunity was important not only as a means for providing access for an underserved population, but also to address enrollment issues."[19]

Putting process and routine before priorities related to students is a matter of necessity in colleges of challenge, not necessarily choice. Many of these colleges depend heavily on state aid and tuition for operating support. A decline in state funding will have an immediate impact on institutions without budgetary slack. The only way out is to raise tuition—an action that has the unintended effect of putting college needs ahead of the needs of its most impoverished students. A college administrator expressed his dismay at having to raise tuition:

> We've had a significant jump in tuition and fees over the last several years and I'm concerned. Community colleges have got to be accessible. Affordability is part of accessibility and we are putting ourselves in a position where it's becoming increasingly more difficult for people to come to even a community college."[20]

Interestingly, this administrator was describing the resource condition of a college with a strong track record of success in serving students. Imagine the effect of a jump in tuition on enrollment in a low-performing institution. Increasing out-of-pocket costs are a problem for students attending any college, but in colleges of challenge they have a potentially devastating effect. Rising tuition leads to problems with enrollment and revenue which, in turn, affect the operating budget leaving the institution with two choices: 1) bring costs into line with revenue by cutting the budget or 2) generate additional revenue by raising tuition even further. Neither choice is palatable, and what began as a short-term problem with enrollment and revenue can quickly evolve into a debilitating cycle of decline unless leaders move deliberately to stabilize the relationship between access, cost, and quality. A failure to do so will accelerate the process of decline by bringing the college to a point where it no longer has the students or the resources to maintain a minimum standard of quality in programs and services.

Another area that contributes to drift in marginal institutions is inadequate resources for technology. When resources are insufficient to purchase industry-standard technology and to train staff, people must be counted on to perform tasks that can more efficiently be handled by technology. Attention turns to process and to operations instead of efficiency and enhancement. Inefficiency prevails, and institutions experiencing difficulty keeping up with student needs and expectations become even less capable of doing so. The effect of dated technology on drift is nicely captured in the words of a president describing his experience in a financially troubled college:

> We have been able to improve the availability of technology to students, but considerable work remains to be done with administrative systems. We're a campus with a Legacy computing system that results in a lot of tasks being done by hand, which is a waste of resources and a drag on our ability to produce data we need to make decisions.[21]

Dated technology and incapacity are a significant problem in colleges of challenge not only because their inefficiency results in effort that must go into producing and processing information, but also because of the message it sends to students who expect organizations to be up to date on technology.

Good and bad reputations build on themselves and are difficult to change. Even with good intentions, colleges preoccupied with their internal environment send a message of complacency to stakeholders. Their most formidable foe is not rival institutions, but inertia within. The problems leading up to the closure of Compton Community College (California) in 2003 were not caused by regional competitors, but by mismanagement and complacency. For colleges of challenge, organizational myopia is the real issue. The marginal capabilities and operational mind-set of people inside these colleges are more formidable enemies than anything outside the institution. For anyone serious about leading or working in a college of challenge, the issue is not one of acquiring more resources to right the ship, but of finding a way to build a healthy culture.

Ineffective Leadership

At their best, leaders perform an uplifting role by crafting and communicating a believable vision of a better future in tough times. At their worst, they paralyze a college by stifling initiative and undercutting morale. Stories about presidents using command and control tactics to steer people and resources in a direction corresponding to their personal interests are not uncommon. Oft observed are sagas of leaders who "ride" institutions with a primary goal of survival. Risk is avoided, decisions are made on the basis of convenience, and opportunities are not pursued because they cannot be seen. Not surprisingly, these leaders insulate themselves from forces that challenge or contradict their view of the institution and their role within it. Much time is spent justifying decisions that have produced poor results and displacing blame to subordinates who are not measuring up. Ineffective leaders ensure that positive outcomes are visible and evident to powerful stakeholders, but they are seldom held accountable for poor results. This enables them to survive and accelerates and perpetuates the cycle of decline that is characteristic of so many marginally performing institutions.

Ethics and Leadership

Colleges of challenge typically suffer from volatility within executive leadership and board positions. The authority of leaders is compromised when boards become difficult to work with or resources are insufficient to move people and the organization forward. Leaders working in difficult environments have a natural tendency to protect their flanks. Survival comes first and actions taken to preserve the authority of office and one's power to act are part of the turf. In extreme cases, even unethical practices are rationalized. The political entanglements encountered by the president of a community college in the Northeast provide a good example of corruption originating outside the executive office requiring the action of a leader taking office.

> My predecessor, as well as other leaders within the college, was more interested in protecting friends and their own futures than guiding the college. Contracts were directed to individuals on a regular basis, consultants were hired for $35,000 that were not needed, and an employee was hired for

$50,000 and not required to come to work. He bought things the college didn't need.[22]

Some colleges are forced to deal with questionable behavior on the part of board members. While most presidents work with boards that are smooth running and effective, CEOs in colleges of challenge are more apt to work with boards given to extreme behavior ranging from disengagement to intrusive meddling. One president spoke at length about the issues that he and past presidents experienced with the board that he inherited. It was commonplace for board members to overstep boundaries in an effort to gain political advantage and financial gain. One instance cited occurred during the search process that resulted in his presidency:

> The board went out on a national search. AACT ran the search and I was selected through that process. Now, there was a lot of behind the scenes manipulation. One of the trustees who considered herself a power broker had convinced a state legislator who served this district, and who had formerly worked for the college, to apply and had assured him that if he applied for the job it was his . . . Well, the person whom the female trustee guaranteed would be hired was not, which led to some interesting dynamics later on.[23]

In this case, unethical behavior was not limited to a single trustee. Over time, other trustees began to pursue personal interests, and a culture developed within the board that supported the actions of trustees working from personal agendas. Consider the plight of an earnest hard-working president in a Mid-Atlantic community college who was victimized by a political initiative on the part of two trustees that eventually spread to an entire board.

The president took over a troubled college that had been through four presidents in six years. In his first year in office he concentrated on putting the college on solid footing—a strategic plan was developed and endorsed by the entire college community, experienced and capable administrators were hired in key positions, new personnel policies were enacted, governance was opened up to faculty and staff, and a premium was placed on open and timely communication. Everything appeared to be going well until a trustee, acting on his own initiative, requested confidential personnel documents directly from the college's human resource officer. The officer deferred to the president, and shortly thereafter the president informed the trustee he would comply with the request, but all further personnel requests should come directly to him.

The infuriated trustee informed the board chair of this experience, and eventually it surfaced in executive session. The chair indicated that the board had a right to personnel information without the consent of the president. The matter was discussed and tabled to no one's satisfaction. Several months passed before the president was approached by the board chair with an informal request to sign an agreement committing the college to sponsorship and support of a community partnership in health education—an agreement that he had turned away days earlier because he felt it was beyond the college's financial means. The chair indicated that signing the agreement would not bind the college to financial support—an understanding the president agreed to. The agreement was signed and eventually turned up as an item on the agenda of a regularly scheduled board meeting per individual trustee request. The president was queried about signing an agreement binding the college to support an initiative that had not been discussed by the full board. The board chair indicated that this was a violation of board policy and called into question the leadership of the president. Within a matter of weeks the board moved to terminate the contract of the president.[24]

Behavior and practices of this type seriously undercut the morale of staff. They are not uncommon in colleges of challenge, and their effect extends beyond the current actions of leaders. People have long memories, and deep scars remain after a breach of conduct. Leaders in troubled institutions, therefore, carry a double-edged sword. Not only can they plunge a college into decline through their decisions and actions, but in doing so they can perpetuate conditions underlying decline. The longer the tenure of ineffective leaders, the more difficult it is for a college to escape its situation.

Limited Connectivity with the External Environment

Detachment from Stakeholders

Community colleges serve many stakeholders—more than most higher education providers. This simple reality makes organizational life both easy and difficult. On the one hand, multiple stakeholders have unrelenting needs—a service of some kind is always needed, and this means opportunity and growth. On the other hand, demand will invariably outstrip capability in tough economic times—a circumstance that mandates difficult choices about what to do and what not to do.

Healthy colleges manage choice by looking outward and anticipating needs. Marginal colleges look inward and focus on the present because that is their operational reality. Waiting for staff each day are poorly resourced operations that need constant attention. To make the best of a tough situation, they narrow their vision to what must be done and adopt a survival mentality. This is referred to in the literature as the "mother of rigidity"—a mind-set active among staff in troubled organizations that opposes change and seeks stability through traditions and countercultures focused on self-preservation.[25]

Working in the best interest of external stakeholders is a must for any college; working outside of them is a tactical error. Consider the example of two colleges in which leaders and staff inverted the service chain by becoming the primary customer of decisions about when, where, and how to deliver educational services:

College A, a small suburban community college in the Northeast, has gone through five executive teams under two presidents in the span of seven years. The college was established in the early 1960s, and for much of its early history was led by one president. The vision of this president was limited to general education and career programs for low-performing, college-age youth from well-to-do families and children from families that could not afford a four-year college. Decision making was top down with the president at the center of every decision—a circumstance that worked to ingrain his vision with faculty and staff. The college embodied this vision by attracting and serving a limited number of students from the surrounding area and, in so doing, reinforced its image as a small transfer institution. The president's vision was sustained after his retirement by the belief system of faculty serving as emissaries to a succession of presidents and executive teams. From past to present, College A has never reached its full potential because of the limited service vision of a founding president that has shackled it to the past.

College B, a multicampus community college, established a prominent place for itself in the educational, social, and cultural landscape of a southeastern city in the 1970s and 1980s through the vision and visibility of its founding president. During his twenty-five-year tenure, an attractive downtown campus was built, and attendance centers were opened in strategically located leased facilities. This delivery system fit nicely with the linear growth pattern of the city. Faculty and staff identified closely with the downtown campus, and over time it achieved community-wide recognition as the flagship for delivery of public postsecondary education in the city.

In the mid-1980s everything changed for College B. The founding president retired, and the city embarked on an aggressive course of growth. Population and economic output exceeded the most optimistic projections, and the city took on the character of a sprawling metroplex. College B was slow to respond and continued on a path of centralized delivery through its downtown campus. An interim president was named who moved the college on a measured path before turning the reins over to a successor who came from a small college background. Within months the new president came face-to-face with a demand-delivery problem that, without decisive action, would escalate into a crisis. College B would need to dramatically expand its delivery system to meet the educational needs of a rapidly expanding population or face the prospect of losing market share to competitors. Faculty and staff did not share this view. They were committed to the downtown campus. They were not interested in expansion or working elsewhere, and distance delivery was not on the horizon as far as they were concerned.

The president initiated a lengthy strategic planning process using external consultants that led to a series of recommendations for expansion of delivery. Among the options were new campus construction, collaboration with profit and nonprofit entities, and flexible approaches to program and course delivery using technology. Predictably, these recommendations met with a wall of resistance. The president had few choices other than to accommodate prevailing sentiment by backing off or marshalling support from movers and shakers in the community. He chose the latter and galvanized community support for a massive bond issue for capital construction. The bonds for construction of four new campuses were approved in a series of elections shortly after completion of the strategic plan, and College B began its metamorphosis into a different institution.

Colleges A and B are in dramatically different places today. One was able to comprehend its situation through the efforts of an unrelenting leader and the support of a carefully assembled network of community power brokers. The other never fully grasped the magnitude of its situation. Leaders did not comprehend the binding power of culture nor did they effectively reach out to the community for help. As a result, College A operates today at a fraction of its true potential.

Limited Awareness of Changing Conditions and Competitors

Powell and Snellman are among many who describe the United States as well-entrenched in a new economic era—a knowledge economy defined by "production and services based on knowledge intensive activities that contribute to an accelerated pace of technological and scientific advance as well as rapid obsolescence."[26] Colleges throughout the nation have experienced the effects of changing employer expectations, advancing technology, and declining public support. Extreme financial pressure on states due to economic slowdowns, job outsourcing, and increasing costs for essential services will force even the most successful institutions to find new sources of revenue. Healthy institutions respond by anticipating the impact of changing conditions and projecting the resources they will need to maintain operations. Colleges of challenge respond by insulating themselves from change. Faced with the constant press of operations, faculty and staff resist change and forward thinking—senior administrators are responsible for solutions to problems.

The price of resistance is high. From an external perspective, a marginal college will be out of sync with its community if it cannot produce outcomes that meet basic needs. This circumstance was captured in the words of an employer describing the difference between his company's workforce needs and what it was actually getting from a low-performing college:

> The gap between the worlds of education and work is greater than I expected. In education you can turn in an assignment late and get credit for it, you can redo a poorly done paper, you can come to class late, you can skip class—all without major consequences. In work, we would not make a profit if our employees skipped a day of work, missed deadlines, or performed shoddy work. There are no "second chances" in business. How much can we reasonably expect from our employees when the practices they are learning in college are different from what we do and expect in work?[27]

Leaders and staff in colleges of challenge have a limited understanding of competition. They are aware of obvious rivals in traditional markets but have difficulty envisioning competitors beyond the immediate horizon. New markets and emerging competitive forces are not on their radar screens; nor are aggressive rivals who rewrite the rules of competition with every innovation. While community colleges have a competitive edge on price, price is not the only thing that students are looking for. They are also looking for quality and value, both of which are questionable commodities in colleges of challenge.

Minimal Engagement in Strategic Activity

Failing to Leverage

Along with leadership, a major difference between colleges in distress and those that are healthy is the ability to leverage. Colleges of challenge lack the capacity to get the most out of their people and their resources. The reasons are many, but they boil down to an inability or unwillingness to invest in people. When money gets tight, cost-cutting measures like retrenchment, reallocation, and consolidation of positions undercut morale by realigning responsibilities and separating staff from colleagues. In normal operating conditions, staff stretched thin by increasing responsibility and diminishing resources rethink their allegiance to the institution. Problems with morale do not necessarily indicate that employees are of lower caliber. Rather, the burden of additional work lowers efficiency and leads staff to focus on self-preservation in contrast to the welfare of others. In the words of a community college president:

> I don't think there is any way that public sources could have kept up with the growth. It strains the system and the colleges and the biggest effect is the strain on the human resource. People are taking on more and trying to deliver it themselves without the resources they need, whether they be technological or whatever to provide a high level of service. They try to provide all the services they can for larger numbers in spite of the lack of resources. There comes a point when you can't do it anymore and it becomes frustrating because they believe they are not doing things as well as they should be. That's when employees break down. When you reach out to help someone, but you are so overwhelmed in your own area, you can't help someone else.[28]

Attempting to stretch people is a difficult endeavor under the best of circumstances, but doing so with an employee base that is under duress and preoccupied borders on the impossible.

Non-Strategic Behavior

Colleges of challenge are more likely to engage in activities that are operational rather than strategic. Strategy is a systematic way of positioning an institution with stakeholders to create value that leads to advantage.[29] The emphasis of strategy is on competitive differentiation and achievement of long-term advantage. By way of contrast, the managerial emphasis in colleges of challenge is on short-term survival. Problems in their immediate world command attention and preclude consideration of the future. Concepts of advantage, differentiation, and value that are vital to strategy are not part of the organizational dialogue. Staff operate selectively—focusing on core responsibilities in their work and pushing away anything that would divert them from time on task.

An important part of the survival mentality of colleges of challenge is aligning resources and costs. Cost efficiencies are consistently sought, and resources are squeezed from every cost center in the operating budget. Paramount in importance is the bottom line and programs, services, and activities are evaluated on the basis of their contribution to the bottom line. Contrary to operating practices in healthy institutions, programs are subject to modification and reduction even if they are performing effectively. Full-time faculty may be offered incentives for early retirement, and nonpersonnel expenditures cut without due consideration of their impact on the future. Indiscriminate cutting is a trademark of colleges of challenge.

Resource Acquisition

The financial difficulty experienced by colleges of challenge is not limited to current operating funds. It extends as well to the ability to acquire funds. Leaders consumed by problems do not pick their heads up long enough to learn how to argue effectively for operating and capital support. Listen to the words of two presidents describing the resource condition of their colleges at the time they assumed the CEO position:

> Two school districts withdrew from the local fund base and left a $2 million hole in the operating budget. The other school districts either would not or could not offset that loss and, of course, they were unwilling to increase their sponsorship. In fact, when I got here the mill levy—the tax rate set by the school district to help the college—had not been changed since 1990. It was at one mill. During that period the assessed home value had dropped rather steeply, as a result of a sputtering economy. All that tax revenue had been lost, so what one mill was generating was nowhere near what it had generated 12 years earlier.[30]

Another president described his college as having space problems. It was growing, its budget was in limbo, and it desperately needed space.

> The college didn't even own its facilities, so it was in deep trouble. There was an excess of a million dollars in leases. One building was actually rented from the public schools. It was a school building built in 1910. We had a student there who was in a wheelchair and when he needed to go to the bathroom they had to push him behind a furnace and he had to urinate in a coffee can. It was obvious that something had to be done. I don't even know how we met code.[31]

While an instance of this type is rare, it underscores the importance of resource acquisition in colleges of challenge. These institutions need to fight for dollars and talent in a swell of opinion often weighted against them. Low esteem in the public eye limits the potential for resource enhancement. This situation would be difficult for any college to navigate, but in colleges of challenge it is the linchpin in a cycle of decline that constrains them from achieving their potential.

SUMMARY

We have applied the designation *colleges of challenge* to institutions that do not have the capacity to leverage the resources available to them. As decribed in Table 5.1., the focus of these institutions is on survival, and their managerial emphasis is on problem solving. The present is more important than the future, and operations are more important than strategy. Leaders are not interested or committed to integrating people into decision making and direction setting. Ineffective leadership is one of the major reasons why these colleges find themselves in a state of challenge.

Table 5.1.

Dimension of Abundance	Colleges of Challenge
Managerial Emphasis	protecting/acquiring resources
Cohesion	void between leaders and staff
Resources	consumed by fixed costs
Resource Perspective	tangible resources
Organizational Architecture	silos and chimneys
Operational Focus	process ownership and control
Risk	avoid risk
Collaboration	unattractive to partners
Competitive Focus	coping with rivals
Performance Objective	survival
Leadership	top echelon of organization
Attractiveness	difficulty in attracting quality staff

When organizations are in distress, they focus inward, become conservative, and protect resources. This mentality prevents leaders and staff from understanding competition and adapting to change. Planning for the future is low in importance when underresourced operations command the attention of staff. It takes a combination of unusual circumstances—dramatic economic shifts, corruption, unethical behavior, ineffective leadership, and more—to push a college into a position of challenge. In the next chapter, a more common niche for community colleges is explored—that of *colleges of choice*. This category encompasses the vast majority of community colleges. It comprises two types of institutions: those with lean resources moving toward abundance through operational efficiency and those with full resources that have squandered opportunities for abundance through poor decision making.

NOTES

1. K. Cameron, D. Whetten, and M. Kim, "Organizational Dysfunctions of Decline," *Academy of Management Journal* 30, no. 1 (1987): 126–138.

2. R. Grant, *Contemporary Strategy Analysis: Concepts, Techniques, Applications,* 4th ed. (Malden, MA: Blackwell Publishers, Inc., 2003), 165.

3. A. Bedeian and A. Armenakis, "The Cesspool Syndrome: How Dreck Floats to the Top of Declining Organizations," *Academy of Management Executive* 12, no. 1 (1998): 58–67.

4. A. Etzioni, "Administrative and Professional Authority," in *Organization and Governance in Higher Education: An ASHE Reader,* 4th ed., eds. M. Peterson, E. Chaffee, and T. White, 441–448 (Needham Heights, MA: Ginn, 1991); H. Mintzberg, *Mintzberg on Management: Inside our Strange World of Organizations* (New York: Free Press, 1989).

5. Interview, community college president, October 16, 2006.

6. Interview, community college president, November 16, 2006.

7. Interview, community college president, October 16, 2006.

8. Interview, community college president, November 16, 2006.

9. Interview, community college president, April 24, 2006.

10. Cameron, Whetten, and Kim, "Organizational Dysfunctions of Decline."

11. W. McKinley, "Organizational Decline and Adaptation: Theoretical Controversies," *Organization Science* 4, no. 1 (1993): 1–9; Interview, community college president, November 29, 2006.

12. Interview, community college president, November 16, 2006.

13. Interview, community college vice president, October 23, 2006.

14. B. Horst, "Organizational Culture and Change," in *Managing Change in Higher Education: Preparing for the 21st Century,* eds. K. Hughes and D. Conner, 67–78 (Washington, DC: CUPA, 1989).

15. D. Rousseau, "Assessing Organizational Culture: The Case for Multiple Methods," in *Organizational Climate and Culture,* ed. B. Schneider, 153–192 (San Francisco: Jossey-Bass, 1990).

16. Interview, community college president, November 16, 2006.

17. D. Rousseau, "Assessing Organizational Culture," 153–192.

18. Interview, community college president, November 29, 2006.

19. Interview, community college president, April 12, 2006.

20. Interview, community college president, April 25, 2006.

21. Interview, community college president, October 13, 2006.

22. Interview, community college president, October 13, 2006.

23. Interview, community college president, November 16, 2006.

24. Descriptive account of trustee/CEO interaction leading up to contract termination provided by a Northeastern community college president.

25. McKinley, "Organizational Decline and Adaptation," 3.

26. W. Powell and K. Snellman, "The Knowledge Economy," *Annual Review of Sociology* 30 (2004): 201.

27. Employer Focus Group Meeting, Clinton Community College, December 10, 2006.

28. Interview, community college president, April 24, 2006.

29. R. Alfred, *Managing the Big Picture in Colleges and Universities: From Tactics to Strategy* (Westport, CT: Greenwood Press, 2005).

30. Interview, community college president, November 16, 2006.

31. Interview, community college president, October 13, 2006.

6

Colleges of Choice

Colleges create opportunity by making smart choices.

Richard Alfred

Once an organization loses its spirit of pioneering and rests on its early work, its progress stops.

Thomas Watson

In contrast to the austerity and incapacity of colleges of challenge, colleges of choice are healthy institutions operating in equilibrium with their environment. While resources are tight for most of these institutions, financial exigency is not on the horizon. These colleges have a capability for choosing among alternatives for one of two reasons: they have ample resources which permit choice, or they have freed up discretionary resources through operational efficiency. In either case, they share attributes of stability, drift, and choice. *Stability* refers to their ability to maintain programs, offerings, and services at a constant level without radical change or innovation. *Drift* refers to their capacity to make adjustments incrementally to continue providing comparable value to stakeholders.[1] *Choice*—the opportunity to choose freely among alternatives because resources are sufficient to permit the simultaneous pursuit of multiple goals—is their signal attribute. This is the basis of their differentiation from colleges of challenge and their threshold for the pursuit of abundance.

Colleges of choice cover a vast terrain between institutions that have little going for them (challenge) and those that have much going for them (abundance). Although they are not in decline, they are not performing at a level that would qualify them as abundant. Three important factors hold them back: an inability to fully leverage their resources, a reluctance to embrace innovation and change, and missed opportunities. Leveraging human and financial resources is essential if organizations are to fully realize their potential. When resources are predictably allocated to an established business model over time, institutions may lose their creative spark. Conversely, when institutions concentrate lean resources on important objectives and work at a high level of efficiency to create choice, the sheer energy required for this effort will limit their capability for innovation. Ultimately, colleges working in both venues must find a way to leverage their resources, to embrace innovation and change, and to pursue opportunity in order to achieve abundance.

DIMENSIONS AND DYNAMICS OF CHOICE

Stretch and leverage are important dimensions of choice and abundance. We can illustrate the role they play by way of a not-so-hypothetical example. Imagine two colleges operating in the same market. Ample Community College has significant resources of every kind—operating dollars, people, talent, technology, facilities, and visibility. These resources, accumulated over time, are the result of favorable location and propitious economic circumstances. Ample's aspiration is to maintain its current position. Its goal is to "grow enrollment at a level and pace that its resources can support." Ample's resources are substantial, but its aspiration modest. It easily has the resources to exercise choice about what it wants to do, but it does not have the drive to stretch beyond its operating resources.

Lean Community College has limited tangible resources in comparison to Ample. It has no choice but to make do with fewer people, a tighter budget, more modest facilities, and a fraction of Ample's discretionary resources. But Lean has a capacity for leveraging that extends beyond its meager resource base. Like Ample, it has the ability to develop and deliver programs and services in response to market needs. To nurture and sustain this ability, Lean's leaders know they must be operationally efficient, embrace innovation and change, encourage staff initiative, reward achievement, invest in activities that will pay off over the long term, and grow at a pace faster than competitors. From the perspective of the bottom line, Lean is the mirror image of Ample: it is able to choose the opportunities it wants to pursue, but it is resource limited and aspiration rich.

The gap between Ample's resources and aspirations can be described as "slack," and the gap between Lean's resources and aspirations "stretch."[2] Armed with this knowledge, one can reasonably expect that the two institutions will employ fundamentally different approaches to resource allocation but will achieve a similar outcome. Ample is better placed to operate strategically—that is, to develop and deliver new programs and services, to spend more than Lean on technology, to allocate more resources to professional development, and to promote itself through aggressive marketing. Ample's slack, however, is the very reason why it will fall short of abundance. Its leaders and staff have a conservatism born of privilege that constrains their capacity for innovation. They will be reluctant to do anything more than what they have done in previous years: allocate resources to new initiatives, hope some of them succeed, and grow incrementally as resources permit. There is little impetus for risk and change. Ample's approach to organizational development is to increase its capacity through the sheer weight of its resources—however inefficient that may be.

Lean Community College has no such luxury. Confronted with the reality of limited resources, it is forced to stretch its operating resources beyond capacity. Leaders and staff think strategically, they make sound resource decisions, and they are constantly looking for opportunities. The majority of staff are able to relate their professional role and responsibilities to the goals of the institution. They understand the contribution of their work to organizational performance. Tight coupling between the individual and the organization enables them to devote full energy to what the institution is trying to do.

Using the example of Ample College and Lean College, let's see how choice plays out in institutions with different resources and capabilities. The names of the colleges in table 6.1 denote their capacity for choice and their position on a continuum toward abundance.

A capacity for leveraging resources is the single most important attribute that distinguishes abundant from less abundant organizations. Static, Bounteous, and Overachieving have incentives and opportunities for leveraging, but they have constraints, as well, that limit their ability to do so. Static's leaders and staff do not have the vision and capacity to leverage its resources. Bounteous has full resources, but a cruise control mentality limits its ability to leverage. Overachieving has the capability to leverage but lacks the resources to put it over the top. Each college has the option of choosing what it will or will not do, but falls short of the capacity for superior performance that is characteristic of abundant institutions. Let's look more closely at these institutions and see what makes them colleges of choice.

Static College

Static College (SC) is located in a rural county within commuting distance of a large city in the Midwest. While the metropolitan area surrounding

Table 6.1.   Continuum for Colleges of Choice

	Static College	Bounteous College	Overachieving College
Resources	Adequate and allocated primarily to operations	Ample and allocated to multiple initiatives	Strategically allocated and leveraged
Capabilities	The vision of leaders and staff is limited, their focus is on the operating unit, innovation is cautiously pursued, and change is incremental	Work is approached from a perspective of guaranteed staff, resources, initiatives receive full support, and people are fixed in place in a milieu of plenty	Operational efficiency is sought by leaders and strategic skills are valued, staff maintain a dual focus on the institution and the operating unit, and innovation and change are aggressively pursued
Leadership	Leaders are focused on operations and control, a premium is placed on problem solving, and stability is the goal	Leaders are focused on maintaining position, they do not invest strategically, and they lay claim to resources rather than leveraging them	Leaders are strategically focused, they embrace risk and change, and their focus is on leveraging people and resources
Overall Position	Static is anchored in Choice	Bounteous is rooted in Choice, but lacks the drive to achieve Abundance	Overachieving is moving toward Abundance from a position of Choice

the city has experienced steady growth, little has changed in the county. Small towns, wetlands, and farms dot its landscape, and business and residential development projected for more than two decades has not materialized. SC's service area now consists of forty-five thousand residents, three high schools, and a moderately developed business infrastructure comprised mostly of small companies. Within the last five years, two employers have moved into the county to take advantage of its location and favorably priced land. One is an outlet mall employing several hundred people, and the other is an automobile parts plant employing five hundred workers from a variety of educational and skill backgrounds. These companies employ nearly 35 percent of the local workforce and have been integrated into the community through outreach efforts by the Chamber of Commerce.

Static has been slow to follow suit. Over time it has pursued a traditional academic mission, and its leaders have assigned limited value to partnerships with business and industry unless they fit within the college's mission. Contracts have been forged with some businesses, but they were initiated primarily at the request of board members connected to local business. The board has hired and worked with three presidents over the past twenty years, each essentially a clone of the others. Each has been a middle-age white male with executive experience in small colleges, and each was hired with a mandate to keep the college on track with its traditional mission. Static's enrollment is comprised primarily of students between eighteen and twenty-five, most coming directly from local high schools, and the majority are interested in college transfer. Its resources are more than sufficient to support a broad array of program and service offerings. Tuition, local tax, and state aid cover all of its operating expenses and permit discretionary expenditures as well. The availability of resources, however, does not equate with enrollment growth and program expansion. Static's enrollment has remained level at four thousand students for several years, and it has added only four new programs over the last decade.

Static College operates like an extended family. Communication between internal stakeholders, including board members, is frequent, fluid, and reinforces shared values. Primary among these values is a preference for small size that binds leaders and staff in a tightly knit culture. Maintaining the culture comes ahead of everything else—a fact readily revealed in staff resistance to new initiatives that would change the college's character. Never was this more apparent than a decision in 2006 by the president to limit growth by selecting the low projection from enrollment scenarios developed as part of its strategic plan. The rationale underlying this decision according to the president was a desire to avoid the disruptive effect of rapid enrollment growth on overburdened staff in the "extended family."

Despite the availability of resources to support growth and change, Static has chosen to follow a tried and true path in its mission and operations. The capacity for choice is secured through its operating resources, but its potential for abundance is lost to inertia and conservative leadership. Static does not seek to stretch beyond boundaries of size, scope, and purpose that are firmly entrenched in its culture. It is not interested in growth, it is almost exclusively focused on internal operations, and it perpetuates culture by hiring individuals who "fit" prevailing norms. Perhaps most telling about Static is the limited interest of leaders and staff in opportunities and partnerships. The boundary between college and community is clearly drawn, and the external environment—customers, competitors, conditions, and circumstances—is interpreted in a manner that is consistent with cultural norms.

Bounteous College

Bounteous College is located in a southwestern border state that has become a destination for retirees and tech-savvy college graduates. The county it serves is one of the fastest growing and most affluent in the nation. Students graduating from high school typically stay close to home because they have multiple choices for college. A research university, comprehensive teaching university, several private colleges, and three for-profit institutions are Bounteous's neighbors. Bounteous has extensive relationships with business and industry, and it is heavily involved in workforce development. It has parlayed its business/industry partnerships and favorable public attitudes toward postsecondary education into a revenue base that is impervious to fluctuations in the economy. Over the past fifteen years—a period in which declining state appropriations marginalized college and university operating budgets—Bounteous has passed a series of tax levies resulting in a 25 percent increase in its operating budget.

Despite its access to ample resources, Bounteous has not achieved a state of abundance. Although its talent pool runs deep and there is potential for creativity and innovation in every part of the institution, the capabilities of its staff are not leveraged. Strategic initiatives begin and end in the executive suite. The president has made significant changes in Bounteous's capital and operating resources, its operations, and its campus climate during ten years in office. He is a visionary who leads by instinct and intuition, but he prefers to work alone. A voracious reader with an uncanny ability to decipher opportunities from massive amounts of information, he uses administrators and staff as "assistants" to execute his ideas. He is as likely to score big as to miss big on an initiative. Recently, he allocated $1 million to upgrade the labs and workshops in the manufacturing technology building to accommodate the expansion of Bounteous's construction sciences program. His aim was not only to expand opportunities for students in the automotive and construction technology programs, but also to attract contracts from local construction companies. His wager paid off handsomely as the college was able to attract new manufacturing firms into the county. However, earlier in the year, he approved $500,000 to expand technology in the student center but neglected to include input from students who would be the prime users of the technology and technical staff who would be integrating the new software. The total cost of the project increased to nearly $700,000, and students were slow to take advantage of the new technology.

There is a large reservoir of untapped tacit knowledge in Bounteous. High salaries and excellent benefits have attracted talented staff, but their capabilities are underutilized because of the leadership style of the president. There are dozens of people brimming with ideas who could create and pursue opportunities but who leave the task of initiation to the president. Locked in by a favorable salary and benefits package and stable work conditions, faculty and staff are doing the same things today that they did yesterday. Leveraging their talent by involving them in planning and decision making and dialogue about the future would open up opportunities for Bounteous that cannot be seen through the eyes of a leader. For Bounteous, the difference between choice and abundance is the capacity for leveraging.

Overachieving College

Located in an expansive but largely undeveloped county in a northwestern state, Overachieving College has had a difficult history compared to other community colleges in the state. Major employers moved their operations to other states in the 1970s, precipitating a loss of manufacturing and agricultural jobs that continues today. Postsecondary education is not high on the radar screen of most county residents, evidenced by the fact that only 30 percent of the adult population has attended college. Overachieving is committed to economic development and has tried to help by partnering with the county in an effort to draw new business into the area. Doing so, however, has put it in a difficult position. A commitment to customize workforce programs and noncredit offerings is required to attract and retain business, but Overachieving does not have the revenue to develop new programs. It has tried on numerous occasions to pass a tax referendum for increased operating support only to see each proposal go down in flames. Worse yet, efforts to educate the citizenry on the vital role played by the college in regional development and the resource needs associated with this role have largely fallen on deaf ears.

Five years ago, the college hired a new president, the first ever who was not an internal candidate. She brought considerable experience to the job through prior appointments in the private sector, as a professor at a public university, and a vice president of academic affairs at a rural community college. Her leadership style is "people-first" in contrast to the political style of former presidents. Upon arriving at Overachieving, she noted that the culture reflected that of an organization in decline. Morale was low, self-preserving behavior was rampant, and individuals were focused almost exclusively on operational tasks. Repairing fractured subcultures throughout the institution became a priority. She approached this task through monthly meetings with the community and internal constituencies and cross-organizational teams to develop creative solutions to pressing problems. The team initiative brought individuals from across the college together and helped diminish protectionist behavior. Organizational commitment increased as staff began to share knowledge across departmental boundaries and focus on problems beyond their individual subcultures.

The new president worked hard to create an environment that valued people. As word spread of her leadership skills, the number and quality of applicants for open positions rose dramatically. The message was clear—Overachieving had developed a reputation as an attractive workplace. By leveraging talent, the president had created choices that would not have been possible at an earlier time. Today, Overachieving has all of the tools necessary to achieve abundance. All it needs to put it over the top are additional operating resources.

IN THE EYES AND WORDS OF LEADERS

The case examples of Static College, Bounteous College, and Overachieving College are drawn from the authors' experience with institutions representing different variations of choice. As was the case with colleges of challenge, the rationale for a designation of *choice* is based on qualitative information gathered from leaders and staff in formal and informal conversations as well as observations during campus visits. Particularly rich as an information source are the informal reflections of leaders during conversations away from campus.

Five prominent themes emerged from analysis of the information gathered from leaders and staff in colleges of choice:

- Appreciation of the importance of the individual
- Organizational dynamics
- Quality and pervasiveness of leadership
- Comprehension of the external environment
- Leveraging people, resources, and performance

Recognizing that colleges of choice represent a continuum of institutions ranging from those that are underresourced, operationally efficient, and fully resourced, we have chosen to describe these colleges in terms of their mainstream capabilities; that is, the capabilities that distinguish them, as a group, from colleges of challenge and abundance.

Appreciation of the Importance of the Individual

Colleges of choice enjoy substantially better leader-staff relations than colleges of challenge. As a group, they have not experienced sustained financial austerity, internal strife, or crises in leadership. They are buffered from shocks in the external environment and pursue change as an incremental process in contrast to an urgent imperative. Leaders and staff are more interested in staying the course with an established direction than pursuing a risky initiative. Lacking a stretch goal or urgency for action, staff settle into comfortable routines that guide their approach to work. Routine is a harbinger of resistance, and it is a primary attribute of choice that deters progress toward abundance.

Strategic Staffing

Presidents affiliated with colleges of choice note that people are the most important resource within the organization. In their worldview, organizations are a reflection of the people who work within them, and performance is dictated by people, not resources. Operational efficiency is also important, and it is best achieved through staff who are committed to their job and efficient in their use of time. Change and innovation are a mixed bag for colleges of choice. Some embrace it and innovate as a way of achieving priorities. Others prefer the comfort of routine. Consider, for example, the tendency of colleges to import new programs rather than create their own, to copy the systems of peer institutions, and to mimic the marketing practices of competitors. For leaders in these institutions, the rationale for borrowing is simple: why spend money on creating something that you can more easily acquire from another college at a level of quality and cost savings you cannot duplicate?

Contrary to colleges of challenge, colleges of choice have the resources and the capability to move forward through strategic staffing. They invest in people, and they are focused on situating competent staff in every part of the institution. New hires play an important role in this effort, but even more important is a commitment to building internal capability by investing in current staff. Prominent in this regard are practices such as encouraging staff to think beyond their current position, continuous professional development, and promoting from within. Moving up in the organization has a dual effect that advantages colleges of choice—it reduces the element of risk in hiring (leaders know exactly what they are getting), and it elevates staff morale.

Growing People from Within

In contrast to colleges that conceptualize professional development as an annual activity built into the contract, colleges of choice view it as a means of growing their own in positions of leadership. A conversation

with the president of a large midwestern college confirmed the importance of "growing people from within":

> For reasons of financial constraint and practicality, we cannot depend on
> outside hires to move us forward. Increasing the quality of human resources
> is a continuing challenge that has everyone's attention. One of the ways that
> we are trying to deal with it is to grow our own—to encourage and promote
> growth that will prepare staff for higher leadership positions and provide
> opportunities for individuals with the hope that they will stay and fill these
> roles for us.[3]

Bringing people along by providing opportunities for growth and
development is critical to elevating performance. It is also one of the single most important attributes distinguishing colleges of choice from those
of challenge. Talent is embedded and leveraged in colleges of choice
whereas it is lacking or incapable of mobilization in colleges of challenge.
Even in difficult times, the commitment to professional development
remains constant. In the words of a president who maintained commitment to professional development even in budgetary crisis:

> We have strengthened the college by continuing our commitment to profes-
> sional development even under the worst of conditions. I'm one of those peo-
> ple who believes in developing staff at all levels in the organization. Even
> when we were trying to get control of the budget, I was increasing funding
> for professional development.[4]

Growing talent from within is not necessarily a smooth ride. To commit to an organization, staff need to feel ownership over something more
than the routine of their work. In colleges of challenge, commitment
begins and ends with the routine of work. In colleges of choice, ownership extends beyond position to the larger organization itself. The meaning of work changes as staff find that the organization is more than a job
or a department. Listen to the voices of two presidents describing actions
they took to increase ownership and, ultimately, commitment to the
organization:

> Some of our managers were resisting changes we wanted to make in our
> recruiting and hiring process. We handed control over to them for determin-
> ing hiring priorities. It took time, but when they began to feel a sense of own-
> ership over the process, trust developed and their commitment increased.[5]

> Working to retain staff, even under extreme financial circumstances, helps to
> increase their commitment. We've had to merge positions, eliminate pro-
> grams, and even retrench activities seen as untouchable, but unrelated to

core mission to adjust to state cutbacks. Yet, staff stayed with us—they were impressed by the integrity and consistency of the president.[6]

Personally Investing in New Staff

Beyond their commitment to developing talent from within, colleges of choice use new hires to fill performance gaps and bring new energy to program and service initiatives. A high level of clarity in hiring practices ensures that staff are employed who quickly and meaningfully fill needs in the organization. Presidents seeking to fit new hires with institutional mission and direction employ deliberate hiring practices that make clear what the institution is looking for and encourage potential applicants to self-select throughout the hiring process. This practice is facilitated by a consistent set of values broadly shared among staff. It is also fueled by leaders who are personally involved in the hiring process:

> I talk to people, I meet with all groups, I have an open door. There is a half-hour interview with the president for every applicant we are in the final stage of considering as a full-time employee. I get to know each employee personally and to greet them on that basis when I see them on campus.[7]

> One of the things that I do, and my colleagues think I'm crazy, is to interview every person that is hired on as a full-time employee in the college. It is the only way I know that quality is maintained. I know that they have made it through the ranks of interviews and committees and that they have the credentials and resumes. I do the interview of the heart. I tell them about the vision of the college and ask why they want to be here. I look for people who don't want just a job because this is not just a job.[8]

Involvement in staff selection is not the preference of many presidents. There are ways, however, to screen and filter candidates. Listen to a president who does not interview candidates for full-time positions but is personally involved in the search process:

> Part of the search process here is that the president visits with the search committee and shares the charge with them. Embedded in that charge are things like diversity and opportunity. One of the things that I always try to slip in there is to choose someone who could become a member of your family. Make it a family member of choice. The aspect of family that you are looking for in an employee is difficult to put your finger on, but it is something that most of us can relate to. So that's the non-specific aspect that we are looking for—someone who can fit into the community college family and, more specifically, into our college family.[9]

Authenticity

In contrast to their counterparts in colleges of challenge, leaders in colleges of choice exhibit a greater tendency for authenticity—that is, openness in thought, word, and deed. Leaders behave authentically when espousing and acting on a set of positive values, behaving in a consistent manner, and treating others with respect. Followers tend to reciprocate authentic behavior and, in doing so, induce a shift to norms of openness, respect, and care for others in the organization. The intersection of leader and follower behavior moves the organization toward transparency—a state in which intentions, actions, and behaviors are clear and deception is minimal.

Authenticity is a feature distinguishing colleges of choice from challenge because the transparency essential for effective communication evolves more easily in colleges that have access to resources. Leaders and staff in colleges of choice are part of an established network of relationships in which individuals understand what the institution stands for, what is expected of them, and what they must do to contribute to performance. They enjoy a relationship that, on the one hand, enables trust to develop while, on the other hand, encourages resistance as a natural form of organizational behavior. These countervailing forces come together in the words of a president describing tactics he uses to engage staff in change. They are the tactics of a leader who is comfortable within himself and whose behavioral tendencies are well known to staff:

> We are very careful not to pick people who are predisposed to be supportive of things going on in the college. I want naysayers to be involved in change initiatives so they can go back to other naysayers and carry the message.[10]

By involving resistors in strategic activities through transparent behavior (certainly the resistors recognized and understood the motives of the president) the college was able to move its change agenda forward. Authenticity is more easily achieved by leaders and staff in colleges that have the benefit of operating in a stable environment. In colleges of choice, it is a privilege of circumstance for leaders and staff.

Organizational Dynamics

Drift

Colleges of choice have the good fortune of having access to resources that permit stability and consistency. Staff occupy positions in a culture that is relatively fixed—one they helped create and intuitively reinforce—on a daily basis through shared values. The extensive period of calm that is part of a stable culture leads to a sameness and sense of order among staff that limits change. In the words of a president taking office in a college of choice:

> We do a number of things because we have always done them that way. There are some things we have done historically that we just don't need to do anymore. We need to look at other ways of doing things to become more efficient.[11]

Why should staff change if business is good and the institution appears to be running smoothly? Why should they adopt new practices when old ones seem to work effectively? Why should they question values that have worked for years and brought the college to where it is today? Organizational dynamics in colleges of choice are about drift—the gradual assimilation of change by leaders and staff based on the immediacy of forces in the environment.[12] By nature, stable organizations drift over time to reliance on norms that suppress change. Means become ends, and staff miss opportunities to pursue new initiatives because they are reluctant to depart from prevailing norms.

Consider, for example, the reluctance of a southeastern community college to adjust its business curriculum to the changing needs of regional employers.[13] Full-time instructors were committed to developing courses that fit their own preferences (advanced courses in international trade, corporate competition, continuous quality improvement, etc.) in contrast to the expressed needs of employers for workers with highly developed cognitive and affective skills. Not until the division dean and key business instructors met face-to-face with employers were they convinced of the need to rethink the direction of their business curriculum. Another example is that of a complacent mid-Atlantic community college that sacrificed an opportunity to contribute to the renewal of a decaying city. By choosing to locate its primary campus operations in outlying suburbs, it removed itself as a player in regional economic development and sacrificed its eligibility for workforce development funds.[14]

In colleges that have the resources to choose among alternatives, organizational drift retards change. It is the point at which leaders and staff internalize behaviors that achieve a reasonable balance between resources and performance and the rate at which the institution must change. Discrete change permits operational consistency, thereby reducing the impact on staff. Fast-paced or "punctuated" change is disruptive because it throws people off balance by challenging established norms. Drift is a protective mechanism that allows people to control the pace of change and customize it to their preferences.

Flexibility

Flexibility is a conduit to change because it encourages staff to embrace new ideas and try different ways of doing things. Conversations with presidents in colleges of choice revealed a dual outlook on flexibility. It is, on the one hand, essential for improved performance.

> Part of our design for the learning environment was to remove the barriers we discovered as we talked with the faculty. What hampers them from being able to do what they want to do and then removing them. In designing class-rooms, we made sure that all of the furniture was movable and flexible. We also made sure that there would be an opportunity for breakout class-rooms—whatever might structurally stand in the way of superior teaching was removed. When you don't have constraints of space and resources, you minimize the need or the ability to say 'I'd love to do that, but I can't because . . .'[15]

On the other hand, it is something that has to be unlocked and lever-aged in institutions bound by convention:

> We initiated an academic reorganization because I was concerned that we had too many layers. We had too much hierarchy in our academic structure from an academic vice president, to the campus provost, to the dean of instruction, to the associate dean (which would be the equivalent of a depart-ment chair in an administrative position), and the faculty. We eliminated the dean of instruction position because we wanted the campus provosts to take greater responsibility and accountability for the academic programs on their campuses. We're trying to put a greater emphasis on academics, but the only way to do it is to streamline the organization by cutting administrative layers.[16]

Leaders in colleges of choice indicate difficulty in creating an environ-ment in which staff have the freedom to embrace and pursue change. They know that lip service to change and the experience of change are two different things. They also know that the first task involved in change is removing barriers to ideas and action. In a midwestern community col-lege this took the form of a "Challenge to Excellence." Each year the exec-utive team would identify and issue an institution-wide challenge. One year it was improving quality, the next it was streamlining systems and processes, then strengthening culture and developing talent from within. Challenges were the foundation on which barriers to flexibility were bro-ken because to achieve them new ways of thinking and doing had to be found.

When this college—we'll call it High Reach Community College—set a goal of 50 percent enrollment growth over a period of eight years, resource limits made the goal seemingly impossible. A more realistic goal might have been 20 percent enrollment growth, but this would have left the college far short of its goal of responding to unmet education needs. High Reach came very close to achieving its goal. The enormous reach implied in its growth target forced leaders and staff to abandon conventional wisdom and to rethink how they were doing business. The challenge could not be met by doing more and working faster within the limits of existing structure, processes, and relationships. It could only be met by doing things differently—by removing the shackles of convention and rethinking processes, roles, and responsibilities.[17]

Bias for Action

An important dimension on which colleges of choice differ from colleges of challenge, and also from each other, is their bias for action. Colleges of challenge do not have the resources or the capability to move to the idea stage, much less beyond it. Colleges of choice have resources and they have capability, but they differ in the pace at which they move ideas to action. Consider the difference between a leanly resourced college and a fully resourced college in moving new programs to market. College A does not have the time or the resources to make mistakes—it must commit to a course of action and make it work. College B has the luxury of working at its own pace because its resources are sufficient to overcome problems of almost any kind. College A will work with an urgency and dispatch beyond that of its fully resourced counterpart. It has a bias for action because its resources are inadequate to permit a wide gap between thinking and doing.

A bias for action is driven by the will of a college to make something happen. This suggests an important difference among colleges of choice, namely the difference between thinking and doing, between reflection and action. Strategic moves by leaders in lean organizations are likely to be predicated on a bias for action; for example, committing to a new opportunity arena on the basis of carefully considered discussions with stakeholders. An executive team working with a new idea might discuss it in cabinet and make a go/no go decision based on answers to questions such as: How many people will be affected by this idea? How important will it be in meeting their needs? Is the market for this idea apt to grow? What is the best case scenario . . . the worst case scenario? What do we have to lose in committing the idea to action? In the words of a president:

> We are a place that is never satisfied with things and we like to be at the leading edge. Innovation is one of our values, so we are always saying, "Can this be done in a different and a better way?" We create a lot of innovation—

for example, accelerated learning started here. We launch a lot of things ahead of other colleges and our pilot ventures impact a lot of people. A number of them are copied by other institutions and end up as state policy.[18]

In contrast, counterparts facing constraints that limit their capacity for action are unlikely to employ due diligence in working with ideas. Listen to the words of a president as she described obstacles that had to be circumvented to bring new ideas to life:

> When you are in a unionized environment such as the one in this state, full-time faculty cannot teach classes that start after 4 P.M. as part of their regular load. That's a real obstacle. I understand why that is so because of abuses in the past, but in a contemporary environment that's a constraint on administrators and faculty.[19]

This college had the capabilities and resources to do just about anything it wanted, but intent was compromised by policy. A college that is subverted from bringing an idea to life because of external constraints or internal obstacles—even if the idea is a sure thing—will also be subverted from achieving abundance. Institutions with a bias for action will not be denied from achieving important goals. Their commitment to action precedes the calculation of the resources they will need for implementation or the resistance they will need to overcome to bring an idea to life. Elapsed time between thinking and doing is minimal in colleges with a bias for action.

Quality and Pervasiveness of Leadership

In colleges of challenge, leadership was described as a drag on the ability of institutions to move forward in pursuit of mission and goals. Issues of trust and commitment precluded leaders from involving people in decisions, and power rested with those at the top of the organization. The context for leadership is different in colleges of choice. Leaders exhibit a greater tendency toward inclusiveness and transparency, and people are viewed as the institution's most important resource. Leaders also know the difference between leading and managing—a capability reflected in their ability to delegate responsibility for operations. One president put it this way when describing her leadership style:

> My style is open and participatory and I am direct in delineating what areas of work are joint or advisory in decision making and those which are the purview of the president or executive team. It is not shared governance, but there is a notion that more heads are better than one, so I would describe it

as open and inclusive. I like to hear from all employees and it is not the title that matters.[20]

Relating to People and Unleashing Talent

Leaders in colleges of choice evidence a commitment to involving staff in decisions that give direction to the institution.

> With staff, it's been great to watch them grow and become involved because we have really engaged them. They have never been engaged or participated in the institution and they've come alive. They're on fire right now in their enthusiasm. Some of it has to do with the culture and climate of the institution. We have good people and a caring environment, but we have to remind folks of that. When I arrived there was definitely a wait and see mindset. You know, "we have a new guy and let's see how it goes"—that kind of attitude. I think some of the actions we have taken in the last 16 months have turned things around. One of them is simply recognizing folk who are doing good things, encouraging cooperativeness, encouraging teamwork, and rewarding positive behavior. We have put a focus on unity and working together while at the same time recognizing the challenges in front of us.[21]

In colleges of challenge, the difficulty of leaders in relating to staff and including them in decisions was singled out as a constraint to high performance. Leaders in colleges of choice generate support for initiatives by involving staff in design and implementation. They spend time building and maintaining relationships not only because they know it is essential for getting things done, but also because it is an investment in their capability to lead. E-mail and written communication are not substituted for face-to-face interaction. Leaders work with staff to make decisions and design initiatives that move the institution forward. In the words of a seasoned president who understands the value and benefits of involvement with staff:

> You have an interest in what they do. You promote what they do and you attend their events. The part that I find most satisfying, knowing that I have a reputation for being hands-on, is that you know what is going on without having to meddle.[22]

Leaders in colleges of choice have more talent to work with than those in colleges of challenge, and they use it. Much of the knowledge in organizations is tacit, and unleashing the talent within people has a lot to do with the success of a college in achieving goals. A midwestern college president described it this way:

All organizations have the capacity to be great. A college needs to have employees who see the big picture—people who can look at the institution beyond their position and day-to-day operational work. So trying to unleash that talent within people requires them to think outside of the box and view the organization as more than a sum of parts.[23]

Efficiency and Convention

Colleges of choice try, but do not always succeed, in exercising the creative potential of staff. They are staffed by skilled personnel who are accustomed to delivering results but limit their potential by placing too much emphasis on efficiency—a circumstance that overburdens staff with operational responsibility. Managers and staff are able to make operational decisions, but their day-to-day responsibilities do not permit time to get involved in strategic decisions. Encouraging staff involvement in strategic management is essential if colleges are to improve performance. It is perhaps the foremost challenge facing leaders who have the raw material of abundance but lack the know-how to leverage it into superior performance.

Meeting the challenge of customers and competitors in an environment of fast change requires an organization with a high capacity for creativity and innovation—attributes that are lacking in colleges of choice. In some colleges, the problem resides with leaders who cautiously approach innovation and change in order to minimize risk. In others, it is a reflection of tight budgets that discourage the allocation of resources to untested venues. Followers watching leaders avoid risk will invariably do the same. The cumulative effect is one of stasis throughout the organization as operating units hunker down in familiar modes of activity. Efficiency and convention become operating dictums as leaders establish norms that determine latitudes of acceptable risk. This circumstance can be described as a "convergence toward the norm," and it is commonplace in colleges that bypass opportunity in favor of stability. Consider, for a moment, a conversation that one of the authors had with the president of a midwestern community college regarding priorities for institutional development emerging from a strategic planning process:

Consultant: Based on information in the external scan related to population growth, economic development, and employer needs for new and replacement workers, it is clear that this community college has enormous potential for growth.
President: Yes, that comes as no surprise. It is what I am hearing in the community. We are being pushed by community leaders to extend

our operations into outlying areas of the county and by employers to develop new programs customized to their needs.

Consultant: I suppose that means that we should develop three scenarios for enrollment growth—low, medium, and high—and recommend that the college adopt the high projection. How does that sound to you?

President: We can't go with a high projection—faculty and staff won't adjust to that pace of growth, and I am not comfortable with it either. What you don't understand is that this college is a family—we are like an extended family all the way from classified staff to the board of trustees. I can't make a case for a high projection without disrupting people and violating the value this culture places on small size and personal touch. So we'll go with the medium projection and grow at a measured pace.[24]

Whole Organization Perspective

While leaders in colleges of challenge are routinely confronted with the problem of staff hunkered down in silos, leaders in colleges of choice work with staff in the framework of the whole organization. Working toward a common goal and institution-wide priorities is an easier task in institutions with resources because job security is not at issue. In the words of a president:

> You can't just operate alone or in cruise control. You have to recognize organizational problems and shortfalls as a collective entity. That is the key—"collectively" we can overcome almost anything. The shared vision of many is better than the vision of a few.[25]

This president was describing the success he had in moving his college toward a shared vision and direction by accentuating positive features of the organization. As part of this effort, he realized that a catalyst would be necessary to get individuals working on the same page. The catalyst was strategic planning.

> We ensured that every single employee—full-time, part-time, and otherwise—had the opportunity to provide input into this plan. We also brought in the community through focus groups. By combining internal and external input we wound up with eight strategic priorities that determined where, as an organization, we are going.[26]

Working with a whole organization perspective, this president intuitively started an epidemic that moved the institution forward on a change agenda. The idea of an "epidemic" is an interesting change dynamic in organizations. It is derived from Gladwell's 2000 book, *The Tipping Point: How Little Things Can Make a Big Difference,* and is premised on the idea that new ideas meet resistance until support from a critical mass tips the balance in favor of change.[27] Leaders working with a whole-organization perspective use the principle of the tipping point to generate support for initiatives. Additionally, they use "kingpins" (organizational leaders) that, like in bowling, hold enough sway that when they are tipped they will bring numerous others with them.[28] The ability to sway, or at least neutralize, resistors is important as a condition for accelerating organizational change. When known naysayers throw their support behind an initiative that would normally meet with resistance, a clear message travels throughout the organization.

Broadening Engagement

In contrast to the managerial tendencies of, and opportunities open to, leaders in struggling institutions, leaders in colleges of choice understand the importance of involving people in change efforts. They know that talented staff are working hard throughout the organization. Staff outnumber administrators, and they play a critical role in determining whether change will be successful. To exclude them from institution-wide change initiatives is to waste a formidable resource; so much so, in fact, that a growing number of colleges are moving to formalize staff roles in decision making and change processes. In the words of a president:

> We have formalized processes that allow people from every employee classi-fication to get involved. They break down lines between faculty, staff, and administrators that exist because they have different jobs. We try to say that each and every individual has an opportunity to affect students' lives and that each, in his or her unique way, is an educator.[29]

Similarly, a president mindful of the increasingly important role of part-time faculty in her college sought to involve them in institutional systems and processes as a way of accelerating the pace of change:

> Our initiative to enhance student retention is almost institutionalized, but we need to get part-time staff in all departments involved. A real focus of our professional development is on our part-time faculty—they are a critical part of our college and an increasingly important part of our capacity to do better.[30]

These presidents understand the critical resource that staff represent for the institution. Including them in activities central to institutional direction and change is a step that not only motivates, but it also engages.

One of the quickest ways to disengage staff is to exclude them from the strategic life of the institution—visioning, planning, budgeting, and big-picture decisions. This element of leadership is deceptively simple, almost to the point of being self-evident, but a surprising number of executives fail to recognize and act on it.

Comprehension of the External Environment

As market conditions shift and change, community colleges like all organizations are running faster to keep up. Rivals defy convention by constantly raising the bar on convenience, and students and stakeholders expect more and better service. The environment in which colleges work is anything but static. Not only is change an everyday event, but the speed at which it is occurring is unprecedented.

Colleges of choice are clearly better positioned to adapt to change than institutions struggling with resource and leadership issues. They have the capacity to undertake initiatives through talented staff and discretionary resources. They do not, however, have the capacity to do everything simultaneously. This is evident in their reluctance to pick and choose among alternatives when responding to stakeholders. For example, rather than prioritizing and sequencing service needs with some targeted for later response, colleges of choice routinely choose to respond to all needs by stretching staff and resources to the breaking point. Thus, while colleges of challenge are hunkered down in problem solving inside the institution, colleges of choice drain resources by simultaneously pursuing too many initiatives with multiple stakeholders.

Reaching Out to Stakeholders

Leaders in colleges of choice indicate that timely and decisive action in responding to needs is key to generating support from constituencies. Needs come with a price tag—it takes time to identify them and even more time to act on them. Consider the effort required of leaders in three institutions to reach out to stakeholders and establish their college as a preferred provider:

College A

> I spent the better part of a year and a half talking to any group of more than three who would let me in the front door. I met with all of the Rotary Clubs, I met with the Lions Clubs in the county, I met with the Daughters of the American Revolution, and a host of other groups. I described to them the economic benefits of college attendance and the college's economic impact

on the community. I talked with them about the variety of programs we have
and the diverse mission of the community college. What I discovered was
that most of these people only knew the college from their own point of contact. So, if they had been involved in workforce training through continuing
education, that was all they knew about us. If they had been enrolled in a
transfer program, that was what they knew about us. If they had been in a
two-year program, that was it. So I was painting a broader picture for them.[31]

The grass roots approach taken by this president helped him understand what stakeholders wanted, needed, and expected from the college.
Information gathering on a face-to-face basis with stakeholders is a direct
route to learning what a college must do to satisfy needs. The superficial-
ity that is part of surveys is avoided, and there is the ability to probe
beyond initial questions to get at the core of an issue. This approach also
broadens community awareness of what a college has to offer.

College B

The high school students in our service area were not going to college. They
are first generation students from low income families. When we looked at
our numbers, only 3 percent of the students were from the public schools. I
thought, wow, what is going on with us. We launched the state's first program designed to increase the high school attendance rate and we have
developed an intensive relationship with the high schools to help students
by doing some of the remediation while they are still in high school. Our
enrollment from urban schools is now about 20 percent.[32]

College C

We have tremendous potential for business and industry development in a
complex that used to be a military base. Some small businesses are in there,
but it was thought that we could attract more business if there was an
industry-specific workforce development program in the area. We developed
a program and it has borne fruit. There is a Canadian corporation that has
announced that it will be moving to the area and it will break ground early
next year. A primary reason this company decided to locate here was
because of the workforce development program we developed.[33]

These presidents moved directly from information to action by restructuring existing relationships or cultivating new relationships with constituencies. Each reached out to stakeholders to determine a course of action
that would broaden the relationship between college and community.
The act of restructuring is an interesting dimension of community
building in colleges that have lost ground with a constituency. It requires
skills that are essentially the same as those in relationship building—an

interest in people, an ability to see and pursue opportunity, strong interpersonal skills, and the tenacity to bring an initiative to completion.

Working with the Community

Leaders in colleges of choice realize that more than lip service is required
to effectively serve the needs of the community. Identifying needs is only
the first step. Beyond this is the important step of operating as part of the
community through active collaboration with players that have a stake in
the college. Getting groups and organizations involved in tangible ways
is good business both from the standpoint of engaging the community
and increasing support. Relationship building, however, is a demanding
task that is never finished, as one president discovered through interaction with influential groups in the community:

> We really had to document for the public that we're a great return on invest-
> ment. We learned to communicate with our publics in a way that was tai-
> lored to their needs for accountability, transparency, and return on
> investment—sometimes in lay language that educators don't often use. We
> had to get to know our audience and deliver what they wanted, so we
> described to them the value we bring. I think our approach to communica-
> tion has paid off in terms of showing that we are very well managed and
> very efficient. Now, we are trying to focus the community and state agencies
> on the idea that quality requires investment as a way of generating increased
> support.[34]

Some leaders have resorted to building community support by creating
citizens' advisory committees that communicate what the college is delivering, or can deliver, to the community. Others have taken the step of
building a vision of what a college can become by taking community
members on visits to fully developed institutions:

> We are taking a group of movers and shakers in our district on visits to look
> at new educational facilities at a community college. A four-year college just
> opened a brand new 126,000 square foot joint use facility, so we're going up
> there in a week or two. A few weeks ago, we rented a van and took them to
> Cy-Fair College. That changed their whole perspective of a community col-
> lege. They now see this as more than just education—it's quality of life and
> its economic development. They're starting to go beyond the "we need our
> own college" thing—it's going to be much more than that.[35]

When a college is moving in tandem with its community, it takes on
the personality of the community. Listen to the words of a president
describing his college's gritty approach to difficult economic conditions:

I think there is something in the nature of people in the region that makes them resilient—makes them pull together and work together. When the base closed, instead of being devastated and wondering what was going to happen now, the community and the college joined hands to recover from this. We work and live together. On that old base there are now more civilian employees than the airbase employed when it was up and running.[36]

Anticipating Challenges

Colleges of choice have reached an interesting point in their development as organizations. Despite the bridge-building efforts of leaders, there is a growing concern about their capacity to meet the changing needs of an increasingly diverse student population. As more and more learners turn to community colleges as the point of entry for postsecondary education, there is a very real danger that capacity may be stretched to the breaking point. Classrooms are filled with learners with widely varying backgrounds, academic abilities, aptitudes, and learning preferences. Most of these learners are taught by part-time instructors who are loosely connected to the institution. In the words of a seasoned academic leader describing the learning environment on her campus:

> One of the biggest challenges we face is the variety of students that we have. We have the very young students still in high school—the millennial generation—and they truly do learn very differently. Then we have the mature student who is in a second career. These populations mix and interact in classes and they demand not only more and better services, but different services as well. We know that many of our students are first generation, but the needs of a 14 or 15 year old—and we have them as young as that—side-by-side with an adult learner? We don't have that worked out yet.[37]

While diversity is a challenge in its own right, its impact on colleges of choice is magnified by competitive pressure from an expanding universe of postsecondary education providers. The reason is simple: when community colleges were the only game in town, learner needs could be efficiently managed without changing the fundamentals of how the institution did business. As competitors entered the market and changed the rules of engagement, community colleges had no choice but to respond or face the prospect of losing market share. For colleges of choice (and community colleges in general), losing market share is not an option. Leaders in some colleges acknowledge pressure from competitors:

> The for-profits, the proprietary schools coming in with medical programs, and businesses getting into the business of education are not a huge problem for us yet in terms of competition. They are a growing concern, however,

because there are more and more of them and it is critically important that we keep our college front and center with the community.[38]

Leaders in other colleges don't dwell on competition, choosing instead to focus on capacity:

> We're inundated with students and are more concerned about finding resources to meet the demand. I wouldn't even know how to go about competing. We put out information about everything we do and students decide whether we're worthy. They vote with their feet.[39]

With demand and capacity on the front burner as an issue for many institutions, new ways of thinking about competition are beginning to emerge. A growing number of leaders in colleges of choice are beginning to view competitors as collaborators through which mutual advantage can be achieved. In the words of a president looking at the future of competition:

> I don't see it as competition. I think students gravitate to the best place for them. Our job is to make sure that they know what we have and to meet their needs. You know, a long time ago four-year colleges thought that community colleges weren't really happy about them because we were going to take each other's students. Over the years what has evolved is that they've become our biggest supporter because they know that many of their new students are going to come through our college.[40]

Leveraging People, Resources, and Performance

Leveraging—the achievement of superior performance through the optimal use of resources—is vitally important in colleges coping with the challenge of limited capacity. People inside organizations make things better or worse depending on their motivation and approach to work. In colleges of challenge, capacity is constrained by personnel working at half speed on the periphery of the organization. In colleges of choice, resources and morale are decidedly better—a condition sufficient to open the door to leveraging.

Working with a resource platform that permits the option of choice, leaders in colleges of choice have leveraged capacity by reaching out to partnering organizations as a means for conserving resources and getting initiatives off the ground.

> We partner not only to increase funding, but also to provide faculty and staff with the tools they need—whether that's physical, human, fiscal, or technological—to do their job well. Instruction and student support come first and

partnering to enhance our capability in these areas is in the best interest of all agencies in our service area. . . . I am always happy to use someone else's money to get work done and I think that partnerships and linkages are now a truism of life and leadership in community colleges. Our mission is community-based. We charge around $2,500 a year. Our 4-year counterparts charge considerably more, but if we didn't have partnerships with them, we would be less and they would be less. So, whether it's with K-12, whether it's with the community, whether it's with business, whether it's with our 4-year counterparts, whether it's with government—everyone needs everybody else.[41]

In colleges of choice, leveraging organizational capability through collaboration is seen as a key to avoiding what has come to be known as the "sponge syndrome"—a circumstance in which individuals take on so many additional responsibilities they cannot absorb any more. Partnerships that accentuate strengths and alleviate weaknesses are seen as good business. This is particularly evident in the words of a leader describing his college's need to solve a capacity problem by collaborating with outside organizations:

We are very strong in workforce development and we are running out of capacity. So we are partnering in some workforce development initiatives in our three counties so we can work and deliver it more efficiently.[42]

And, in the words of a president who worked for years to develop relationships with business in a high-tech industry and succeeded in positioning his college as a leader in job training:

The state has a huge priority in developing its technical base, so math, science, engineering, and so forth have become target points for investment. We read the early signals in this area and through multiyear government grants made some strategic investments in the high-tech industry. Now the state has become a high tech hub and a number of companies have attracted major contracts in which we have a stake. Our high-tech programs are perfectly positioned to work with these companies.[43]

By leveraging resources through partnerships, these colleges put themselves on the road to abundance by enhancing their capacity, conserving their resources, and elevating their performance. More importantly, they invested in their staff by off-loading operational responsibility to, and simultaneously acquiring knowledge and expertise from, outside organizations.

SUMMARY

The designation *colleges of choice* applies to institutions with the potential to achieve abundance but without the resources or the wherewithal to do so. There are many reasons for this incapacity, but they boil down to three deficits: leadership capability that is not fully deployed throughout the institution, a reluctance to embrace innovation and change, and missed opportunity borne out of a lack of urgency. As illustrated in Table 6.2, the performance objective of these institutions is growth and resource acquisition, and their managerial emphasis is on building capacity. Competing with rivals and winning is important—growth, after all, is a function of market share. Collaboration is gaining recognition as a strategy for increasing efficiency and building capacity.

Table 6.2.

Dimension of Abundance	Colleges of Choice
Managerial Emphasis	building capacity
Cohesion	segmental relationship of leaders/staff
Resources	adequate to full—enabling choice
Resource Perspective	tangible and intangible resources
Organizational Architecture	interactive silos
Operational Focus	improving efficiency
Risk	selective approach to risk and change
Collaboration	growing network of partners
Competitive Focus	competing with rivals and winning
Performance Objective	growth and resource acquisition
Leadership	punctuated leadership
Attractiveness	capable of attracting quality staff

When organizations are adequately resourced, urgency for change is constrained. Creativity and innovation occur on the basis of individual initiative, not organizational sponsorship, and doing more with less is an operational priority. Colleges of choice have the resources and talent to invest in staff by developing their strategic capabilities. They do not, however, have the incentive to do so because of a lack of urgency. In the next chapter, a special group of colleges that has everything going for them—talent, resources, capability, and leadership—will be described. We call these institutions *colleges of abundance*. They occupy a niche to which all community colleges should aspire.

NOTES

1. M. J. Hatch, "The Dynamics of Organizational Culture," *Academy of Management Review* 18, no. 4 (1993): 657–693; T. Schumacher, "West Coast Camelot: The

Rise and Fall of an Organizational Culture," in *Cultural Complexity in Organizations: Inherent Contrasts and Contradictions*, ed. S. A. Sackman, 107–132 (Thousand Oaks, CA: Sage, 1997).

2. Hamel and Prahalad, *Competing for the Future*, 151 (see chap. 1, n. 2).

3. Interview, community college president, December 15, 2006.

4. Interview, community college president, April 23, 2006.

5. Interview, community college president, October 23, 2006.

6. Interview, community college president, November 29, 2006.

7. Interview, community college president, November 14, 2006.

8. Interview, community college president, November 29, 2006.

9. Interview, community college president, November 14, 2006.

10. Interview, community college president, November 16, 2006.

11. Interview, community college president, November 14, 2006.

12. Hatch, "The Dynamics of Organizational Culture," 663.

13. Employer Focus Group, Community College Strategic Planning Project, October 1995.

14. College Strategic Planning Project, September 2000–December 2001.

15. Interview, community college president, November 29, 2006.

16. Interview, community college president, April 25, 2006.

17. This illustration is drawn from our experience working with the executive team of a midwestern community college between 2002 and 2007.

18. Interview, community college president, November 29, 2006.

19. Interview, community college president, October 23, 2006.

20. Interview, community college president, November 29, 2006.

21. Interview, community college president, November 14, 2006.

22. Interview, community college president, April 24, 2006.

23. Interview, community college president, April 24, 2006.

24. Community College Strategic Planning Project, 1995–1996.

25. Interview, community college president, November 14, 2006.

26. Interview, community college president, November 14, 2006.

27. M. Gladwell, *The Tipping Point, How Little Things Can Make a Big Difference* (New York: Little Brown, 2000).

28. W. Kim and R. Mauborgne, "Tipped for the Top: Tipping Point Leadership," *INSEAD Quarterly* (2004): 3–7.

29. Interview, community college president, November 14, 2006.

30. Interview, community college president, November 29, 2006.

31. Interview, community college president, November 26, 2006.

32. Interview, community college president, November 29, 2006.

33. Interview, community college president, November 14, 2006.

34. Interview, community college president, November 29, 2006.

35. Interview, community college president, November 20, 2006.

36. Interview, community college president, November 14, 2006.

37. Interview, community college president, November 29, 2006.

38. Interview, community college president, April 25, 2006.

39. Interview, community college president, April 24, 2006.

40. Interview, community college president, April 24, 2006.

41. Interview, community college president, April 23, 2006.

42. Interview, community college president, November 14, 2006.

43. Interview, community college president, November 29, 2006.

7

Colleges of Abundance

Positive organizational dynamics are significantly and positively related to effectiveness.

Kim Cameron

Organizations that are truly empowered have moved out of the old paradigm of negative competition and beliefs in limitation and scarcity.

Shelli Bischoff-Turner

In chapter 4 we introduced abundance as a condition or state of being that exceeds a normal or healthy condition. Abundance is a fluid state that people and organizations work vigorously to achieve; it is not a permanent state they occupy. At the individual level, it is a condition of psychological well-being manifested in positive feelings, facilitating behavior, and personal satisfaction. At the organizational level it is a condition of extraordinary performance captured in words like "excellent," "flourishing," and "optimal."[1] Abundant organizations focus on the positive; they achieve superior results by leveraging resources and capabilities beyond a reasonable level of expectation.

Our objective in this chapter is to bring abundance to the world of practice by describing attributes that mark its presence in community colleges. Abundance defies easy understanding. One does not readily pick it up from theory and research on organizational behavior, and institutional success stories are always suspect because what appears to be best practice may, in fact, be clever marketing. For this reason, we think that practitioners will most easily understand the concept through the experience of leaders and staff on college campuses.

201

We introduce the concept by profiling the experience of two community colleges that have moved from choice to abundance. These colleges, one in the Midwest and the other in the Northeast, have been labeled Vitality Community College to signify an institution that has reached a state of abundance and Ascendant Community College to denote an institution on the threshold of abundance. Next, we use the words and actions of leaders to identify attributes that mark the presence of abundance. We close the chapter with a compendium of attributes that practitioners can use to determine whether or not, and to what extent, their colleges are abundant.

CASE ILLUSTRATIONS OF ABUNDANCE

Vitality Community College

Located in a midwestern industrial state, Vitality Community College is situated in a service region that is equal parts urban, suburban, and rural. Up to the mid-1980s, the history of the college was largely nondescript. Vitality developed and delivered programs and services in response to identified stakeholder needs. Its operating mode was one of a college of choice—it did what it had to do to fulfill its community-based mission, but within limits imposed by operating resources and the preferences of leaders and staff. Vitality confined its reach to partnerships that would be expected of a community college anywhere. It maintained working relationships with the largest employers in the region, community agencies, and with K–12 schools. For the most part, its reactive approach to the community was accepted as typical of the manner in which institutions operated in the postsecondary education industry. With the board of trustees and the Chamber of Commerce, however, a feeling prevailed that Vitality was a sleeping giant—an organization only scratching the surface of its potential.

Following the lead of influential board members, forward thinking staff, and the Chamber of Commerce, a new president was hired in 1987 and charged with developing the college to its potential. Rather than moving quickly to transform the institution by putting "his people" in key positions, the president studied the culture and worked with staff in a variety of circumstances that would test their potential. At the close of his first year in office, some employees were moved into positions that better suited their capabilities, others were coached into professional development programs to develop new capabilities, and those who could not or would not keep pace with change were moved toward retirement.

The president did make some strategic hires, but the majority of personnel changes involved relocation of existing staff.

The president's early work with Vitality's human resources and culture was only a harbinger of what was to come. A significant event early in his tenure—the failure of a local tax levy—provided the impetus to step out of role and take a calculated risk. Conversations with internal and external stakeholders in focus sessions convinced him that Vitality lacked the shared commitment, external linkages, and organizational architecture to unleash its true potential. To speed the pace of change, he reduced the administrative hierarchy from five levels to three levels; disbanded the president's council and replaced it with a weekly meeting involving vice presidents and leaders from faculty, staff, and student organizations; and opened membership on operations committees to faculty and classified staff. He also opened communication lines with companies and corporations not using Vitality's workforce development programs. Customized professional development opportunities were initiated for faculty and staff. All of these changes were accomplished within three years of his appointment.

During this time, Vitality established a new vision statement crafted by a committee comprising equal representation of administrators, faculty, and staff. Principles in the vision statement were tied directly to the budget and focused on turning working relationships with external organizations into "intensive partnerships" premised on shared benefits and open communication. The president worked to enlarge Vitality's presence in the community by creating a "network" of partners including business and industry, K–12 schools, agencies of local government, and civic organizations. He brought the idea of the network to fruition through three steps: providing incentives for staff to become involved with networks, expanding membership on strategic and directional committees, and establishing a summer leadership institute attended by administrators and representatives of all employee groups. Additionally, the president worked with business and industry to implement a continuous improvement culture affecting all parts of the organization. Staff were given an opportunity to understand their jobs in the larger context of the institution. In the process, he became an authentic leader drawing on innate goodness, and an acute sense of timing to cultivate a committed workforce.

Two decades after the arrival of the new president, Vitality barely resembles its former self. Before the president arrived, it had only a handful of partnerships and was rarely approached to develop working linkages with outside organizations. Today, Vitality is approached to partner on a weekly basis and is the hub of an expansive network of profit and not-for-profit organizations. Within this network are small and large business employers, K–12 schools, community organizations, agencies of local government, hospitals and health care providers, colleges and universities, social service agencies, and influential citizens. The president is viewed as the driving force in the network, but integral to its success are Vitality's senior and middle administrators who carry much of the responsibility for building and maintaining relationships with partners. An example of Vitality's prowess in partnering is the stunning contribution it has made to workforce development in the region and the state. In 1990, manufacturing jobs constituted 45 percent of total number of jobs in the service region. Today manufacturing constitutes 15 percent of the jobs and workforce development is key to the well-being of citizens. Vitality has developed partnerships that account for 15 percent of all contact hours for workforce development delivered by colleges and universities in the state.

The partnerships developed by Vitality have enhanced its capability and placed demands on its operating resources. Consider, for example, the time, energy, and operating resources required to initiate and maintain regional business incubators, a university center involving eight four-year colleges and universities offering thirty-five baccalaureate degree programs and twenty-four masters degree programs, and a regional one-stop center with the Chamber of Commerce. Vitality is the only community college in the state to offer a University Partnership Program that enables learners to earn baccalaureate and master's degrees from several universities without leaving campus. It is also the largest provider of e-learning programs in the state; a national leader in Six Sigma training and certification; the first college in the state to build an Advanced Technologies Center for business and industry; and one of the first community colleges in the country to integrate academic, continuing education, and training resources into a seamless delivery system.

"Growing leaders from within" is at the core of Vitality's evolution into a high-performing institution. Professional development has taken on a new meaning as 100 percent of administrators, 75 percent of full-time faculty, and nearly 40 percent of classified staff participate in theme-based professional development programs each year. Over the past five years it has filled 35 percent of its administrative openings from within, even holding one senior administrative position open for two years while a midlevel administrator completed her doctoral degree. The reputation of the college has grown to a point where individuals from other colleges wait for job openings.

Every three years Vitality reassesses its strategic direction. This process involves structured conversations with internal staff and external stakeholders—regional employers, government agencies, K–12 schools, college and university leaders, civic organizations, influential citizens, and social service providers. Vitality engaged more than 1,200 people (not including internal staff) in its mission reassessment process in 2006–2007. While only 5 to 10 percent of college operations are impacted by, or directly linked to, future planning, the involvement of citizens is tangible proof that the college is committed to providing exceptional value to its stakeholders.

At the heart of Vitality's evolution into an abundant organization is a belief embodied in practice that intangible resources—people, tacit knowledge, and culture—are the foremost asset the college has. Exposure over time to consistently positive behavior on the part of leaders and inclusion in strategic activities generates positive feelings in staff which, in turn, lead to replication of positive behavior throughout the organization and, subsequently, to an elevation in performance.

Ascendant Community College

Located near a heavily populated corridor in the Northeast, Ascendant Community College serves 3,600 full-time students through two campuses, one of which is urban and the other suburban. Public support for community colleges has waned over the past decade in a state that has historically placed four-year colleges and universities at the top of the postsecondary education pecking order. Challenges to Ascendant's stability were rooted not only in forces external to the college, but in its infrastructure as well. The managerial style of the president and executive team over two decades preceding the appointment of a new president in 1996 was "command and control." Innovation was stifled, decisions were top down and rarely questioned, and staff were encouraged to keep their nose to the grindstone. The earlier president's legacy was one of minimal interest in collaboration, limited investment in professional development, and neglect of stakeholder needs and expectations. Ascendant was a model of "institutional Darwinism"—conflict prevailed and the strong survived while the less advantaged got weaker.

When the new president arrived in 1996, he quickly determined that only a dramatic cultural shift would move the college from a marginal state to one in which it could assess its strengths and weaknesses and work to develop its potential. He likened Ascendant to a conglomeration of "hardened silos" where individuals practiced warfare by "lobbing verbal grenades to see what they could stir up." A catalyst for change was needed to establish a modicum of trust, and strategic planning seemed the best way to go. The president proposed a structured planning initiative in which individuals throughout the college could table new ideas, consider new directions, suggest new structures, and advocate for what the college ideally should be. Staff resisted involvement in the early stages of planning by declining to provide suggestions and refusing to be part of the effort. The conditioning they had received during the previous president's tenure was too much to overcome. The president persisted and eventually was able to convince individuals that providing suggestions would not lead to public humiliation or retaliatory acts. After nearly two years of slowly dismantling the protective armor of staff, a strategic plan was crafted. It could hardly be described as a fully developed strategic plan, but the twelve operating principles it contained became the cornerstone for culture change.

The evolution of the strategic plan and its final product culminated in a discovery for the president that changed his outlook on organizational development. Planning was subordinate to culture. As a leader experiencing an epiphany, he concluded that "culture eats strategy for breakfast." Planning can yield a successful outcome, but only if it is supported and valued by the culture of the institution. The twelve operating principles that constituted the end product stood for something that was beyond the original goal of planning. The process and product were a way to get people out of their bunkers—to create a feeling of trust that the college could be shaped to pursue important goals, to nurture and support people, and to cultivate talent. In short, the president realized that the best way to break down silos was to create processes that enabled staff to reinvent their support systems while becoming comfortable with a different way of doing business.

Twelve years after the appointment of a new president, Ascendant has been transformed from a reactionary institution under authoritarian leadership to a proactive organization guided by participatory management and decision making. It has used strategic planning to guide its development but has varied the approach to meet its needs and circumstances. The 1999–2002 strategic plan employed a comprehensive scanning process with internal and external stakeholders; the 2003–2006 strategic plan involved a nine-month process of intensive discussion among faculty, staff, students, and the community about priorities for development; and the 2007–2010 strategic plan used the process of appreciative inquiry to chart a course of action for the future. A one-day college and community summit attended by more than two hundred individuals in May 2007 forged statements of core values, vision, and strategic direction that departments and offices used to develop operating goals and performance benchmarks.

Growth and enrollment goals are not a prominent part of Ascendant's future. Its foundation rests on deeply held values related to student engagement, collaboration, personal and professional growth, respect, diversity, access and opportunity, and excellence. Most important is the way in which planning is conducted at Ascendant. The entire college community is engaged in information gathering and analysis. The plan is not complete until it is approved by the total college community.

Ascendant is listed by a national search agency as one of its top destinations for talent. Perhaps the most tangible indication that participatory leadership is the coin of the realm, however, is the approach that Ascendant has taken to redesigning its internal processes and systems using systematic process management methods. Process management is a set of tools and a philosophy of improvement designed to efficiency and effectiveness. It is also a strategy for culture building because of the premium it places on cross-functional involvement of staff in problem solving. Beginning in fall 2004, instructors and staff at Ascendant identified more than twenty areas (ESL retention, program review, financial aid, student success, college readiness, student assessment, etc.) requiring process improvement. Cross-functional teams gathered and analyzed data, identified areas for improvement, and made operational decisions. The systemic effort required in process redesign not only resulted in improved efficiency—it also reinforced a culture of collaboration and engagement as staff from different operating units worked together to make decisions based on data, rather than instinct, politics, or personal relationships.

Further evidence of Ascendant's progress toward a cultural goal of engagement and collaboration is the work of a cross-functional committee called the Strategic Directions Committee that is responsible for working with the college community to identify priorities for college development. With the exception of budget issues, priorities are recommended to the president and approved without changes.

Ascendant has taken steps to broaden its leadership base by training instructors and staff to serve as facilitators in diversity and tolerance, total quality management (TQM), continuous quality enhancement, and process management. The result is an organization in which the "whole" is more important than any of its "parts." As individuals have taken steps to cultivate relationships across units, Ascendant has enhanced its capacity to build external relationships. Over a ten-year period, the number of workforce contracts has increased tenfold, reserves in the Foundation have significantly increased, and private revenues have increased exponentially. Nearly one-third of the operating budget now comes from private sources.

INDICES OF ABUNDANCE

The case examples of Vitality and Ascendant illustrate the broad dimensions of abundance. The devil is in the details, however, and what these illustrations do not do is to provide specific indices of abundance—

indicators that can be used to determine the extent to which a college is more or less abundant. Discerning practitioners will know that the moves made by the presidents of Vitality and Ascendant are not unique to them, their institutions, or their approach to leadership. They will ask: Did these moves actually work to enhance performance by fundamentally altering internal dynamics? How did the behavior of leaders contribute to abundance? What forms of behavior are associated with it? When does leader behavior impede the achievement of abundance? What steps can leaders take to accelerate an institution's progress toward abundance?

To uncover the specifics of abundance, we use the attributes presented in chapter 4 to identify indices that can be used to determine the extent to which a college is more or less abundant. Before we do this, it is important to issue a caveat: Abundance *is not* an all-or-nothing proposition. It exists to a greater or lesser degree in every organization. Therefore, an institution labeled as "abundant" is not expected to possess every attribute of abundance, and an institution labeled as "less abundant" will not be totally devoid of abundance. Abundance is a continuum on which the position of an institution is constantly changing. It is not a finite state.

Attributes of Abundance

The characteristics of organizations that exhibit abundance are deceptively simple. They derive from the literature on positive psychology and peak performance. When applied to community colleges, a compendium of twenty attributes that distinguish abundant from less abundant institutions can be identified. These attributes cluster into four dimensions of organizational behavior as shown in table 7.1. *Attributes of Culture* encompass the integrated pattern of attitudes, values, beliefs, and behavior that motivate leaders and staff toward high performance. *Attributes of Architecture* refer to the way in which structural properties of an institution are organized to facilitate innovation and change. *Attributes of Capability* refer to the presence of individual and organizational traits conducive to leveraging and high performance. *Attributes of Performance* refer to outcomes or results that distinguish an institution as operating at an optimal level.

Implicit in these attributes is a difference in organizational performance attributable to the presence of abundance. Change is a gradual process in abundant organizations. It is prolonged and it is measured in terms of qualitative change in intangible resources—talented and motivated people, virtuous behavior, and a healthy culture. In less abundant institutions, change is measured in terms of tangible resources—more students, more money, more facilities, and more of everything. One of the dominant themes throughout this book is that to achieve their full potential, community colleges must strive for the best in people, in the organization, and the world around them. If people are motivated to do their best, a

Table 7.1. Attributes of Abundance in Community Colleges

Attributes of Culture
Abundant Colleges:

- build upon strengths and value assets
- emphasize intangible resources (people, tacit knowledge, and culture)
- develop and support leaders throughout the organization
- embrace and reward risk and change
- develop strategic capabilities in staff
- attract and retain talented staff

Attributes of Architecture
Abundant Colleges:

- work in teams bound by common purpose
- emphasize the whole institution
- forge enlightened collective strategic decisions
- reduce challenges and problems to simple organizing ideas
- establish, manage, and operate in networks

Attributes of Capability
Abundant Colleges:

- create exceptional resources through leveraging
- anticipate change through continuous scanning
- seek information about best practices
- collaborate with rivals for mutual gain
- identify and pursue opportunity
- design and manage change effectively
- know the value they deliver to students and stakeholders

Attributes of Performance
Abundant Colleges:

- view stretch and leverage as the index of exceptional performance
- deliver exceptional value to students and stakeholders

tipping point will be reached, and the organization will perform at a higher level. The real question then becomes: *how do institutions become abundant?* More specifically: *how do leaders motivate people and create a climate where abundance is a natural outcome of behavior?*

ATTRIBUTES OF CULTURE

Build upon Strengths and Value Assets

Abundant colleges search for the best in people, the organization, and the world around them. There is an emphasis on achievement, assets, unexplored potential, strengths, innovation, opportunities, high points, strategic capabilities, and visions of desired futures.[2] Taking all of this into account, abundant institutions work from the "positive" and assume that staff have the talent to make things happen. They make their employees feel valued and empower them to create, regardless of their position in the organization. In the words of a president:

> We have a classified staff council. I meet monthly with the leadership and it really makes a difference. It's been great just to watch the staff because we have really engaged them. A few years ago they were a fairly negative group. Now they produce their own newsletter, they do fund-raising for scholarships through the classified council, they develop salary and benefit proposals, and they share with administrators where they would like to see salary and benefits go.[3]

Another president, realizing the importance of making people feel valued, decided to formalize staff recognition:

> We established a celebrations and ritual committee, because even at an institution that is 30 years old, someone would ask, "When are we going to recognize classified staff?" I said, "Why don't we get together and formalize this a little bit because we are doing everything ad hoc. Let's determine what we want to recognize, when we want to do it, and how we want to do it." They started meeting regularly, and became the focal point for the community. So it's a matter of formalizing things that enable people from every employee classification to get involved.[4]

Giving staff the freedom to create and removing barriers to innovation is an effective strategy for building on existing strengths and promoting new capabilities. Bureaucratic barriers can drain excitement from a good idea. When asked why so many people wanted to work at Cy-Fair College (Texas), President Diane Troyer answered:

> It's the chance to have barriers taken away so that you can, in fact, do what you like. Part of our approach was to remove the barriers described to us as we talked to faculty about an academic design for the college. We asked: "What hampers you in being able to do the things you want to do?" I think a lot of people were drawn to an environment in which constraints are removed. So overall, we've got lots of people who have lots of creative ideas who want to try new things and who really expect to be involved in a lot of things. The campus life from day one has been one of the richest I've ever seen, with cultural events, theatre, and a film series. That kind of energy . . . our faculty and staff do it all . . . is exciting.[5]

Cy-Fair sought to find staff that would fit its envisioned culture—one that was to be exciting, fast-paced, and imbued with a can-do attitude. To attract personnel who would fit this culture, it tried to create a positive workplace made up of creative and generative images embedded in understanding what staff would value and experiences they would like in the workplace. In this way, the problem-focused approach to management and change that is so common among institutions was broken. Cy-Fair focused on what it would need to do to become a great place to work. The tangible result of its inquiry process was a series of principles that described what the institution stood for, what it wanted, and where it wanted to be based on strengths and capabilities it valued in staff.

Emphasize Intangible Resources

When Tom McKeon became president of Tulsa Community College in 2003, he took over an institution that had room for improvement in staff satisfaction and morale.[6] Under the leadership of two long-serving presidents, Tulsa had become enormously successful in carving out a niche for itself in the regional higher education market. It embarked on a thirty-year cycle of almost uninterrupted growth and morphed into a four-campus system enrolling twenty-four thousand students in credit courses. The top-down leadership style of McKeon's predecessors worked in the early stages of Tulsa's development but became a disadvantage as the institution matured and faced a different set of challenges. Staff morale suffered as decisions were made by a chosen few and communicated to the many.

Beginning with his first day as president, McKeon and his team invited the full participation of faculty and staff. Their focus was on building the resource they believed to be Tulsa's most formidable asset: its *people*. They modeled and reinforced inclusion in virtually every strategic activity of the institution. New statements of mission, vision, and core values were created through cross-functional teams representing every part of the institution and crafted in the language of faculty and staff. Each statement was subjected to continuous review by full-time staff and went through multiple iterations before receiving college-wide approval. The executive team used the same approach to develop institution-wide strategic priorities; a college-wide facilities master plan; college-wide councils in academics, student services, enrollment management, diversity, technology, and operations; a staff, professional, and organizational development program; and a compensation program designed to achieve parity and recognize different degrees of performance.[7]

Perhaps the most telling example of the importance assigned to staff was the selection of twenty-five facilitators drawn from the ranks of faculty and staff to provide training in strategic thinking to staff throughout the institution. The objective was to equip staff with "big picture" thinking skills—skills that would enable them to gauge the implications of information for the institution and act on the basis of an informed perspective. The attraction of McKeon and the executive team to this program was the leveraging effect it would have on institutional performance by equipping staff with skills that would enable them to more fully participate in the strategic life of the institution.

Like McKeon, leaders in abundant institutions build on the strengths of staff and value the assets they bring to the table in the form of capabilities and tacit knowledge. They provide staff with opportunities to participate in strategic activities and imbue them with skills that enable them to participate on an even keel with senior administrators. Most importantly, they empower staff to think critically, to make decisions, and to design new ways of doing things—all factors that advantage the institution by stretching its capacity.

Develop and Support Leaders throughout the Organization

Shared governance has not been a developmental legacy of most community colleges. In recent years, however, the shape of governance has begun to change. Increasing size and complexity have encouraged institutions to add administrative tiers—deans, associate deans, directors, coordinators—and distribute responsibility for decision making. While formal authority remains firmly in the hands of top administrators, there is a difference in span of control between abundant and less abundant institutions. Leaders in abundant organizations have been identified, nurtured, and developed throughout the organization, and they are empowered to make decisions at the point of contact with stakeholders. In less abundant institutions, decision making remains centralized in the hands of leaders at the top of the organization.

Leaders in abundant colleges are comfortable with who they are and are capable of relaxing the need for authority in decision making. Although there is a natural drive to retain control over decisions that have traditionally been the province of senior management, there is simultaneously an understanding of the need for staff to be involved in the strategic life of the institution. Astute leaders know that engagement in decision making encourages commitment to the organization. They also know that decisions informed by those closest to the point of contact are less prone to backfire because of incomplete information or unanticipated consequences.

The experience of Joe Forrester at Community College of Beaver County (CCBC) in Pennsylvania is a good example of inclusion by loosening the reins of authority. CCBC began preparation for reaccreditation in 2004 in the wake of a successful quest to gain county support for operations. The team leading the self-study was caught by surprise when President Forrester did not censure sections of a self-study report that were critical of the college. Interestingly, he invited the team to be *more* critical. Knowing that Middle States would mandate that CCBC produce a collectively developed strategic plan, he used the opportunity of accreditation to deliberately involve staff in the development of a strategic direction for the college.

> I had carefully selected a group of people to be trained. A mix of faculty, administrators, and support staff because it was my intention to give everyone in the college a voice. We were very careful not to pick people who were predisposed to be supportive of things that were going on at the college. We talked about what we wanted them to do and I indicated that they would be leading the effort to develop a strategic plan. We were going to do this by going out and talking to the community and by bringing in focus groups of alumni and current students—we were going to talk to everybody. . . . For all intents and purposes, I spent a period of six months sitting on the sidelines while this group coalesced. When I entered the process, rank had no privilege. I knew we were on safe ground when one of the people we trained, a clerk in our admissions office, looked me right in the eye in one of the first sessions and told me why I was wrong. . . . I talked to the Board ahead of time and said I would like this group to present the strategic plan. They made the presentation and absolutely blew the socks off the Board members. By the time we got finished, the Board had bought in completely because they saw the level of commitment coming from the people who were involved in the process. . . . Looking back, we were engaged in a process of compression planning that was carried out under the auspices of what we jokingly refer to as the Kumbaya circle. When we got everyone on the planning team together with the Board and asked them to talk about the total experience, there wasn't a dry eye in the room. Me, the Board members—everyone had tears in their eyes. You had faculty members saying: "I never believed we could do this." "I never believed we could turn this college around." "I was not prepared to believe the president." "I was not prepared to believe the Board, but you're serious about this." It just laid the whole thing out. It was an amazing moment. It was one of those defining moments in the direction of the institution.[8]

CCBC began the transition from choice to abundance by giving staff the opportunity and the resources to lead. Coming on the heels of a failed presidency and difficult political circumstances, the planning team was initially skeptical about its role. After working with the president and observing consistency in his actions and words, the team came to believe that the president was earnest in his commitment to participatory leadership. This would prove to be a monumental tipping point in the evolution of the college.

Embrace and Reward Risk and Change

Think for a moment about how an experiment might turn out in your college. What if you were to pull together a couple of teams and charge each with putting together a new initiative? The initiative could be a business plan for a new academic program, a delivery system for a new service, a new partnership with regional employers—something innovative that will require imagination and resources. Charge one team with developing the specs for a new program based on finite information. Provide baseline information about the annual budget that the program should operate within, the ratio of full-time to part-time instructors that can be hired, the availability of space, and information related to other operational aspects of the program. Inform the team, as well, that a review and adjustment process will take place after its work is complete and that final approval will not be certain until action is taken by the board of trustees.

Give the second team an open charge for developing the specs for a new service. Inform its members that the president's cabinet and board of trustees are interested in the best possible design for the service—a design that will deliver superior value to students. Indicate that it is always important to consider the budget in designing a program or service, but quality and student impact are the primary consideration, not cost. Indicate, as well, that 1) you have complete confidence in the team and that its work will receive the full attention of the cabinet, 2) its report will move quickly to the board of trustees for action, and 3) the final report that goes to the board will reflect the best thinking of the team and the president's cabinet.

What do you think the result of each team's work will be? If you set a $950,000 operating budget for the first team, it is likely that you are going to get $950,000 worth of thinking, not a penny more. You are also going to get a marginal program. You might as well tell the team to not waste its time. "We don't trust you to do this the right way and we're not really interested in your ideas about program design. Just do it our way and get it done on time." The chances of a superior design from the second team are much higher. The committee has been empowered to get out of the box in its thinking and to take risks. It has also been informed that a new way of doing things is desirable, creative thinking is valued, its work will make a difference, and the time interval between proposal completion, approval, and execution will be short.

Abundant organizations embrace and reward risk and change. By providing opportunities for staff to get involved in new ventures and to experiment with different ways of doing things, they make it possible to leverage capabilities to their fullest potential. If leaders are perceived as uncomfortable with change, risk aversive, or disinterested in navigating uncharted waters, why would anyone take a chance on something new or different? If leaders aren't willing to take risks, how would colleges like Rio Salado in Arizona and Anne Arundel in Maryland craft the innovative approaches to educational design and delivery that have made them exemplars of innovation and change? Consider for a moment the transformation Rio has undergone to become one of the most vibrant colleges in the nation under its president Linda Thor.

Rio is about PEOPLE DEVELOPMENT—supporting individual, team, and organizational learning through a system of people development. People Development is the first of eight goals in Rio's 2012 Strategic Plan for Innovation, Improvement, and Growth; it is accompanied by goals that invest in people.[9] Note the people element embedded in operational strategies for five of Rio's eight 2012 strategic goals:

People Development

- Create a comprehensive system for development of core competencies for all employees
- Develop a comprehensive plan for adjunct faculty development that supports Rio's service standards
- Develop technology skills in staff that support their job performance

Innovation

- Identify, maintain, and expand those innovative processes that are responsible for Rio's continued growth
- Explore new opportunities with existing partners

Blue Ocean

- Encourage and facilitate innovation
- Expand current models to new partners and markets

Rio Advantage

- Identify and improve upon what internal and external customers experience, and what they value most at Rio
- Apply the Rio Advantage and customer astonishment concepts to internal customers

Communication

- Improve communication processes that build an atmosphere of inclusiveness and foster interdepartmental engagement

- Create a physical environment that promotes key characteristics of the organizational culture.[10]

How does Rio make these goals happen? Its leadership team places a deep emphasis on anticipating change in external conditions, customer needs and expectations, and competitor behavior.[11] This emphasis is repeatedly communicated and reinforced with employees individually and collectively through multiple channels: formal and informal communications, Rio's staffing model, its approach to operations, and its reward system. Breakthrough ideas that stretch the capabilities of staff, depart from customary ways of doing things, and extend beyond what customers expect or competitors are doing are constantly sought. These ideas can come from anywhere in the organization and when they arrive in leaders' hands, the interval between consideration, action, and implementation is very short. The speed at which ideas move from thought to action gives a clear message to staff: *we value your ideas and it is through you that change is initiated and executed.*

A similar commitment to risk and change is evident at Anne Arundel Community College. In 2000, Anne Arundel accelerated its evolution into a learning college by reducing the number of vice presidents to three and changing the titles of each to reflect a focus on learning.[12] The leadership of the three vice presidents—vice presidents of learning, learner support services, and learner resources management—was supplemented by: 1) a learning response team (LRT) with responsibility for the performance of administrative and management structures and systems in meeting emerging learning needs in a timely and effective manner and 2) learning design teams (LDTs) with responsibility for organizing and implementing initiatives identified by the learning response team.[13] Integral to the work of the LRT and LDTs is a continuum of lifelong learning with lines blurred between credit and noncredit instruction to achieve the goal of producing learning in students regardless of their age, educational aspirations, or mode of instruction.

The learner response team is comprised of administrators while the learning design team includes representatives from all work groups in the college. Much of the work in carrying out a change agenda, however, rests with faculty and support staff in direct contact with learners. To engage them in change, Anne Arundel has altered its instructional staffing model to include three categories of personnel: full-time instructors, instructional specialists, and trainers. It also recruits and hires new faculty under a flexible job description that allows instructors to meet contractual obligations in a number of ways other than teaching the standard five three-credit courses per semester. Faculty are encouraged to accept assignments to support business and industry contract training, to teach continuing education courses, to serve as mentors to other faculty, and to work in teams providing outreach services to the community. In this way, Anne Arundel has encouraged instructional personnel to become involved in change by giving them personal choices about change—the when, where, and how of becoming involved.

Develop Strategic Capabilities in Staff

Abundant institutions invest in staff by gauging the extent to which strategic capabilities are in place and developing programs to enhance these capabilities. In 2004, thirteen community colleges formed a network—the Strategic Horizon Network—the purpose of which was to assess their strategic readiness and, where lacking, find ways to enhance the capabilities of staff.[14] The results of assessment revealed strengths and deficits in specific areas of strategic capability:

Strengths	*Deficits*
Awareness of student needs	Strategic thinking
Commitment to serving student needs	Knowledge of value created for stakeholders
Meeting changing needs through innovation	Understanding of organizational culture
Commitment to developing leaders	Change design and management
Process management	
Communication	

Armed with this information, colleges in the Network organized teams to design and create learning modules that could be used with staff for developing strategic management skills. Cross-functional personnel (including the president and a senior administrator) from multiple colleges formed the nucleus of each team. After two years of work, the teams developed learning modules in five areas: *Strategic Thinking, Process Management, Communication, Designing and Managing Change,* and *Developing Leaders.*[15] These modules were pilot tested with Network college personnel in 2006 and 2007 and shortly thereafter released for use with staff in campus-based professional development programs.

Professional development as a conduit for developing skills and capabilities that leverage performance is a hallmark of abundant institutions. Richland College in the Dallas County Community College District has developed and implemented an approach to professional development that enhances the knowledge and skills of every employee, whether full- or part-time.[16] Full-time faculty and staff participate in a thirty-six-hour program of professional development each year in Richland's Thunderwater Organizational Learning Institute (TOLI). Twenty-six hours are devoted to prescribed content such as Richland's Quality Enhancement Plan, Intercultural Competence, and college-wide activities specifically focused on strategic planning priorities (SPPs). The remaining ten hours are comprised of elective courses and activities determined in accord with department and unit priorities. Beyond the thirty-six-hour core program, professional development is focused on building new competencies that are necessary to help students succeed. For example, Thunderbolt—an electronic learning component of TOLI—regularly offers courses on Blackboard, communication, soft skills, MySpace and YouTube, and podcasting for full- and part-time faculty.

Newly appointed full-time faculty, administrators, and staff at Richland are expected to participate in a ninety-hour professional development program throughout the duration of a three-year contract.[17] Their commitment is affirmed when the initial contract for employment is signed, which includes required participation in structured professional development programs to facilitate assimilation into Richland's culture of *teaching, learning,* and *community building.* Among the programs offered are: Visions of Excellence, Intercultural Competence, a Poolside Chat Series with the College President, Meetings with Mentor and Supervisor, Quality Enhancement Plan, and Technology Skills. Part-time instructors are included in professional development as part of an effort to develop a core of instructors who are involved in the college community. They are expected to complete an online orientation, participate in college-wide convocations, and enroll, when possible, in TOLI courses. Additionally, Richland has developed an Adjunct Faculty Certificate Program offering a core curriculum of professional development activities in Cooperative Learning, Intercultural Competence, E-Learning, Socratic Pedagogy, Learning Styles, Media Cart/Power Point, and Conversation-Based Teaching and Learning.

The sun has set on the day of lifetime employment with a single employer. Today, talented staff demand and expect professional development opportunities that have value not only in their current job, but also in the general job market. To stay competitive with rivals, abundant colleges work hard to determine what their employees want and value and help them develop accordingly. Tom McKeon, president of Tulsa Community College, describes Tulsa's investment in the individual:

> The most important thing when hiring people is to look at the whole employee. We try to look at it from the employee's perspective—what is important for them personally. It's not about the institution, it's about you and your growth as an individual. We're committed to giving employees skills that will help the college, but also help them individually. It's a subtle

shift in thought, but I think it's an important one—particularly with the generational differences we're seeing now in workers who are coming to the College. Younger workers are not as fixed on the organization as much as they are fixed on their development. There's not an allegiance to the "corporation" as there once was. So training programs and development programs are increasingly important to attract and retain talent and to ensure a strong faculty and staff. Beyond that, employees need to be engaged. An engaged employee is going have a more fulfilling job and do a better job. If you're processing applications at a registration desk, that's going to get pretty mundane; but if you feel like you have a voice and you can do some things in your department, then you have a role in the future of the organization beyond the registration office. That is when you're going to feel more valued and you're going to have greater job satisfaction.[18]

Attract and Retain Talented Staff

Abundant organizations have signature experiences that set them apart from other organizations. By identifying and explicitly communicating what makes them unique, they dramatically improve staff engagement and performance. They also enhance their ability to attract and retain talented staff. In the quest for talent, most colleges rely on name recognition to match or exceed competitors' resources—offering better compensation and benefits, professional development opportunities, work schedules, and so forth. While these tactics may be useful in bringing job candidates to the door, they may not bring the right people across the threshold—talented staff who are capable of leveraging resources and performance.

The idea of a "signature experience" is important for any organization trying to distinguish itself through its personnel. Erickson and Gratton describe it as a visible distinctive element of an institution's overall staff experience—the "bundle of everyday routines and processes" that are a symbol of an organization's culture and values.[19] Signature experiences are difficult to imitate because they evolve in-house and reflect the institution's heritage and the leadership team's ethos. Examples of signature experience are most readily evident in companies with highly engaged, mission-aware employees.[20] These organizations excel at attracting and retaining top talent because they know who they are, and they effectively express what makes them unique. They vividly demonstrate who they are with stories of actual practices and events.

At Whole Foods Market, potential hires are informed that each department in each store (meat, vegetables, bakery and so on) comprises a small, decentralized entrepreneurial team whose members have complete control over who joins the team.[21] After a four-week trial period, team members vote on whether a new hire stays or goes; the trainee needs two-thirds of the team's support in order to join the staff permanently. This signature experience corresponds with Whole Foods' profit-sharing program. Thirteen times a year, the company calculates the performance of each team and awards bonus pay to the members of high-performing teams. The bonus pay is explicitly linked to group rather than individual performance, so team members choose their trainees carefully—they want coworkers who will perform, not friends. This signature experience weeds out low-performing employees and conveys a strong message about Whole Foods' core values of industriousness, collaboration, and decentralization.[22]

Trilogy Software, a rapidly growing software and services provider in Texas, uses a "trial under fire" orientation experience to attract employees and ground them in corporate values. New employees go through a three-month immersion process in which top management, including the CEO, oversees their every step.[23] In the first month, new recruits participate in fast-paced creative projects in teams of twenty under the mentorship of an experienced manager. In the second month, project teams are shuffled and split into smaller "breakthrough teams" charged with inventing a product or service idea or creating a new business model. In the third month, the recruits are required to demonstrate their capacity for personal initiative either through the team or on their own. Upon completion of the program, recruits undergo rigorous evaluation and receive detailed feedback on their performance.

Trilogy's orientation experience serves as the company's primary R&D engine. It also serves as a proving ground for Trilogy's next generation of leaders. Most important, however, the orientation experience provides a compelling illustration of life in the firm.[24] A candidate who prefers a clear-cut, well-defined work environment will almost certainly withdraw after learning the details of the immersion process.

Whole Foods Market and Trilogy Software are abundant organizations. They have successfully created and communicated signature experiences that attract and retain the kinds of people who will fit comfortably into their culture. The closest parallel we could find to a documented "signature experience" in community colleges is the system for targeted hiring, career development, and succession planning in place at Richland College.[25] Recognizing the need to be increasingly agile in meeting student and community needs in a rapidly changing economic, social, and political climate, Richland uses a multifaceted approach to identifying, attracting, and hiring talented staff. Four tactics under the banner of *Strategic Staffing* are particularly important because they communicate Richland's signature as an organization deeply committed to continuous staff development.

Strategic Direction Staffing

Richland's executive leadership team uses ongoing environmental scanning to identify areas of emerging need and moves quickly to adopt programs or services to meet the need. An EXPLORE program is launched in consultation with Human Resources (HR) and administrative supervisors to identify internal candidates with training and experience in the proposed program area. Simultaneously, the executive leadership team appoints program-related advisory teams to elicit assistance in finding suitable candidates from the external community.[26]

Strategic Succession Staffing

To assist in forecasting retirement-related turnover among administrative, instructional, and support staff, Richland's HR and institutional research offices annually provide the executive team with an analysis of retirement eligibility in each employee category. Data from a career and succession-planning questionnaire completed periodically by employees are then matched with retirement forecasts to identify the strength of the internal candidate pool for positions projected to come open. As staff indicate plans to separate from Richland through retirement, relocation, or career moves, succession activities are initiated.[27]

Faculty Succession Staffing

Faculty and administrators promote the quality of Richland's work environment nationwide through professional networking, conferences, and associations—a practice that results in a nationwide pool of quality candidates who apply for openings. The president can delay a competitive search and offer a Visiting Scholar position for up to two years if a promising prospect is found internally or externally who needs additional experience prior to becoming a candidate in a competitive search. This enables Richland to "grow its own" talent.[28]

Leadership Staffing Succession

All full-time faculty, staff, and administrators annually complete a confidential survey indicating interest they may have in advancement, leadership opportunities, or professional development. This information is shared with the executive team for the purpose of succession planning. Armed with this information, the executive team identifies and allocates funding for a customized program of professional development for individuals whose interests and skills align with Richland's strategic planning priorities. Opportunities for professional development are extensive and include community leadership development programs; the North Texas Community College Leadership Consortium; national community college leadership development programs such as NILD, NACUBO, NCSD, and National Chair Academy; internships and formal job shadowing opportunities; and quality examiner training through Baldridge.[29]

Richland's approach to strategic staffing underscores the importance of developing and communicating a "signature experience" in the quest for talented staff. Experience tells us that this aspect of abundance is overlooked in all but the most creative institutions. Abundant colleges have the ability to attract and retain the right people—staff who are excited by what they are doing and the environment they are working in. These individuals are likely to be deeply engaged in their work and less likely to chase after better salaries or benefits elsewhere. Their commitment has a ripple effect on continuing and prospective staff and makes the organization as a whole more attractive.

ATTRIBUTES OF ARCHITECTURE

Work in Teams Bound by a Common Purpose

David Hartleb encountered a broken college when he was named president of Northern Essex Community College (Massachusetts) in 1997. Faculty and staff worked in silos that could be likened to bunkers, and the senior management team was anything but a team. Operating units commanded the allegiance of staff, and rancor and discord marked the relationship between people.[30] On a good day Northern Essex could be called a "sum of parts"; most days it was a dysfunctional organization.

Over a period of ten years, Northern Essex has transformed itself into a college with many attributes of abundance. It has done so through nothing less than a cultural transformation by getting new and continuing staff to work together around a common purpose. Much of the credit goes to Hartleb. From day one, he recognized that discord is rooted in a lack of coherence—a problem that diminishes when a critical mass of people are engaged in pursuit of the same goals. In the insightful words of Jim Collins, "Most organizations build bureaucratic rules to manage the small percentage of wrong people on the bus, which in turn drives away the right people on the bus, which then increases the percentage of wrong people on the bus, which increases the need for more bureaucracy to compensate for lack of discipline, which then further drives away the right people, and so forth."[31] The problem at Northern Essex, as Hartleb discerned, was not a preponderance of the wrong people on the bus, but good people thrown off track by conflict and mistrust that are part of an unhealthy culture.

Hartleb knew that an alternative existed: put the right people in positions of leadership, get the right people on the bus, open channels of communication, put everything on the table, involve staff throughout the organization in strategic activities, and insist that leaders and staff work together to achieve identified priorities.[32] Getting on the same path, however, is one thing; staying on it is something else. To reinforce his early success in getting people to work together, Hartleb and the executive team created a framework for collective engagement in strategic activities that would shape the direction of the college and its approach to business. Three activities requiring broad engagement were pursued: 1) creation of a new statement of vision and core values, 2) beginning-to-end involvement in developing a comprehensive strategic plan, and 3) involvement in process management—a practice that assists colleges in continually improving internal processes and systems to better serve stakeholders.[33] All of these processes promoted team building and collaboration among faculty and staff, and all were directly tied to institutional goals and priorities.

The beauty of Northern Essex's approach to transforming culture can be found not only in its multipronged approach to getting people to work together, but in how it used collaboration to appreciate strengths and find new ways of doing business. Through shared understanding of institutional vision and priorities, leaders and staff developed an appreciation of Northern Essex's capabilities. By adding new staff and new ideas to a cohesive culture, they discovered new ways of doing things and forged an entrepreneurial spirit. This creative duality now runs through every aspect of Northern Essex's organization, and it is woven into the fabric of its culture. On the one hand, it can be observed in new staff who bring new ideas and a freedom to question existing ways of doing things. On the other hand, new staff have had to commit to culturally reinforced goals and priorities and to tailor what they do to prevailing norms. In Collins's words "they have freedom, but freedom within a framework."[34] Through its commitment to collaboration, Northern Essex exemplifies a key attribute of abundant organizations: *cultural coherence* created and sustained by people working toward a common purpose.

Emphasize the Whole Institution

From the perspective of external stakeholders, community colleges are "safe" organizations perceived as operating in the best interests of citizens and communities. The upside of favorable public perception is support for institutional initiatives. The downside is growing demand that can strain institutional resources by requiring an institution to move in simultaneously contradictory directions. The impact of the downside is captured in the "all things to all people" idiom that has shadowed community colleges for more than two decades. This idiom is captured in the words of a president decrying the need for cuts:

> I am used to adding things, not cutting them. Cutting is difficult because there are so many things the community needs, how are you going to tell them "no." If you really want to do something, you'll find a way to do it. That's what I told my staff and that's what we're going to do.[35]

Abundant colleges cultivate a clear conception in stakeholders of what the institution is and what it stands for. Their focus is on the whole organization and clear messages about what the organization does for stakeholders. Savvy leaders use college and community engagement in strategic decisions to build and maintain focus. Roy Church and the executive team at Lorain County Community College in Ohio use a structured process of engagement to provide college staff and community stakeholders with a voice in planning and decision making. The conduit for engagement is a strategic-visioning process called Vision 2015 that involves college-wide staff and community stakeholders in a structured conversation about the community's "College of the Future."[36] This process has four phases.

Phase I. Listening and Learning

Strategic Visioning begins with face-to-face engagement with external constituent groups through a series of structured conversations to gather building block ideas for the College of the Future.[37] Over an eighteen-month period in 2006–2007, a series of forty-five internal Listening and Learning sessions were held with college faculty and staff involving 360 individuals—roughly 75 percent of Lorain's full-time staff. Over the same period, 104 sessions involving 1,435 individuals were held with external community constituents. The product of these conversations was a broad-based pool of ideas about Lorain's future that would require winnowing in Phase II.

Phase II. Building the Vision

A one-hundred-member Vision 2015 Council comprising college and community constituents reviewed ideas generated through the Listening and Learning sessions in combination with environmental scanning data to winnow down to a manageable number of initiatives.[38] The Council met on five occasions between September and December 2006, each focused on a specific topic (Orientation, Education and Economy, Culture and Community, Strategic Priorities, and Strategic Initiatives). Electronic voting technology was used to select themes for development into initiatives.

Phase III. Sharing the Vision

A six-month process involving college faculty and staff between January and June 2007 was undertaken to confirm institutional strategic priorities and finalize a list of possible initiatives.[39] The outcome of this process was six priorities that Lorain elected to pursue to achieve its desired future:

- Raise the community's participation and attainment of higher education
- Prepare globally-competent talent to compete in the innovation economy
- Accelerate business and job growth to enhance regional competitiveness
- Connect Lorain County with regional priorities and partners
- Serve as a catalyst for enhanced community life
- Build the college's resource capacity

Phase IV. Acting on the Vision

Beginning in September 2007 internal teams were assigned to monitor each initiative. Through Vision 2015 and similar approaches to engaging college and community constituencies in strategic decisions, Lorain has built a compelling conception of the institution that is widely shared by a lot of people. The visioning process—real time involving people inside and outside who count—worked to imprint the college as a living organism in the minds of stakeholders. Stakeholders can get a lot of information about a college from Web sites and marketing materials, but nothing can substitute for firsthand experience in forging a relationship with an institution. Constituents have no choice but to identify with a college because it is their creation.

Forge Enlightened Collective Strategic Decisions

Ask an instructor or lower-level administrator in your college, "Where are we trying to get to as a college?" The answer you receive will likely be worded in the form of vague ideals ("to help learners reach their potential") or short-term operational goals ("to enroll more students," "offer more programs in response to community needs," or "improve our financial position through private giving"). In many colleges, staff do not share a sense of purpose above and beyond that of short-term unit performance. Lacking a compelling sense of direction, only the most venturesome individuals feel a sense of responsibility for competitiveness. Most won't go the extra mile unless they know where they are heading.

Abundant organizations employ decentralization and empowerment as tactics for overcoming problems with inertia.[40] Recognizing that decentralization and empowerment work best when a clear and compelling direction is in place to guide staff effort, these organizations strive to engage people in a collective process of strategy development. General Electric is a good example of a "boundaryless" organization where cross-unit collaboration is used to make big decisions. The closest parallel in community colleges would be institutions like Lorain County Community College, Northern Essex Community College, and Tulsa Community College where large-group processes involving representatives of all employee groups are used to make strategic decisions about institutional vision, values, and priorities. These processes are in the early stages of use, and they are still evolving. They are, however, an essential building block for developing the strategic capabilities of staff and, hence, an important attribute of abundance.

Reduce Challenges and Problems to Simple Organizing Ideas

Borrowing from the Hedgehog Concept introduced by Collins in *Good to Great*, abundant organizations know how to reduce challenges and complex circumstances into simple organizing ideas that improve performance.[41] Leaders and staff in these organizations focus on a basic principle or concept that unifies and guides everything that they do. It doesn't matter about the pace of change, the degree of complexity in the environment, or how difficult circumstances become—everything is reduced to simple organizing ideas.

The trap of complexity was never more apparent than a recent meeting involving the senior author and information officers from ten community colleges. The objective of the meeting was to develop an interinstitutional approach to external scanning that would save time and reduce cost— essentially, a network that would make scanning easier by distributing responsibility for the function among institutions. The meeting progressed nicely, and the group was on the cusp of a simple design when one of the players came up with a brilliant idea: why not use sophisticated technology to amplify the amount of information that could be scanned, organize it in an elaborate matrix, and issue detailed reports? In other words, make the scanning process more sophisticated to fit the complexity of the information that would be part of the process. Naturally, this idea provoked an avalanche of new ideas about how technology could be used to improve the scanning process. After thirty minutes of intense discussion with one idea topping another, the group hit the wall. A simple process had been turned into a procedural nightmare that no one could, or would, implement. The group had lost sight of the simple goal and, like the proverbial fox seeing all of the possibilities and looking for ways to pursue them, the means had become more important than the end.

Consider the example of Illinois Central College (ICC) and how it has used the philosophy and methodology of Six Sigma to simplify its approach to business.[42] Six Sigma is a philosophy of excellence and continuous improvement methodology used by many organizations to improve performance. Developed by Motorola and launched in 1987, it gives organizations a way to compare performance against customer/constituent expectations and achieve enhanced targets for performance.[43] Significant costs are associated with poorly designed and executed processes. Six Sigma puts the customer first and uses facts and data to drive decisions. The objective of Six Sigma is to create a culture of collaboration by encouraging staff to work together to design processes that better meet the needs of the people they serve. Six Sigma also enhances the collective intelligence of an institution as it works to solve its most pressing challenges.

Illinois Central adopted Six Sigma in spring 2003 as a way of building interunit cooperation and accelerating improvement throughout the institution. By 2008, it had trained 512 employees in Six Sigma methodology, and 20 employees had attained the status of trainers.[44] In a five-year period following adoption, ICC has used Six Sigma methodology to redesign processes in twenty key areas, including new student orientation, course quality approval, minority retention, initial student advisement, prospective student follow-up, student refunds, student advisement, financial aid, and college travel.[45]

In classic hedgehog style, Illinois Central is tackling some of the more difficult challenges it is facing by reducing them to a simple organizing idea: put customers first and design processes that better meet their needs. It has created a culture of collaboration built on a principle of superior service to customer needs. If a process in any part of the college is identified as falling short of customer expectations, it is flagged for redesign using Six Sigma methodology. Think about it—512 employees have been trained in Six Sigma methodology. ICC's full-time staff numbers four hundred, so this number is considerably beyond the tipping point required to make change stick. Its logic is simple: more staff committed to Six Sigma will lead to more processes being identified for improvement which, when multiplied times satisfied customers, will 1) attract more customers to the college and 2) make ICC an attractive employer for prospective staff with an interest and skills in Six Sigma. The cumulative effect over time will be a deeply ingrained philosophy of excellence that sets Illinois Central apart from competitors.

Establish, Manage, and Operate in Networks

Abundant colleges create and work in networks that make them a nexus for the community. A network is an interconnected group of organizations tied by one or more types of interdependency such as values, vision, ideas, financial benefit, expertise, and so on.[46] Networks operate on many levels from units in organizations working together to achieve a common objective up to the level of organizations themselves partnering to achieve mutually beneficial goals. Surprisingly little has been written on the role of networks in community colleges, but we know that they play an important role in the way organizations are run, the way decisions are made, and the extent to which institutions succeed in achieving their goals. Listen to Eric Reno describe the connection between college and community at Northeast College in Texas:

> This is where we want people to come for their recreation, culture, and their training—academic opportunities, educational opportunities, and programs for all ages. That's the logic underlying our partnerships. We want kids coming from the youngest age to the library, to the YMCA, to the theatre, as part of a natural progression. They won't be intimidated by higher education, because they've been coming on campus their whole lives, and know that this is a resource for the whole community. That's why we have the Center for Civic, Domestic, and Economic Education—a venture designed to bring people together to teach them the things they need to do to be happy and successful. Being a part of a family, being a parent, is a difficult job. There are things that people need help with. And, there is the civic part in all of these communities. People run for office, for school boards, for city council, whatever, and some people need help with the nuts and bolts of being an elected official.[47]

Cy-Fair College (Texas) was opened in 2003 with a promise to design and build a college that would be a hub for the community. Shortly after bonds were approved for the new college, Cy-Fair's executive team met with residents of the Cypress and Fairbanks school districts to organize a system for gathering information about their preferences for campus design. A series of one hundred focus group meetings were conducted with citizen groups; employers were surveyed; meetings were held with the Chamber of Commerce, CBOs, and civic organizations; PTOs and school principals were consulted; and high school and college students were canvassed.[48]

What came back was a preference for a collegiate campus (a "real" college) that would also be a hub for the community. Cy-Fair would become a gathering place for the community, and it would do so through blended services with community organizations—a learning commons doubling as the county library and Cy-Fair's Learning Support Center, a fire station and training complex providing fire and emergency services to the county, and countless networking projects carried out by faculty and staff (income tax preparation, Habitat for Humanity, etc.).[49]

The networks established by Cy-Fair and Northeast College demonstrate the capacity of abundant colleges to leverage resources through working relationships with external organizations. These relationships ease financial pressure by offsetting costs. More importantly, they build organizational capability by contributing expertise, improving linkages, and attracting new resources. Why build a learning resource center using operating dollars when a partnering opportunity can be forged with local government to build a joint-use facility? Why purchase sophisticated technology when a high-tech partner can underwrite all or part of the cost? The economic incentives for network building are aptly described by Tom McKeon, president of Tulsa Community College:

> We work very closely with the Career Tech Center. Our administrative building, where my offices are, was jointly purchased with the Career Tech Center and we each have half of the building. We left the top floor open and jointly decided to make that into a training center for K–12 teachers as well as college and university tech faculty, focusing on how to integrate technology into teaching and learning. We have over 25 colleges, public schools, and private schools that are part of this consortium and we operate it with the Career Tech Center. It's a wonderful partnership. We have our aviation program at their campus and we run our professional pilot school at their campus. We do the first two years and the four-year universities do the last two years and that's been a unique opportunity to think creatively about how we bridge between K–12 schools, four-year colleges and universities, and jobs.[50]

Networks are about much more than cost savings, as illustrated by Burt's seminal analysis of social networks.[51] Organizations with strong ties to partners are more resilient to external shocks and enjoy an advantage in securing resources. Listen to a savvy president describe the importance of community partners in advantage building:

> It may sound a bit Machiavellian, but I make sure that we have partnerships with all the big players in the city and representation on all the important

county committees. That way we have inside information on important changes going on and we always have someone pulling for us. In an environment as political as this, you don't want to get caught unaware.[52]

Networks are not easy to create or to maintain. They require constant vigilance from leaders, and there is an opportunity cost in the form of time and effort. McKeon describes the personal investment required for community partnerships to work:

> You really have to work at it. It's all about relationships with people. We wouldn't have partnerships with our universities if the presidents of those institutions and I didn't have strong personal relationships, know each other as friends, and not look at each other as competitors. That's why the Tulsa model is working. There are communities where colleges don't even talk to one another, and so it's all about the personal relationships. We're friends— you have to establish that and, if you don't, partnerships can unravel quickly.[53]

Interestingly, while priorities spelled out in strategic plans often refer to competition between community colleges and alternative providers, our research revealed that abundant colleges focus more on creating partnerships than outperforming competitors. Sandra Kurtinitis, president of Community College of Baltimore County, put it this way:

> Certainly the potential for competition is always present, but I think the way to approach it is to enhance what you already do well—that is, to craft partnerships and linkages that make sure that the institution is on everybody's radar screen relative to what we can do. We need to work hard at not being a threat to anyone, but to being everybody's best partner.[54]

The future of networks will be an extension of the present. Look for colleges to assume the role of hub and add new players to existing networks. Abundant colleges are not merely passive members of networks— they take a leadership role in bringing partners together and establishing strategic direction. In time, we are likely to see the rise of "network colleges" which take the form of umbrella organizations integrating the activities of network partners in order to effectively deliver core activities.

ATTRIBUTES OF CAPABILITY

Create Exceptional Resources through Leveraging

Resource constraints are not an impediment to the achievement of superior performance outcomes in colleges of abundance. Owens Community

College is one of the fastest growing colleges in Ohio despite a resource base marginalized by low tuition and austere state support.[55] Owens does not have local taxing authority. It leverages resources by raising the numerator in productivity ratios (number of students served) rather than reducing the denominator (number of staff delivering service). With a goal of reducing expenditures for specific outcomes, denominator-focused institutions are more about reducing resources than leveraging resources. Numerator-focused institutions like Owens are constantly looking for ways to deliver more and better service without committing additional resources—collaborating with partners to expand technology on a standstill operating budget; creating additional space for instructional and service delivery through shared facilities; building visibility through cost-effective approaches to marketing; and redesigning processes and systems to serve students better and faster.

Leaders and staff in abundant institutions are continually on the alert for new, less resource-intensive means of achieving strategic priorities. They know that in tough economic times advantage comes down to the capacity to leverage resources rather than the capacity to acquire more money and outspend rivals.[56] They measure capacity for leveraging by determining the ratio of growth to dollars spent on activities designed to generate growth. Thus, while a fully resourced competitor may possess more capacity for making strategic investments, it may be no better than average in terms of resource leveraging. Through alliances and joint ventures, Owens can avail itself of resources and skills outside of its capacity. By sharing a partner's resources, Owens not only gains access to its tangible resources, but also to its intangible resources—people and skills. Over time these skills are learned from a partner, and the resource base of the institution is leveraged. Learning is a more efficient way of acquiring new skills than buying people or consulting. When buying, an institution must pay for both the skills that it wants as well as the skills it may already have or deem inadequate. There are also problems of cultural integration and harmonization of new personnel that are much higher in acquiring new talent than in collaborating with a partner.[57]

A vice president in an urban community college expressed the simple logic of leveraging through collaboration with partners. "Why create something new when you can acquire a quality product or service by working with a partner?"[58] In other words, the partner does the resource-intensive work of product design and implementation, and the institution leverages its operating resources by acquiring the product. Tapping into the creative capabilities of partners is a critically important source of resource leverage. Leaders in abundant colleges know that the absorptive capacity of their institutions is as important as their inventive capacity. In the future this capacity will take a myriad of forms: sharing development risks with partners, acquiring resources from less expensive markets (for example, working via the Internet with low-cost software programmers and tutors located in India), or participating in interinstitutional consortia. Whatever the form, the motive will be the same—to supplement resources with those outside the boundaries of the institution.

Anticipate Change through Continuous Scanning

The work of community college leaders and staff is information intensive. They are exposed to vast amounts of information from a wide range of sources and must make difficult choices about what to use in day-to-day decisions and long-term planning. Institutions operating from a deficit perspective tend to employ an *inside-out* approach to information use. That is, they narrow the focus in management to internally generated information that is used to solve problems. In contrast, abundant institutions employ an *outside-in* approach to information use. They systematically collect and analyze information from internal and external environments to enrich the basis on which operating decisions are made.

Grand Rapids Community College (GRCC) in Michigan uses a continuous multimodal scanning process to generate information for decision making at all levels in the institution. Its *GRCC Dynamic Scan* systematically draws and assembles information from the Internet in six "landscapes"—demographic, economic, educational, technological, social, and political trends—which are used by staff to plan for the future. A second scanning process, *Focused Scan*, zeroes in on information related to a special topic, such as technology or health care in response to a request from faculty, staff, or a community group. GRCC integrates information acquired from scanning in a convenient e-mail, *The Future GIST*, distributed with attachments to faculty and staff to help create a future's mindset and to stimulate dialogue. Text in the e-mail contains the author's thoughts about a specific trend, issue, or condition, and attachments contain detailed information—an article, an abstract, or a trend picked up in GRCC's continuous scanning process.

Anticipating change is more than a process of scenario planning or forecasting using available data. Abundant colleges prepare for change by mining information about the external environment to determine what could be and then work back to what must happen for that future to be realized. It is this type of foresight that fuels Lorain County Community College's drive to achieve double-digit enrollment growth each year for the next ten years. It is this type of foresight that drives Owens Community College's quest to provide the best value for postsecondary education in Ohio. It is this type of foresight that underlies Northern Essex Community College's view of quality as embedded in a culture of continuous improvement.

Anticipation of change is informed by deep insight into trends in lifestyles, demographics, economics, and technology, but it rests as much on imagination as prediction. To undergo change toward a desired future, a college must first be capable of imagining it. Abundant colleges do this by developing an ambitious visual representation of what the future could be using multiple source scanning data. To borrow from Disney, what they do is "imagineering."[59] They imagine a future state in which the institution is everything that it can be. Lorain has assembled a vision of what it will look like in the future based on college and community input. Northern Essex has developed a webcast of its long-range development priorities formulated through a process of appreciative inquiry.

What is the fabric of an enlarged sense of change and future possibilities? In our experience with abundant institutions, it grows out of ambition shared by leaders and staff, unbounded energy, and a willingness to take risks. Anticipation is the product of eclecticism, of imagination, of the pursuit of opportunity, and of a genuine empathy with stakeholder needs.

Seek Information about Best Practices

A college is a reservoir of experience. Every day leaders and staff come into contact with stakeholders holding unique expectations, organizations employing a variety of business practices, and rivals competing for the same students. What differentiates abundant from less abundant institutions is not so much the depth of experience of leaders or the tacit knowledge of staff, as their capacity to mine learning from experience. Put simply, abundant colleges are capable of extracting more learning from experience inside and outside of the organization than other colleges. They are also more likely to open themselves up to learning outside the organization by studying the best practices of high-performing organizations. The capacity to mine ideas for innovation and change from experience is a critical component of leveraging.

Member institutions in two organizations—the Strategic Horizon Network (SHN) and the Continuous Quality Improvement Network (CQIN)—have advanced organizational learning by studying the best practices of organizations outside of education. Within the Strategic Horizon Network, colleges have used reputational indices to identify leaders in the manufacturing, service, health, travel, and entertainment industries.[60] Visits are arranged and packaged around an agenda designed to inject college staff directly into the mechanics of best practices. Industry-leading organizations like Marriott, Caterpillar, SAS, Oracle, Whole

Foods, Northrop Grumman, Southwest Airlines, Honda, Disney and start-up organizations like Skybus are eager to share their best practices. These organizations, and others like them, are interested in forging partnerships with community colleges that provide a good starting point for sharing accumulated wisdom.

Abundant colleges use best practice information to improve or redesign their own practices. They know the principles that underlie exemplary customer service are the same regardless of where the service is delivered—a hotel, an airline, a hospital, an automotive service center, or a college office. They know that innovation and change are part of life in any successful organization, and practices that appear disruptive today could become standard tomorrow. Lorain County Community College and Northern Essex Community College, for example, are using best practices from Honda Motor Company (quality enhancement) and Southwest Airlines (corporate culture and talent attraction and retention) to redesign systems for staff recruiting, selection, and retention. Both institutions are capable of mining ideas and experience from cutting-edge organizations at a pace and volume vastly beyond their less abundant counterparts.

The capacity to learn from other organizations depends, of course, on many things: the number of staff who are well-versed in strategic thinking, the extent of staff involvement in strategic decision making, and their interest in learning from other organizations. Interestingly, unlearning—a willingness to think outside current practice in order to do things differently—must often take place before learning can begin. What determines the capacity of community college leaders and staff to learn from external organizations is, as much as anything else, their flexibility and ability to forget.

Collaborate with Rivals for Mutual Gain

Abundant colleges supplement their resources with those of competitors to multiply the value they deliver to stakeholders. This is the very essence of leveraging, and it involves a number of capabilities that collaborating organizations must share:

- New product imagination
- A culture that supports and engages in change
- The ability to envision and accept competitors as collaborators
- A capacity to embrace paradox—to partner and compete with rivals simultaneously

Primary examples of mutual gain collaboration with competitors are the university center and middle college concepts that have altered community college boundaries with four-year colleges and K–12 schools. Partnerships established with universities for the purpose of delivering baccalaureate and graduate programs on community college campuses are popping up in many states. The University Center at Macomb Community College (Michigan) was one of the first partnerships, and it is prototypical of how they work.[61] Approved by voters in 1988 and up and running in 1991, Macomb's University Partnership offers students the ability to complete their entire education from associate degree to graduate degree without leaving campus. It does this through eight university partners offering more than sixty baccalaureate and graduate degree programs. Credit for enrollment and state aid is equitably divided between Macomb and its university partners with all players benefiting from the collaboration because enrollment that would normally be contested is shared.

The concurrent enrollment program between Macomb and Oakland University illustrates the extent to which collaboration between competitors can create a win-win situation for all parties.[62] Named Macomb 2 Oakland (M2O), the program enables students to apply to both institutions simultaneously with one application. Students can take courses at one or both institutions at the same time, coordinate financial aid at both institutions by combining credit through concurrent enrollment, expand course selection, coordinate advising and course planning, and access on-campus resources at both institutions. Similarly, an alliance between Macomb and Franklin University enables students to earn a Bachelor of Science degree online from Franklin without leaving Macomb's campus.[63]

K–12 school districts are not viewed as competitors by community colleges except in extreme financial circumstances when both must vie for shrinking state dollars. The growing popularity of dual enrollment programs in many colleges has changed the boundary between secondary and postsecondary education. Even more prominent are charter programs on community college campuses that keep youth in school and engage them in college. Labeled "middle colleges" or "technical middle colleges," these programs enable students to graduate from high school while completing a certificate at the community college. The number of students that can be accommodated is limited, but the implications for boundaries between service providers are enormous.

The ability to collaborate with rivals is a signature attribute of abundant organizations. It requires a capacity for compartmentalizing thinking so that competition and collaboration can coexist. It also requires a capacity for big-picture thinking and an understanding of trade-offs. From the standpoint of the big picture, leaders and staff know that growth will come through many portals, among them collaboration with competitors. Collaboration is a desirable alternative when the costs associated with generating growth outweigh the revenue it brings in. It is also a smart alternative to competition when rivals are working with deep pockets.

Identify and Pursue Opportunity

Leaders and staff in abundant institutions envision and exploit opportunities using capabilities that less abundant institutions do not have. Busy leaders have a tendency to concentrate on market space and opportunities that are right in front of them. Time and resources do not permit looking beyond the visual horizon, and convenience determines what receives attention. Convenience is not an acceptable alternative when it comes to opportunity. When leaders substitute convenience for curiosity, they unknowingly cede market leadership to competitors more actively engaged in the pursuit of opportunity.

How do abundant colleges identify and pursue opportunity? Leaders in these institutions encourage staff engagement in innovation and risk taking. Eric Reno put it this way when reflecting on the early days of his presidency at Red Rocks Community College in Colorado:

> It was intimidating to follow someone who was beloved, not just at the institution, but throughout the community. What could I do to improve upon the great work that she did? . . . I laid out a menu of initiatives—international education, an honors program, service learning, learning communities—and I asked people who were interested in those areas to get involved. Obviously you're going to get people who say they're interested. I gave them some money, gave them a year to explore, go to conferences, visit other institutions, and come back with a recommendation about what to formalize within the institution. Not to my surprise, a number of people got excited and wanted to do it.[64]

Reno knew that staff would come forward with new initiatives, but his goal was not to create new services and activities. His aim was to engage staff in the pursuit of opportunity by removing the threat of risk or failure and increasing commitment to innovation through ownership.

Although most leaders acknowledge the importance of innovation and change, few assign value to these concepts through their actions. We have described colleges of challenge and choice as being operationally focused—as mired in orthodoxy. Yet the people working inside these institutions do not see themselves as any less imaginative than those who work in abundant institutions. It is the complexity, multiple levels of authority, and the lack of personal freedom that bottle up the innovation.

To minimize orthodoxy, leaders in abundant organizations have devised ways to free staff from the shackles of bureaucracy through incubator projects, Six Sigma management techniques, rewards for entrepreneurs, and so on. These techniques are not the exclusive province of abundant institutions. Some or all of them have been tried in less abundant institutions, but with only mixed success. The difference can be attributed, in part, to the flexible architecture of abundant institutions that enables innovation to bubble up quickly inside the organization.

We can illustrate the difference using the hypothetical example of two colleges: "Fast Track College" and "Tradition Bound College." Fast Track has profited enormously from the fact that a neighboring college, Tradition Bound, has squandered opportunities for innovation because of its suffocating bureaucracy. Hierarchy and routine rule everything that Tradition Bound does from marketing and recruiting to course scheduling and service delivery. Fast Track's faculty and staff had only to listen to adult learners describe the inconvenience of Tradition Bound's course offerings and service delivery to know that opportunity was at hand. Seizing the initiative, leaders at Fast Track implemented a flexible entry approach to instruction with classes starting weekly at convenient times for adult learners. They also devised a system for accelerated development of distance delivery courses and 24/7/365 delivery of services on the Internet. The result: Fast Track captured market share from Tradition Bound by virtue of the importance it assigned to opportunity and its architecture which moved ideas quickly to action.

Design and Manage Change Effectively

In *The Heart of Change,* Kotter observed that "people change what they do less because they are given analysis that shifts their thinking than because they are shown a truth that influences their feelings."[65] Change is a personal journey, and learning from leaders of abundant institutions can be reduced to a few simple lessons. Chief among them is the stark reality that trust is a precursor to change. Leaders who inspire trust are capable of initiating, leading, and finishing change. Change is an altogether different journey in institutions with poor leader-follower relationships—it is a winding road laden with pitfalls.

Earn the trust of staff before proposing significant change. Leaders face the tension of external pressure for, and internal resistance to, change. Yet, presidents who manage change effectively establish trust as a first step.

When asked about his approach to enacting large-scale organizational change, Eric Reno used a symbolic example to make a point.[66] When he came to Red Rocks Community College, the institution had a history of frugal spending. This mentality extended to the furnishing of the president's office, in which desks were created out of planks of wood with cinder blocks and plywood. Reno was concerned that the office would look unprofessional to potential donors he was planning to woo. Instead of buying the new furniture, he tabled the issue as an item at the end of semester meeting. At the meeting he said, "I just want to let you know that I am meeting with people on campus about supporting the college. I want to make the President's office look more professional, so I'm going to order some new furniture. 'Oh, ok.' No big deal. I never heard another word, but if I hadn't done that, I guarantee you, someone would have made a big deal of it."[67] By building trust through consistent action and by vetting ideas with staff, Reno built the trust necessary for larger changes in the future.

Create a sense of urgency in key staff. In abundant institutions, "key" staff are larger in proportion to the whole institution than is the case in less abundant institutions. In colleges of challenge, leaders tend to restrict the change agenda to core decision makers, thereby excluding staff from the design and initiation of change. By bringing a significant number of staff into change at an early stage, leaders in abundant institutions build a basis for understanding the need for change and create an urgency for action.

Build later success on earlier success. In *The Tipping Point*, Gladwell describes the outcome of change as uncertain until it reaches a critical mass of support at which point it becomes inevitable.[68] Trust, timing, and tipping points are crucial in change. Staff are more likely to engage in and support change when prior experience with it has been positive. Leaders in abundant institutions build a track record of early success by 1) limiting the number of change initiatives pursued at any one time and 2) pursuing initiatives that are small in scale and less taxing on resources.

Vet ideas with multiple stakeholders to establish consensus for change. Leaders do not always have the luxury of choosing popular change initiatives. Upon her appointment as president of the Community College of Baltimore County, Sandra Kurtinitis was charged with completing a transformation from a district with three colleges to a single college with three campuses. This process involved a dramatic change in organizational structure that was disruptive to faculty, staff, and culture. Kurtinitis eased the transition by informing stakeholders early of proposed changes and involving the college community in implementing the change process:

> This is an institution that has gone through a reorganization du jour almost annually. So the way to approach the huge task of executive restructuring, which by the way has played to almost universal campus approval, is to talk with a lot of people. I started in November, but I came in August to deliver a speech and meet my new college community. They didn't really know me and I certainly didn't know them. I used that opportunity to give some personal, intellectual, and professional philosophy—a biography. Really, to sort

of lay out the landscape that included some very simple, but very crucial philosophic premises that are important to me. In January, when the college community came together again for a professional development day, I made a definitive statement about the restructuring that I was going to propose. I followed that in March with a meeting of the Board in executive session. We spent a couple of hours on the restructuring proposal and when I left that meeting I put in place a month long, college-wide vetting of the proposal. I personally not only attended forums on each campus, but had an all college meeting where I presented the entire proposal. The meeting was videotaped and put on our daily posts. The first thing you see when you open up your computer every morning is the daily post, so nobody in the college would have any reason to feel as if they had not heard about this. My intent was and is to structure college-wide mechanisms whereby people can weigh in. So through the college senate, governance structure, open forums, in whatever way possible, if you're going to do something big, you don't want to do it in a dark room at 11 o' clock at night.[69]

Eric Reno and Sandra Kurtinitis ascribe to an inclusive approach to organizational change in which culturally reinforced venues and processes are used as a mechanism to communicate change. This approach provides resisters with a forum to voice their dissent and to reconcile their arguments against change with factors supporting change. The result, more often than not, is compromise that recognizes valid points—both for and against—that must be considered in the design of change.

Make change stick through constant reinforcement. Finally, leaders in abundant institutions make change stick through constant reinforcement and encouragement. A clear understanding of what is involved, why it is necessary, and what it will lead to develops among staff through consistency of word and action.

Know the Value Delivered to Stakeholders

Abundance is not simply a state of being; it is also a product of performance. A college must make a substantial contribution to student and stakeholder perceived value to be considered abundant. To make a contribution of this magnitude, it must first know the value it delivers to stakeholders. Awareness is a precursor of leveraging—value rises in direct proportion to the resources (tangible and intangible) directed to it by savvy leaders. The difference between more and less abundant institutions rests, in part, on a distinction in what they know about their customers. All institutions gather information from students about goals and attendance plans, but few probe deeply beneath the surface to determine their deepest wants, needs, and expectations. Fewer yet probe deeply into the world of experience to understand how students feel about what they are getting from college; how this stacks up against what they want; and their innermost feelings about the extent to which their goals are being met.

Abundant colleges care deeply about creating a meaningful experience for students, and they exert great effort in trying to understand what they value. They also build relationships with them through one-on-one engagement inside and outside of class. For example, learning coaches are used to intensively monitor student progress on a case-by-case basis instead of academic advisors who engage in arms-length transactions. When a college is earnestly working toward student success, its efforts can be easily noticed. Most students can readily describe why the experience at one college is better than another. Likewise, they can tell you specifically what they like about customer service at one college and not at another, or technology access, or private space on campus, or the attitude of instructors. A college that cares is a significant entity for students. Its capacity for caring depends on the depth of its knowledge about what students want and what they are getting.

Learners are the ultimate judge of value. What is unique about leaders and staff in abundant institutions is that they are driven to ask themselves if a particular activity or application makes a contribution to "value received by the student." Questions they routinely ask and answer include the following: What is of value in this course, this service, or this activity? What are the students wanting or expecting to get? What are they actually getting? Can students get more value somewhere else? What elements of value are most important and thus make the largest contribution to satisfaction? These questions ensure that leaders and staff direct their energy (and their resources) to things that make a difference for stakeholders.

ATTRIBUTES OF PERFORMANCE

Use Stretch and Leverage as the Index of Performance

Abundance is grounded in a different understanding of performance than is characteristic of most colleges today. To achieve optimum performance, a college's architecture and its approach to management and decision making must be grounded in a deep understanding of stretch and leverage. Its ambition should stretch far beyond its current resources and capabilities. Unfortunately, conventional performance criteria channel the thinking of leaders and staff to tangible evidence of execution that lies within the range of currently available resources. What is immedi-

ately attainable—*growth*—drives out what is ultimately desirable—
stretch—as the index of performance.[70]

In contrast to their less abundant counterparts, abundant institutions
move beyond *growth* as the primary measure of performance to *stretch*:
the extent to which resources and capabilities have been optimized.[71]
They know that growth as an indicator of performance is essentially an
"acquisition index." It is a tool for making the case for more resources to
support more growth, but it says nothing about how effectively resources
are being used. When growth is the measure of performance, leaders ask
questions about *volume*: Do we have sufficient resources to support
growth? How much more (money, staff, space) will we need? How much
more are we likely to get? How much can we grow given the resources
we are likely to get?

When stretch is the measure of performance, leaders ask questions
about *achievement*: What do we need to accomplish? How high should we
set our goals? How far can we stretch our people and resources? Is our
performance target high enough or should we set the target higher?
Growth is used to acquire more resources when the resources needed to
grow are not at hand. Stretch is used to leverage current resources based
on the knowledge that resources are scarce and need to be used
effectively.

Growth and stretch are equally important as indices for performance.
On the one hand, smart leaders do not forego growth because they do not
have the resources to support it, nor do they create growth targets that
are outrageously out of line with resources. On the other hand, ready
acceptance of resource limits without a consideration of how far the institution can stretch to achieve ambitious performance goals is not an
option. What happens if a college lowers the bar on its performance target
because it does not feel that resources will be available to support
growth? If Lorain County Community College had been "realistic" in the
1990s, it would have compressed its ambition to live within its available
resources. Its enrollment today would be much smaller, it would be working with significantly fewer partners, its physical and technological
resources would be considerably less than they are today, and it would
be a bit player in the county and the state.

Leaders and staff in abundant institutions do not allow what is feasible
to drive out what is desirable. What is feasible seldom does more than
project the present forward incrementally.[72] The goal of stretch is to fold
the future into the present. It forces people to ask, "What must we be
doing differently today if we want to achieve a superior level of performance tomorrow?" A view of performance as stretch and leveraging helps
bridge the gap between what is available today and what can be achieved
tomorrow. Stretch and the creativity it engenders are the fuel for growth

and vitality in abundant institutions. This is why leaders and staff in these institutions purposefully create goals that dramatically exceed their resources—that create a misfit between where the institution is and where it wants to be.[73]

Deliver Exceptional Value to Stakeholders

Beyond knowing the value they deliver to stakeholders, abundant institutions deliver *exceptional value* to stakeholders. They focus on five elements that work together to enhance value:

- *Awareness:* deep knowledge about stakeholder wants, needs, and expectations
- *Enhancement:* ideas for service that meet or exceed stakeholder needs
- *Execution:* actions that deliver exceptional value
- *Evaluation:* determine the extent to which value delivered meets stakeholder needs
- *Leveraging:* reinvention of service to deliver greater value

Value ultimately depends on the relationship between benefit received and needs and expectations at the individual level. Ideally, this relationship will be balanced or weighted on the positive side—that is, the value delivered would match or exceed that which is expected. Unfortunately, value is not well understood in colleges and universities, and we are bereft of real world examples to illustrate the concept. What follows is an account of what a college would need to do in an ideal world to deliver unparalleled value to stakeholders.

A college with a plan for managing value would start by gathering *deep* information from stakeholders about their needs and expectations and plot them against current practice. It would identify gaps between what it is doing and what stakeholders want, and devise ideas for turning gaps into positive steps. That is, it would alter current practice to deliver equivalent or better value than stakeholders expect. The time lag between idea generation and execution would be short with ideas being implemented on a rolling basis as they are generated. Evaluation would be continuous with a variety of methods used to query stakeholders about their perception of the relationship between what they want and expect and what they are getting. If performance gaps are detected for any reason (upward shift in stakeholder expectations, service outcomes falling short of identified needs, etc.), staff would go back to the drawing board to redesign practice to leverage value beyond stakeholder needs.

SUMMARY

As an organizational type, *colleges of abundance* have the capacity to leverage resources available to them into superior performance outcomes. The performance objective of these institutions is stretch and leveraging, and their managerial emphasis is building on strengths and valuing assets. Achieving ambitious goals in the future is more important than incrementally managing the present. Primary emphasis is on intangible resources (people and tacit knowledge) in contrast to tangible resources. Leaders in abundant institutions are committed to developing strategic capabilities in staff and to nurturing leaders throughout the organization.

Table 7.2. Comparison of Models

Dimension of Abundance	Colleges of Abundance
Managerial Emphasis	building on strengths; valuing assets
Cohesion	leaders/staff bound by common purpose
Resources	exceptional resources through leveraging
Resource Perspective	intangible resources
Organizational Architecture	holistic organization; tightly integrated
Operational Focus	system and process innovation
Risk	embrace and reward risk and change
Collaboration	college is hub of an expansive network
Competitive Focus	collaborate with rivals for mutual gain
Performance Objective	stretch and leveraging
Leadership	leaders throughout the organization
Attractiveness	desirable workplace; magnet for quality

Leaders and staff in abundant institutions possess an ambition that stretches beyond their resources and capabilities. They do not allow what is feasible and convenient to drive out the desirable but difficult. In these colleges, the goal of stretch and leveraging is to fold aspirations for superior performance in the future into execution in the present. Stretch and the creativity it engenders are the fuel for growth and vitality.

NOTES

1. Cameron, Dutton, and Quinn. *Positive Organizational Scholarship* (see chap. 1, n. 10).
2. Cameron, Dutton, and Quinn. *Positive Organizational Scholarship*.
3. Interview, community college president, April 25, 2006.
4. Interview, community college president, April 24, 2006.
5. Interview, community college president, November 20, 2006.
6. Interview, community college president, April 25, 2006.

7. Interview, community college president, April 25, 2006.

8. Interview, community college president, November 16, 2006.

9. Rio Salado College, *Rio Salado College Web site,* http://riosalado.edu (retrieved October 19, 2007).

10. Rio Salado College, *Rio Salado College Web site.*

11. Interview with Linda Thor, president of Rio Salado College, April 14, 2007.

12. M. Smith and A. Meyer, "Institutionalizing the Commitment to Learning: Evolution, Not Revolution," *Learning Abstracts,* Phoenix: League for Innovation 6, no. 6 (June 2003).

13. Smith and Meyer, "Institutionalizing the Commitment to Learning."

14. R. Alfred and P. Carter, *Creating the Future of Leadership and Management in Community Colleges,* Strategic Horizon Network Concept Paper (Ann Arbor, MI: Center for Community College Development, 2004).

15. Center for Community College Development, *Assessment of Strategic Capabilities in Horizon Network Colleges* (Milan, MI: Center for Community College Development, February 2005).

16. Richland College, *Richland College Web site,* http://rlc.dcccd.edu (retrieved September 26, 2007).

17. Richland College, *Richland College Web site.*

18. Interview with Tom McKeon, president of Tulsa Community College on April 25, 2006.

19. T. Erickson and L. Gratton, "What it Means to Work Here," *Harvard Business Review* (Boston: Harvard Business School Press, March 2007), 104–112.

20. Erickson and Gratton, "What it Means to Work Here," 104–112.

21. Erickson and Gratton, "What it Means to Work Here," 104–112.

22. Erickson and Gratton, "What it Means to Work Here," 104–112.

23. Erickson and Gratton, "What it Means to Work Here," 104–112.

24. Erickson and Gratton, "What it Means to Work Here," 104–112.

25. Richland College, *Richland College Web site.*

26. Richland College, *Richland College Web site.*

27. Richland College, *Richland College Web site.*

28. Richland College, *Richland College Web site.*

29. Richland College, *Richland College Web site.*

30. This illustration is derived from our strategic planning experience with Northern Essex Community College in Haverhill, Massachusetts in 1996–1997, 2001–2002, and 2007.

31. Strategic planning experience with Northern Essex Community College.

32. Strategic planning experience with Northern Essex Community College.

33. Strategic planning experience with Northern Essex Community College.

34. J. Collins, *Good to Great: Why Some Companies Make the Leap—and Others Don't,* 1st ed. (New York: HarperBusiness, 2001), 123.

35. This description of a president's perspective on budget reduction and stretch was obtained by the senior author as part of a series of discussions with a midwestern community college president between 2004 and 2005.

36. Lorain County Community College, *Lorain County Community College Web site,* http://lorainccc.edu (retrieved August 2, 2007).

37. Lorain County Community College, *Lorain County Community College Web site*.

38. Lorain County Community College, *Lorain County Community College Web site*.

39. Lorain County Community College, *Lorain County Community College Web site*.

40. Hamel and Prahalad, *Competing for the Future*.

41. Collins, *Good to Great*, 90–93.

42. Illinois Central College, *Illinois Central College Web site*, http://icc.edu (retrieved January 11, 2008).

43. Illinois Central College, *Illinois Central College Web site*.

44. Illinois Central College, *Illinois Central College Web site*.

45. Illinois Central College, *Illinois Central College Web site*.

46. W. Powell, K. Koput, and L. Smith-Doerr, "Interorganizational Collaboration and the Locus of Innovation: Networks of Learning in Biotechnology," *Administrative Science Quarterly* 41, no. 1 (1996): 116–145.

46. Interview with Eric Reno, president of Northeast College, on April 24, 2006.

47. Interview with former Cy-Fair president, Diane Troyer, on November 20, 2006.

48. Interview with former Cy-Fair president, Diane Troyer, on November 20, 2006.

49. [AQ30: the entry for endnote 49 is missing.]

50. Interview with Tom McKeon, president of Tulsa Community College, on April 25, 2006.

51. R. Burt, *Structural Holes: The Social Structure of Competition* (Cambridge, MA: Harvard University Press, 1992).

52. Interview, community college president, November 16, 2006.

53. Interview with Tom McKeon, president of Tulsa Community College, on April 25, 2006.

54. Interview with Sandra Kurtinitis, president of Community College of Baltimore County, on April 23, 2006.

55. This illustration is derived from our strategic planning experience with Owens Community College in northwestern Ohio in 2003–2004.

56. Hamel and Prahalad, *Competing for the Future*, 159.

57. Hamel and Prahalad, *Competing for the Future*, 159.

58. Interview, community college vice president, October 23, 2006.

59. The concept of "imagineering" was described to the senior author by personnel at the Disney Institute in Orlando, Florida as part of a conference program in November 2006.

60. Center for Community College Development, *Strategic Horizon Program*, http://cfccd.com (retrieved November 18, 2007).

61. Macomb Community College, *Macomb Community College Web site*, http://macomb.edu (retrieved December 10, 2007).

62. Macomb Community College, *Macomb Community College Web site*.

63. Macomb Community College, *Macomb Community College Web site*.

64. Interview with Eric Reno, president of Northeast College, on April 24, 2006.

65. J. Kotter, D. Cohen, and NetLibrary Inc., *The Heart of Change: Real-Life Stories of How People Change Their Organizations*, p. xiv, (2002): Available from http://www.netLibrary.com/urlapi.asp?action = summary&v = 1&bookid = 79102. P. 1.

66. Interview with Eric Reno, president of Northeast College, on April 24, 2006.

67. Interview with Eric Reno, president of Northeast College, on April 24, 2006.

68. M. Gladwell, *The Tipping Point: How Little Things Can Make a Big Difference* (Boston: Little Brown, 2000).

69. Interview with Sandra Kurtinitis, president of Community College of Baltimore County, on April 23, 2006.

70. Hamel and Prahalad, *Competing for the Future*.

71. Hamel and Prahalad, *Competing for the Future*.

72. Hamel and Prahalad, *Competing for the Future*, 145.

73. Hamel and Prahalad, *Competing for the Future*, 145.

Part III

LOOKING AHEAD

8

Thinking Differently

Abundance is a desirable state for any college. Who would deny that qualities of trust, happiness, and satisfaction make a college a better place to work? Who would disagree that people are a college's most important resource—its most critical asset? Why would someone want to work in a college where conflict is rampant, resources are woefully inadequate, and leadership is ineffective? The simple truth is that most people would prefer to work in an environment that is harmonious and fulfilling—a college of abundance.

Looming underneath the ideal of abundance, however, is a fundamental reality about people and organizations: an ideal state is easier to talk about than to achieve. It is possible to build and be part of an abundant organization—one that embodies trust, happiness, and virtuousness. The real question is how to create this organization—how to make your college abundant.

This chapter tries to answer this question by asking you to look at your college and think about it in a different way. It begins with a series of questions that gauge the extent to which your college is abundant. Using this information as a threshold, we shift the horizon of the reader beyond convention by framing different ways of looking at community colleges as organizations. Four dimensions of organization are examined—performance, resources, the organization itself, and leadership—and current modes of thought and action are challenged. Finally, we present a case study of a college moving toward abundance to illustrate the importance of thinking and acting differently in creating momentum for change. The chapter closes with eight questions about the future.

IS YOUR COLLEGE ABUNDANT?

Let's open the discussion about thinking differently by asking you to place your college on a scale of abundance. Look at your college. Think about where it is today and how it got there. Think about its capabilities and how people feel about it. Ask yourself: do we have a clear conception of what the college is and what it would look like at its very best? Do people feel valued? Do they understand how their performance contributes to the overall success of the college? These are not rhetorical questions—get a pencil and rate your college.

1. Which of the following gets more attention from leaders in your college?
    Solving problems   *Promoting growth*   *Employee growth and development*

2. In visioning, a healthy organization builds commitment by developing shared images of a desirable future. Do leaders and staff share a clear and compelling vision of the future?
    Yes   *Don't know*   *No*

3. Do leaders and staff share a collective view about what your college would look like at its very best?
    Yes   *Not sure*   *No*

4. With which of the following levels of organization do people in your college most readily identify (which is "home" to them)?
    Whole institution   *Department/division*   *Close associates*

5. Leadership encompasses strategic thinking, planning, and decision-making. Where are leaders found in your college?
Throughout the institution   *In selected positions*   *At the top of the organization*

6. To what extent do leaders and staff collaborate in pursuit of common objectives?
    Often—in pursuit of   *Occasionally—on*   *Only when required*
    common obectives   *important issues*

7. Which of the following is more important to people in your college?
    Intangible Resources   *Tangible Resources*
    (people and ideas)   (money, space, positions, technology)

8. Do leaders devote as much time and energy to developing staff as to promoting institutional growth?
    Yes   *Don't know*   *No*

9. How do people in your college view change?
    They embrace it   *Depends on the initiative*   *They avoid it*

10. Are they willing to take risks?

    Yes   *To some extent*   *No*

11. How open is your college to changing established policies, processes, and procedures?

  It is always seeking to improve   *As problems occur*   *We tend to keep things as they are*

12. Given the resources available to your college, it performs:

    Beyond expectation   *At an expected level*   *Below expectation*

13. Stretch goals are goals that lie considerably beyond your college's resources. To what extent do leaders and staff pursue stretch goals?

    It's a way of life for us   *Often*   *Seldom*

14. To what extent do staff understand the relationship between their work and the institution's overall performance?

    Most of the time   *Some of the time*   *Rarely*

15. How aggressively does your college seek to collaborate with other organizations?

    It is aggressive   *It partners selectively*   *Only when approached*

16. How do leaders look at competitors?

   As potential collaborators   *As rivals for students*   *Pay little attention*
      for mutual gain   *and resources*   *to them*

17. To what extent do leaders and staff reach out to other organizations (inside and outside of education) to learn about best practices?

   A considerable extent   *Some extent*   *Not at all*

18. Which of the following best describes your college's outlook on performance?

   Create superior outcomes   *Meet stakeholder needs*   *Grow as much and as fast*
    by leveraging resources   *and expectations*   *as possible*

19. How much do leaders and staff know about the value your institution delivers to stakeholders?

    A lot   *Some things*   *Very little*

20. Do leaders and staff possess a deep sense of urgency about the future?

    Yes   *Not sure*   *No*

If most of your marks fall on the left side of the chart, your college is well on the way to abundance. If they fall to the middle or the right of the chart, its strategic capabilities are limited and fundamental change will be necessary before it can claim abundance. When leaders and staff have a clear and collective vision of where they want to take a college and what it would look like at its very best, the cohesion necessary to pursue abundance exists. When their focus is on intangible resources and valuing people, the outlook needed to leverage resources is present. When they embrace risk and change and pursue stretch goals, the motivation needed to elevate performance is in place. This adds up to an institution-wide capability for leveraging resources into superior performance—the defining characteristic of abundance.

In the process of our work with community colleges, we frequently ask campus leaders about their view of the college through three interrelated questions: Where are you taking this college and why? What is the optimum for this college in terms of performance—what would it look like at its very best? What is unique about this college—what makes it different from other institutions? The answers we receive reveal campus leaders' conventional thinking about leadership and management. Leaders and staff spend a lot of time on problem solving and operations. By experience and training, they are pragmatic decision makers rather than enabling progenitors. Experience has taught them that the best way to handle problems in the short term is by directing tangible resources to practical solutions. Abundance, by contrast, is an organizational state requiring a different approach to leadership—it develops over the long term through leveraging intangible resources.

THINKING DIFFERENTLY

If the goal is abundance, a college must be capable of leveraging its resources; to leverage resources it must be committed to building strategic capabilities in staff. Working longer and faster will not get your college to abundance, but investing in people and working differently will. To work differently, however, leaders and staff must first think differently about four aspects of the organization: performance, resources, the organization itself, and leadership.

We did not develop baseline elements of the analyses that follow exclusively on our own. We had help from Gary Hamel and C. K. Prahalad and the marvelous ideas about organizations in turbulent times that they put forward in *Competing for the Future*.[1] For more than a decade, Hamel and Prahalad have helped leaders navigate change by looking at organizations as portfolios of core competencies. In so doing, they have made strategy an important part of every organization's business. Core constructs of performance, resources, the organization, and leadership in the pages that follow are derived from the work of Hamel and Prahalad and adapted for application in community colleges.

Thinking Differently about Performance

Performance is a growth industry. Leaders try to improve it, legislators debate it, coordinating boards and budget offices measure it, and stakeholders weigh it in decisions they make. It is typically couched in information that tells an institution how well it is doing compared to another institution or how much better or worse it has done than it did in the preceding year. When the measure of performance is growth rather than stretch, the key construct is gain or loss—change in numbers that count, like enrollment and revenue. This makes assessment easy because it involves less work, the numbers are easy to obtain, and reporting is simple. The problem, however, is that information about gain or loss says very little about the value a college is delivering and how effectively it is using its resources. Performance is about much more than positive numbers. It is about aspiration and ambition, about stretch and leverage, and about people and value.[2] Let us explain.

College leaders have long focused on growth as the measure of success. The abiding interest in growth delivers a multitude of insights about performance—the relationship between size and legitimacy, the correlation between market share and resource acquisition, and the dynamics of accountability. The upside of growth is that it makes institutions look good to stakeholders. The downside is that excessive attention to it obscures ways of looking at performance that could put a different perspective on the contribution of community colleges. By placing the emphasis on growth, colleges adopt a truncated view of performance that diverts attention from a fundamental strength of abundant organizations—the ability to leverage lean resources into high productivity.

In abundant organizations, doing more with resources already at hand is as important as acquiring more resources. For example, we are aware of colleges that tout their ability to generate continuous enrollment growth but fail to come up with substantive answers to inquiries about qualitative aspects of performance—learning outcomes, general education competencies, employer satisfaction, student satisfaction, and the like. Additionally, leaders make short shrift of performance when they tie it to tangible resources and indicators of growth. Public officials watching treasuries evaporate in the most troubled economy in three decades are asking tough questions about resource use. Colleges are expected to do more with less, and words like "efficiency," "sustainability," and "economy" are taking on new meaning and importance. High performance is now as much a matter of setting and achieving "stretch goals" and leveraging lean resources as it is generating growth and new resources. Inattention to this dimension of performance will prevent community colleges from adequately preparing for a future market in which success in underresourced institutions will be as much about stretch and leveraging as about growth.

Prevailing views of performance also emphasize external stakeholders at the expense of internal stakeholders. The first order of business in any organization is to gather intelligence about client needs as a means of ensuring that key stakeholders get what they want. Information about growth may be good for board members and policymakers because it provides an indication that the institution is doing something right. What it does for people inside a college, who are shouldering all of the work to generate growth, may be another matter. Putting the needs of external customers above the needs of staff constrains performance by unbalancing the relationship between effort and reward and devaluing the contribution of staff.[3] Externally driven performance criteria are more about tangible evidence of change (growth) while internally driven criteria are about intangibles (engagement and satisfaction) that make an institution work more effectively.

In sum, we are concerned that the emphasis on growth has shaped the way leaders and staff think about performance and argue for a broader perspective on performance, which begins with the human element in our colleges. A perspective that addresses what staff want and need should be used as a threshold for leveraging lean resources and producing superior results. Understanding the human roots of high performance, therefore, is a prerequisite for the pursuit of abundance.

Thinking Differently about Resources

Throughout this book we have argued that leaders and staff need to think differently about resources. In our view, people, culture, and tacit knowledge contribute more to the attainment of abundance than any tangible resource. Why is it that in so many colleges the perspective on resources is limited to acquiring more money, more technology, and more stuff, instead of investing in people and ideas? Why is more time spent addressing the symptoms of problems than in addressing the underlying causes, which are generally rooted in people? Why is professional development more akin to an annual ritual linked to the contract and punctuated by an investment of funds to accomplish noble ends than a strategic investment in people? The cost of limited investment in people is a loss of capacity for optimizing lean resources. To optimize resources, leaders need an understanding of resources that extends beyond lines in a budget.

Resources as People, Capability, and Leverage

In most colleges, resources boil down to planning, budgeting, and the allocation of dollars to activities. Typically, budgeting is a process of allocation that treats resources as fixed commodities limited to their face value. A primary focus is on costs for personnel—what is spent on people in contrast to what is achieved through them. The focus is on getting and using more, and the units of analysis are operating dollars. Not surprisingly, thinking about resources in this way is almost always incremental/decremental—more operating dollars, fewer full-time staff, more part-time staff, lower operating costs.

In our way of thinking, an incremental/decremental view of resources fails to promote a deep understanding of the contribution of people and capabilities to an organization. It fails to uncover the creative potential of people. It fails to encourage thinking about ways in which people and resources can be stretched to achieve seemingly unachievable goals. This perspective almost always starts with "what is" on the basis of existing tangible resources in contrast to "what could be" on the basis of leveraged intangible resources.

The distinction between the incremental perspective on resources and the leveraged perspective stands out starkly when we compare elements of the two models in table 8.1.[4]

Table 8.1.

	Incremental Perspective	Leveraged Perspective
Focus	Tangible resources (money, positions, and commodities)	Intangible resources (people, capabilities, and knowledge)
Goal	Acquire new or additional resources	Leverage existing resources
Process	Formulaic and incremental	Open ended
	Set realistic targets for allocating resources	Set ambitious targets for elevating performance
	External forces shape organizational goals and outcomes	Organizational goals and results are driven by leaders and staff
	Use growth as a vehicle for acquiring new resources	Invest in staff as a vehicle for leveraging current resources
	Seek congruence between growth and resources	Seek congruence between capabilities and opportunities
Outcome	Performance is linear/gains are incremental	Performance is leveraged/gains are exponential

To achieve ambitious goals (and move toward abundance), leaders need to see resources in a different way. They need to ask questions about how resources can be leveraged. What performance target do we need to set to reach our full potential? What kind of investment in people do we need to make to achieve this target? What will be our return on investment? Leaders need to learn more about intangible resources and their potential for leveraging finite sums into flexible assets.

Resources as Stretch

In their fullest expression, resources are exponential; that is, they are capable of growing at a rate that exceeds expectation. To see how this works, try an experiment. Ask for a meeting with the executive team in your college. Tell them you need $500,000 to develop a far-reaching program to enhance the strategic thinking capabilities of faculty and staff. If you are part of a college of *challenge* or *choice*, the response from members of the executive team will likely focus on front-end concerns about the cost of the program and short-term outcomes—in other words, on finite numbers related to cost and benefit that indicate whether or not there will be a return and that make a go/no go decision easy. The executive team in a college of abundance is more likely to focus on long-term outcomes that the program would bring, such as the ability to envision and pursue opportunity as a result of enhanced staff capabilities—in other words, on the contribution of the program to the achievement of *stretch goals*.

"Stretch" doesn't mean immediate return or taking big risks. It means setting an ambitious long-term goal and then leveraging staff capabilities to achieve the goal. Leaders in abundant institutions find ways to moderate the threat of risk by investing in people and ideas.[5] Stretch implies risk only when there is orthodoxy in thinking about how to craft and achieve goals. For example, if leaders at College X invest massive resources and use industry best practices to design a new approach for student intake, they very likely believe that the initiative will succeed. The problem is that the initiative could fail if leaders and staff are constrained by conventional thinking—that is, if there is no elasticity or "stretch" in the thought process going into the initiative.

From the perspective of stretch, the job of leaders is not only to set ambitious performance goals (stretch), but to equip staff with capabilities that increase the likelihood of achieving these goals (leveraging). The reader will, of course, want to know what these capabilities are. A list of competencies is provided below that when fully developed will enable community college faculty and staff to contribute to institutional performance in ways that are decidedly strategic.

Faculty and Staff in High-Performing Institutions

- Comprehend, and assign importance to, the impact of external forces, changing customer needs, and competitor practices

- Regularly acquire intelligence about competitor practices and intentions
- Seek and use information about best practices from organizations inside and outside of education
- Possess deep knowledge about the value they deliver to students and stakeholders
- Have an informed understanding of institutional culture and climate
- Understand change and how to make it work

When a critical nucleus of faculty and staff possesses these capabilities, a college will be able to leverage resources in a way that will lead to abundance.

Thinking Differently about the Organization

The need to think differently about performance and resources cannot be divorced from the need to think differently about the organization. Just as limitations in the prevailing conception of performance and resources will constrain a college from achieving abundance, so, too, will shortcomings in the conception of organizational design and change.

Community colleges have reached a point in their development where size and complexity mandate continuous attention to organizational structure. To generate and manage growth, they have decentralized responsibility for hiring and supervision of staff, enlarged the sphere of responsibility for operations, added specialized administrative functions, and elaborated the structure of the organization. In doing so, they have created a *distributed organization* in which multiple organizations— literally "colleges within a college"—execute the purposes of the institution.[6] These "colleges" operate in ways that simultaneously integrate and divide. On the one hand, institution-wide policies, systems, and processes bind them to core purposes of the organization and ensure consistency. On the other hand, they operate independently from one another as a confederation of loosely connected silos serving uniquely different markets. This dualism has built-in advantages and disadvantages. The advantage is that of speed and flexibility: loosely coupled units move quickly and are capable of generating and managing growth. The disadvantage is that of constraint: uniform systems and processes get in the way of operating units serving different markets.

The distributed organization is the antithesis of the centralized, top-down organizational model that was the community college three decades ago. The old model had many problems, not the least of which was a lack of employee empowerment. Before we praise the new and bury the old, however, it is fair to say that the distributed organization may have as many, if not more, problems than the old model. There is a growing divide between leaders and staff. Size and complexity have reshaped culture and put a different spin on what it means to work in a community college. Excessive numbers of part-time personnel have taxed the system by adding new responsibilities to faculty and staff. The insatiable need for information and shorter response time has made communication a vexing problem on most campuses. And, pressure to do more with less has cut deeply into the physical and psychological capacity of staff. There is a cost attached to efficiency, and it is growing incapacity as people become mired in operations and problem solving. There is simply no time to think or plan, which is not a healthy prescription for the future.

We believe that the speed of growth and change in community colleges has marched leaders and staff into a corner in terms of their thinking about organizational structure. Pressure to manage growth, to provide more and better service, and to pay bills with lean resources has encouraged colleges to morph into loosely coupled organizations in which work is done by individual units disconnected from the whole.[7] This design, as shown in table 8.2, while efficient in getting things done, has features that stand in stark contrast to attributes described as desirable by leaders in abundant organizations.

The evolution toward a distributed organization has benefited community colleges by enabling them to grow. It has hurt them by eroding the infrastructure needed to pursue a clear and collective agenda for change. Decentralized units pursue their own goals at their own pace according to the preferences of the people who work within them. To achieve abundance, a college must succeed in developing a critical mass of people who can work in simultaneously contradictory ways: *independently* from one another, but with a *shared sense* of organizational core values that enable change to reach a tipping point.

Table 8.2.

Prevailing Approach: Distributed Organization		*What is Needed:* Abundant Organization
Operating units	*Focus*	Whole organization
Individual action	*Work Dynamic*	Collective action
Formal organization	*Emphasis*	Informal organization
Organization	*Architecture*	Network

From Operating Units to Whole Organization

In many colleges, one cannot speak meaningfully of an overarching institutional strategy because strategy is little more than a sum of the tactics of operating units. Activities that involve the whole organization are episodic and ritualistic, with the time and attention of staff devoted almost exclusively to operating units. If the reader has doubts about the accuracy of this assertion, think back to last year's opening convocation and recollect the faces of faculty and staff who couldn't wait to move from the morning general session to department meetings in the afternoon—the real focus of their work. Staff take on the mind-set of the people they work with. When the institution is viewed from the narrow perspective of the work group, the whole organization takes a hit. Opportunities are missed or go unexploited and organization-wide goals are neglected as people and units pursue independent agendas.

We are not suggesting that distribution of responsibility to departments and administrative units for operating decisions is incorrect or counterproductive. In rapidly growing organizations it is essential. Nor are we suggesting that everyone in the institution should be an architect of change. That is simply not realistic. What we are suggesting is that leaders should refocus the vision of staff on the *whole organization* by crafting a clear and compelling picture of what the institution is and what it is trying to become.[8] This picture should be created through collective action, and it should be simply stated. Rio Salado College's declaration "We astonish our customers!" is a good example of a vision statement that means business.[9] At Cy-Fair it is their "Signature Statement."[10] Only by painting a picture of the institution in bold strokes and bright lights can a college hope to achieve the value that comes from collective attention to a common goal.

From Individual to Collective Action

A lesson that leaders have learned through atrocity tales about ineffective CEOs and institutions that have fallen on hard times is that bureaucracy and hierarchy squelch initiative and creativity. Empowered employees deliver better results and growth is more readily accomplished when individuals have the freedom to act. Empowering individuals, however, is not an all-or-nothing proposition. Hierarchical behavior constrains active dialogue about organizational challenges and direction, and it uses position and authority rather than broad discussion and analysis to make decisions.[11] The goal of empowerment, in its fullest sense, is to enable individuals to design their own jobs, to improve their own processes, and do whatever it takes to improve performance.

It is hard to argue against empowerment—it is clearly the right thing to do in a progressive organization. Yet there are limits to "delayering," decentralizing, and empowering. We believe that individual action, if not carried out within the rubric of a shared sense of direction, can limit performance by directing resources to activities that are not productive. While bureaucracy can have a negative impact on performance, so too can independent operating units and empowered, but unaligned, individuals who are working at cross purposes. Hamel and Prahalad put it this way in *Competing for the Future*:

> Empowerment implies an obligation and an opportunity to contribute to a specific end. The notion of a shared direction, what we call a "strategic intent" reconciles the needs of individual freedom and concerted, coordinated effort. As tempting as it might be, senior management can't abdicate its direction-setting role. Employees want a sense of direction just as much as they want the freedom of empowerment.[12]

In our view, community college CEOs and executive teams have not defaulted on their responsibility for "direction-setting," but they have not allocated adequate time to this important task. The urgent drives out the important as individual attention to immediate problems crowds out collective action on strategic matters. As a result, institutions sacrifice integrated thinking and collective behavior to the compartmentalized needs and interests of individuals working in units.

From Formal to Informal Organization

In recent years many colleges have become interested in organizational culture and climate and made efforts to measure and improve climate. There is a reason behind this, and it has to do with the realization that the informal organization—people, culture, climate, and the like—have more influence over what happens in a college than its formal administrative structure. The informal organization makes things happen—no one would dispute that—but there is a danger in relying too heavily on something that is not well understood. For example, it does not make sense to allow cultural norms to shape the design and mechanics of a change initiative if these norms are clearly not conducive to supporting change. Similarly, ramming an initiative down the throats of staff using one's position in the hierarchy is a waste of resources.

Abundant organizations motivate people to get behind change and see it through to a successful conclusion. To accomplish this, leaders *and staff* work hard to understand the informal organization—the makeup of culture, values of people and groups, norms that guide behavior, modes of communication, political behavior of opinion leaders, and so on. These insights are not uniform across the organization. For example, what is perceived to be acceptable or unacceptable political behavior depends, in part, on one's place in the organization. Behavior that is necessary and functional for senior administrators, and thereby accepted, may not be functional for middle administrators. Alternatively, there may be elements of behavior that are uniformly accepted or rejected irrespective of one's position in the organization. Leaders and staff in abundant institutions understand the makeup and dynamics of the informal organization and effectively use these dynamics to design and carry out change.

One dimension of the informal organization that is currently off the radar screen of leaders and staff is the divide between work groups—senior administrators, full-time faculty, middle administrators, classified staff, and part-time faculty. As colleges have grown larger and more complex, specialization in responsibilities and role expectations has diminished understanding of work done in areas outside of the work unit. Instructors do not understand what administrators do and, of course, the converse is true. The result is a degree of fragmentation that has hampered communication and constrained the capacity of institutions to achieve core goals. A lack of sensitivity to the demands of different work roles could result in expedient decisions that overlook important role dynamics. For example, faculty could disengage from institution-wide activities as a result of frustration with administrators who are perceived as out of touch with challenges they face in the classroom. Likewise, support staff could direct their energy exclusively to the operating unit as an expression of their discontent with faculty and administrators who are perceived as undervaluing their contribution. When faculty and staff sense that leaders understand what they do and value their contributions, positive feelings and virtuous behavior mark their orientation toward work. These are essential ingredients of abundance.

Community colleges desperately need leaders who care about and understand work role dynamics. One needs only to look at the vast number of part-time faculty who are central to the teaching mission of colleges, but peripheral to governance and curriculum management, to understand the implications of a disconnect between role and voice. If the goal is to leverage increasingly scarce resources through the capabilities and commitment of staff, leaders will need to be vigilant about, and maintain an abiding interest in, the needs of staff.

From Organization to Network

Partnering and collaboration are practically automatic in high-performing colleges. Whereas most colleges judge their capacity for growth in terms of personnel inside the organization, progressive institutions forecast growth in terms of people inside and outside of the organization. More and more colleges are finding that networks are capable of producing benefits (service expansion, cost efficiency, and quality enhancement) that leverage performance in ways that surpass the internal organization. Leaders of abundant institutions provide testimony to the importance of networks through their efforts to forge partnerships. Ask any president about the number of partnerships that were in place ten years ago and how many are in place today. Leaders in abundant institutions exhibit a much greater propensity to establish and maintain partnerships than their less abundant counterparts. This leads us to question the effectiveness of the sacred cow we know as the *administrative organization*. Is it possible that the structure of the network(s) a college is part of is more important than its administrative structure?

Leaders who have the foresight and imagination to invest in and grow networks are likely to be more effective in leveraging their institutions to appreciably higher levels of performance. Restricting development to the capabilities of personnel who are part of the organization will leave leaders with less to manage and control, but it will also result in marginal growth. Adopting a more expansive view of development as accomplished through players inside and outside of the organization opens up multiple possibilities, not to mention opportunities and new resources. If Rio Salado College had not dramatically changed its approach to educational delivery, its growth would have stalled long ago. If Lorain County Community College had not developed strong partnerships with business and industry, regional universities, K–12 school districts, and government agencies, it would bear no semblance to what it is today. Sticking to the confines of the internal organization limits a college's opportunity horizon and its potential for creating new "market space." The boundaries of the future for community colleges will be determined by the opportunities in their networks, not the structure of the organization.

Thinking Differently about Leadership

How does your college gauge its success? Most leaders would answer that question with one word—*growth*. The common belief is that students and stakeholders vote with their feet—more people wanting more things from a college means that it must be doing something right. Yet when we talk with leaders of abundant organizations, we hear that a telling aspect of success is the capacity to transform people by becoming a remarkably human enterprise—that is, by adopting a business model that puts people at the center of everything the organization does. The key to accomplishing this goal is building leadership "engines" that invest in people.

Leadership in abundant organizations begins and ends with *people*:

- Leaders and staff look at the college as a human community, not a growth machine.
- Leaders and staff are committed to developing strategic capabilities.
- Leaders and staff draw heavily on a shared understanding of institutional mission and vision as the basis for their work.
- Leaders and staff balance problem-solving and people-valuing activities to build a capability for leveraging.
- Leaders and staff collectively adhere to values governing human aspects of the organization—civility, wellness, virtuousness, forgiveness, risk, vitality, etc.
- Leaders and staff work together to foster a vibrant institutional "core" culture, while simultaneously respecting individual differences.
- Leaders and staff actively think about the meaning of what they do in terms of the wider world in which they live.
- Leaders and staff believe that the primary outcome of education is societal value.

Notice in each item we put leaders and staff together as partners in the business of leadership for these items. Sharing responsibility is an important part of thinking differently. The savvy reader will, of course, argue that responsibility for leadership has always been shared, particularly in progressive institutions, and does not constitute "thinking differently." Lip service to shared responsibility, however, is one thing, and behavior and action are something else. Marginal investment by leaders in developing the strategic capabilities of staff indicates to us that leadership is, in fact, not a shared responsibility on college campuses. It is the province of senior administrators who, through inaction, invest marginally in staff and, in so doing, constrain institutional development.

If leadership is truly a shared responsibility, strategically capable staff administrators will be just as important as strategically thinking administrators.[13] In a world of profound change, incremental thinking is unlikely to add much educational or societal value. Imagine a world in which the things we take for granted today can no longer be assumed in the future. Water can only be used in small amounts, and it is restricted by law. Oil is shockingly expensive and in limited supply, and use of a car is permissible only on certain days and at specified times. Concerns over global warming and national security have reached a point where massive resources are being diverted from education and social programs, thereby halving operating and capital resources for public colleges and universities. States compete with one another and nations go to war over natural resources. Consensus is difficult to achieve on critical policy issues because of a polarized citizenry that cannot agree on anything.

Imagine being a college president in a community experiencing all of those problems. Citizens and community leaders are looking to you to take the lead in bringing people and organizations together to find solutions. Do you have the intuition and imagination to generate ideas, to forge alliances, and to craft creative solutions? Do you have the wisdom and courage to know that you cannot do this alone? Are capable leaders and strategically skilled staff in place throughout your college to help?

Leaders in abundant organizations share leadership responsibility by investing in the strategic capabilities of their staff. They get the right players on the team by acquiring talent, but they also build it from within. They know that if the players under contract lack talent, the team will fall short of its goal. They also know that if these players have talent and aspiration, the team will not only achieve its goal, but it will get better over time. The team analogy illustrates an important point about leadership. A foremost task of leaders is to guide an organization in pursuit of important goals, and this is done by getting the right players on the team and investing in their creative potential.

MOVING TOWARD ABUNDANCE

Thinking differently is not just about words and ideas. It is about behavior and actions—what leaders and staff do inside organizations to enhance performance. To illustrate the effect that changes in leader behavior and organizational learning can have on people and institutions, we describe the journey of a college from challenge to abundance. The experience of this college is real. It is a very different institution today than it was in 2000.

With the appointment of a new president in 2001 and a vision of pluralistic leadership, Transformation Community College (TCC) engineered a fundamental shift in culture from a climate of divisiveness and distrust to a spirit of openness and collaboration.[14] Established in 1967 as a technical college, Transformation is a multicampus institution in the Midwest serving twenty thousand students on two campuses. The larger of its campuses serves a region of the state hit hard by global competition, particularly in the manufacturing industry. The second campus was established in the 1980s to serve a more rural community and has grown into an institution with an identity of its own. Transformation has more than doubled its enrollment after transitioning from a technical college to a comprehensive community college in the mid-1990s. Lacking local tax support, it has used stretch goals and leveraging to achieve dramatic enrollment growth against a backdrop of declining state appropriations.

Bottoming Out in Challenge

When Transformation's new president took office, she stepped into an institution with a bureaucratic structure and a top-down hierarchy. The faculty unionized in the early 1990s—a step that ushered in a rocky relationship with the administration. Choosing to avoid conflict by managing from a distance, the previous president withdrew to his office, consulted with a handful of direct reports, and made decisions by fiat. The outcome was a climate of distrust and fragmentation that placed individuals in favor or disfavor by virtue of the extent to which they were perceived as cooperating with the leadership team.

Bureaucracy, hierarchy, and leader behavior were not the only factors contributing to the climate of distrust at Transformation. Growing pains accompanying expansion triggered a series of reorganizations that undercut morale. The college's human resource capacity failed to keep pace with growth resulting in problems with employee turnover and dissatisfaction. By 2000, these problems had reached a level of severity that was readily apparent to outsiders, including a visiting Higher Learning Commission accreditation team. In its report, the team commended Transformation for its growth and responsiveness to regional educational needs. A ten-year accreditation was granted, but the exit interview recommended a focus visit in 2003–2004 to assess "communication participation by faculty and staff in governance."

Strained relationships between faculty and administrators and poor communication deepened already existing silos within Transformation. Relationships with outside organizations were as tenuous as relationships within as the college gained recognition and notoriety for its aggressive competitive practices with neighboring institutions. With this as a background, the former president retired in 2001, and the board of trustees searched for a leader who would provide a new direction.

From Challenge to Choice

Under the leadership of its new president, Transformation moved quickly to evaluate its position through a college-wide strategic planning process. The president used the recommendation of the accreditation team to engage faculty and staff in intensive dialogue about the future. Previous planning efforts had been limited in scope and were impeded by minimally engaged campus constituencies: new planning process was entirely different. The goal was to collectively determine a direction for the future, but also to begin the process of transforming Transformation's culture. This would be accomplished by putting people at the center of the planning process. Every step in planning engaged the college community, beginning with the selection of a coordinating task force that would be purposefully grassroots in nature, including individuals from every major work group in the college. Beyond this, individuals and groups had a voice in planning through focus groups that would provide a forum for discussion of current operating problems and future directions.

The result, after several months of intensive and sometimes heated dialogue in dozens of focus groups, was the creation of a new mission and vision for Transformation, which reflected a collective ideal of what it would look like at its very best. The task force completed its work and presented a strategic plan to the board of trustees in March 2004. The plan included six priorities and forty corresponding objectives to guide the college's development. Two features of the plan provided a critical departure point from the past: 1) development priorities were collectively determined and embraced by leaders and staff and 2) the plan was a living document that bound personnel to a clear development path. To ensure timely movement from thought to action, a full-time planner was hired to monitor progress, and priorities were assigned to the vice presidents for implementation, monitoring, and support.

Significant staffing changes were also initiated in the first year of the president's tenure. Senior administrators were recruited in student services, continuing education and corporate training, human resources, and dean of the second campus. New revenue markets were opened, and existing resources were leveraged by adding positions in external relations and partnerships. New positions were created in marketing and communications, public relations, government relations, and community outreach. In addition, the resources and activities of the college foundation were enhanced through supplemental funding, and an alumni outreach program was initiated to bolster Transformation's nexus with the community. These steps resulted in significant dividends through improved relationships with local school districts, political leaders, community groups, and business and industry.

While the executive team worked to broaden connectivity with the external community, a concerted effort was underway to revitalize the college's culture by rebuilding trust between college leaders and staff. Additional resources were provided to hire full-time faculty and enrich professional development opportunities. Equity pay increases were granted to nonbargaining unit staff. Numerous awards and recognition programs were initiated to acknowledge and celebrate the hard work of faculty and staff. The president and executive team held regular town hall meetings in which employees were given up-to-the-minute reports on campus priorities and were provided with an opportunity for dialogue and questions. To demonstrate a commitment to recognize and promote talented employees, the president initiated a leadership development program, which has since become a national model. Overall, the early years of the president's tenure were aimed at giving employees and community partners a voice in college development and laying the foundation for Transformation's evolution into a high-performing organization.

Moving toward Abundance

The revitalization of Transformation is not complete, yet signs abound that the institution is progressing steadily toward abundance. The college has embraced a more rigorous standard of performance evaluation through the Academic Quality Improvement Program (AQIP) of the Higher Learning Commission—a performance improvement process that requires broad campus involvement. It has also substantially increased the number of organizations it is partnering with, and is experimenting with a new governance model that fully incorporates faculty into decision making. This model will help Transformation move away from historically confrontational faculty negotiations to an approach where bargaining is based on mutual benefit for all groups.

The evolution to a culture of mutual gain has created an environment in which faculty and staff are able to focus on the ultimate beneficiaries of the college—students. This is in stark contrast to a "growth at all costs" culture in which enrollment was the primary concern of leaders. Growth became an all-consuming goal as a conduit to increased state support with people moved around to accommodate it. In Transformation's evolving culture, growth is a natural outcome of a "Students First" service ideology, designed to help students navigate every facet of their educational experience. This inversion in service ideology encourages and empowers faculty and staff to act in ways that would not have been possible a decade ago. It is the signal achievement in an evolution that will morph Transformation from an insular organization into a virtuous institution capable of leveraging deep commitment of leaders and staff, into unparalleled benefit for students.

EIGHT QUESTIONS ABOUT THE FUTURE

Our goal in this book has been to portray abundance as a desirable future state for community colleges and to provide a map for getting there. We started with a college challenged in almost every aspect of its operation and closed with a college clicking on all cylinders. If you can visualize your institution in the profiles of colleges of challenge, choice, or abundance, you will be a step ahead in the progression toward abundance. We believe that every college possesses attributes of abundance—the important questions are which attributes and to what extent.

Now that you are familiar with the concept of abundance, here are some questions about your college and its potential for the future. Look closely at your college one more time, and rate its capacity to achieve abundance. A simple "yes" or "no" answer for each question will give you a general sense of where your institution is today and what its unrealized potential might be.

- Is your college pursuing audacious goals and priorities given its resources?
- Do leaders and staff share a clear and compelling perspective on what your college looks like, or would look like, at its very best?
- Is there a significant amount of *stretch* in that perspective—that is, does it exceed current resources by a significant amount?
- Do intangible resources (people, knowledge, and skills) receive as much attention as tangible resources (money, technology, and space)?
- Do leaders have an agenda and clearly articulated program for developing the strategic capabilities of staff?
- Do staff have the freedom and wherewithal to pursue opportunities that lie beyond current policy, programs, and operations in your college?
- Does your college have a capacity for collaboration and partnering that significantly extends its operating resources?
- Do leaders and staff share a deep sense of urgency about the future?

These questions capture the essence of abundance—it is an approach to institutional development which emphasizes stretch more than growth, strategic thinking more than problem solving, people more than money, leveraging resources more than allocating resources, and opportunity more than continuity. It is a way of looking at an organization as a difference maker in people's lives.

We have sketched a formidable challenge for community colleges and those who lead them. A conventional approach to thinking and doing will not be enough; at least not for colleges with ambitious goals and lean resources. Abundance will be achieved by colleges that value people and invest in them. We see these colleges as made up of leaders and staff who are authentic in word and deed, with skills that come from a deep interest in people. We see them as embracing change and as being actively in pursuit of competencies that need to be nurtured and developed to achieve "stretch" goals. Finally, we see them as possessing extraordinary ambition and a capacity for leverage that turns ambition into reality. These colleges are not for everyone. They are for people who want to make a difference in the lives of others by creating deep meaning and opening every possible avenue for personal contribution.

NOTES

1. Hamel and Prahalad, *Competing for the Future,* (see chap. 1, n. 2).
2. Hamel and Prahalad, *Competing for the Future*, 267–260.
3. Hamel and Prahalad, *Competing for the Future*, 289–294.
4. The framework for the incremental and leveraged perspectives on resources is derived from Hamel and Prahalad in *Competing for the Future*, 283.
5. R. Alfred, *Three L's for Abundant Organizations: Learning, Leading, and Leveraging,* Center for Community College Development, June 2007.
6. R. Alfred and P. Carter, "New Colleges for a New Century: Organizational Change and Development in Community Colleges," *Higher Education Handbook of Theory and Research*, vol. XIV (New York: Agathon Press, 1999).
7. Alfred and Carter, "New Colleges for a New Century."
8. Alfred, *Three L's for Abundant Organizations*.
9. Information derived from the Web site of Rio Salado College, www.riosalado .edu (retrieved November 2007).
10. Information derived from the Web site of Cy-Fair College, www.lonestar .edu (retrieved November 2007).
11. Hamel and Prahalad, *Competing for the Future*, 290.
12. Hamel and Prahalad, *Competing for the Future*, 290.
13. P. Carter, L. Terwilliger, R. Alfred, D. Hartleb, and B. Simone, "Developing Strategic Leaders," *Community College Journal*, August/September 2002 (Washington, DC: American Association of Community Colleges), 22–25.
14. The case illustration for Transformation Community College is adapted from our experience in strategic planning with a large, multicampus midwestern community college between 2004 and 2005.

About the Authors

Richard Alfred is professor of higher education in the Center for the Study of Higher and Postsecondary Education at the University of Michigan. The author of more than 150 books, articles, and monographs on organizational strategy, leadership and management, effectiveness, and change management, his award-winning 2005 book *Managing the Big Picture in Colleges and Universities: From Tactics to Strategy* ushered in a new way of thinking about management in colleges and universities. Dick spends a lot of time with executive teams on community college campuses. Over a forty-year career, he has worked with several hundred colleges in designing strategy, strategic plans, institutional effectiveness models, and transformational strategies to enhance organizational performance. Prior to coming to Michigan, he served as a senior administrator in community college districts in New York City, Kansas City, and Cleveland.

Christopher Shults is a doctoral recipient and Rackham Merit Scholar in the Center for the Study of Higher and Postsecondary Education at the University of Michigan. He has authored several books and journal articles on organizational strategy, effectiveness, and leadership and contributed in important ways to practice through leadership models and development tools created in partnership with NAFEO and the Strategic Horizon Network. Chris has served in a consulting capacity with a number of national agencies and associations and is currently working on an interassociation African-American Male Initiative designed to enhance access and success in postsecondary education. Prior to embarking on doctoral work at Michigan, he served as research associate with the American Association of Community Colleges.

Ozan Jaquette is a PhD candidate in the Center for the Study of Higher and Postsecondary Education at the University of Michigan. In 2003 he was awarded a fellowship for study at the University of Oxford where he concentrated on funding policy for colleges of further education in England—the English counterpart to American community colleges. He has authored several journal articles relating to community college funding policy and has a deep interest in policy initiatives affecting access to college and student and institutional performance. Ozan has bridged policy to practice through service in a resource capacity to community college presidents and executive officers. In 2005 he developed a series of policy briefs for the Michigan Council of Community College Presidents and in 2006 he served as executive intern at Hudson County Community College in New Jersey.

Prior to entering the doctoral program in higher education at the University of Michigan, **Shelley Strickland** worked for more than a decade in collegiate communications and development. She has taught at community colleges and universities, including developing a curriculum in philanthropy and development for Michigan undergraduates. Her research focuses on fund-raising and the community college presidency. She has an MA from the University of Virginia and a baccalaureate from the Lee Honors College at Western Michigan University.